Through the Rearview Mirror

Through the Rearview Mirror

Historical Reflections on Psychology

John Macnamara

WITHDRAWN

A Bradford Book
The MIT Press
Cambridge, Massachusetts
London, England

This book was set in Sabon on the Miles System by Achorn Graphic Services, Inc., and was printed and bound in the United States of America.

First printing, 1999.

Library of Congress Cataloging-in-Publication Data

Macnamara, John.
  Through the rearview mirror : historical reflections on psychology / John Macnamara.
        p.   cm.
  "A Bradford book."
  Includes bibliographical references and index.
  ISBN 0-262-13352-0 (hc : alk. paper)
  1. Psychology—History. 2. Psychology and philosophy. I. Title.
  BF105.M33   1999
  150′.9—dc21   98-50264
                                                      CIP

Contents

A Word to Readers   vii

Editor's Note   ix

Preface   xi

Acknowledgments   xvii

1   Introduction: Three Very General Observations on Psychology and Its History   1

2   Plato on Learning   9

3   Plato on Truth and Knowledge   17

4   Aristotle on Knowledge and Understanding   25

5   Aristotle on Perception: Three Questions   35

6   The Book of Genesis and Psychology   45

7   The Impact of Christianity on Psychology   53

8   St. Augustine of Hippo: Christian Platonist   63

9   St. Thomas Aquinas on Individuals and Concepts   73

10   St. Thomas Aquinas and Dualism   85

11   Duns Scotus and William of Ockham: The Cusp of the Middle Ages   95

12   Thomas Hobbes: Grandfather of Modern Psychology   105

13   René Descartes: Medieval Man of the Renaissance   115

14   John Locke: A No-Nonsense Developmental Psychologist   125

15   Gottfried Leibniz and Necessary Truths   135

16 Bishop Berkeley and the Consequences of Nominalism   145

17 David Hume: Some Consequences of British Empiricism   157

18 Thomas Jefferson and the Declaration of Independence   167

19 Immanuel Kant and the Foundational Stance in Psychology   177

20 John Stuart Mill: A Contemporary Psychologist   185

21 Charles Darwin: The Newton of Biology   193

22 Wilhelm Wundt: The Founder of Experimental Psychology   203

23 Franz Brentano: Intuition and the Mental   213

24 Sigmund Freud and the Concept of Mental Health   225

25 John B. Watson and the Behaviorists   235

26 Some Notes on the Gestalt Movement   243

27 Extroduction   253

Notes   267
Glossary   269
References   275
Index   281

A Word to Readers

When he fell terminally ill, John was working on still another version of his "Reflections on the History of Psychology." The version we give here to the public is the last one, with two exceptions: a paragraph in chapter 4 was changed back to the text of the previous version and a paragraph of chapter 27 was suppressed altogether.

The changes that the author made in the last version were major ones. He had started to doubt Aristotle's clear-cut distinction between perception and cognition on the basis that even in perception the "alternative of truth and false may apply." His last talk (at the Center for Logic, Language, and Cognition on January 13, 1995) was in fact on the "Language of Vision."

At the end of his life, and following a suggestion of one of us, John worked on a mathematization of the relation between perception and cognition by means of functors (i.e., functions that preserve the category structure) between two categories: the category of gestalts (the domain of perception) and the category of kinds (the domain of cognition). However, a category may also be viewed as a language whose formulas are capable of having truth values. In particular, this is so for the category of gestalts. Thus Aristotle's criterion for distinguishing perception from cognition seems violated: the alternative of truth and falsity applies even in perception.

Such a modification, as he put it, "sent ripples throughout the whole book," and he expressed the desire to rewrite those portions that were affected by the change. He had hoped to advance his work on perception to achieve this aim. Unfortunately, death prevented him from finishing this revision. Nevertheless, on the morning of his last talk, he added a whole paragraph on his views on perception and cognition in chapter 27. We have decided to keep a paragraph of the next to the last version of chapter 4 and delete the added paragraph in chapter 27. On the other hand, we have added two postscripts: one to chapter 4 that consists of the revised paragraph in question and another to chapter 27 that consists of the deleted paragraph of the last version of that chapter. We hope that this will indicate the direction in which his thought was developing.

Gonzalo Reyes, Marie La Palme Reyes, and Albert Bregman

The manuscript of this book lay hidden in the computer through all of 1995. It was so close to completion, yet a great deal remained to be done before it could be sent to the publisher. Zsuzsana Makkai spent many hours on the computer to give us the final text. Marie La Palme Reyes integrated the many revisions to give the "final" text. Both she and Gonzalo Reyes read the text carefully and wisely. Al Bregman's many keen and insightful questions made the text a better one. Geert-Jan Boudewijnse was present at the beginning of the book; he was John's teaching assistant for three years and strongly urged him to write up these notes in book form. He also gave generously of his time to prepare the references, a time-consuming task. Betty Stanton of the MIT Press was an encouraging and enthusiastic supporter. These friends gave of themselves without reserve. It was truly a labor of love. For their selfless and devoted work, John and I will always be grateful. Thank you all.

Joyce Macnamara

Editor's Note

The material in square brackets was added by Marie La Palme Reyes, Gonzalo Reyes, and Albert Bregman at places where some early readers had found the original manuscript to be unclear. Geert-Jan Boudewijnse checked over and completed the bibliographies. A note by John M. O'Donnell, S.J., was added to chapter 7 in response to criticisms that the author's drawing implications about the human mind from the Bible were unjustified from a strict scholarly reading and that his inferences were an attempt to reconcile his Catholicism with his views of the human mind. O'Donnell argues that the author's arguments derive from his reading of the Bible from the perspective of the Catholic tradition as a whole, and not from the bare words of the Bible.

Preface

This book is for people who would like to explore what the history of ideas has to offer us today in our attempts to understand the human mind. I wrote it in the first instance for psychologists, believing that many among them would welcome a closer look than they are usually offered at the psychologists of earlier ages and their relevance for current theory building. One aim, in which I take a particular delight, is to show that the major writings on the mind over the past two thousand years are not museum pieces; they are often as rewarding as the very best to be found among the contemporary books and journal articles that clamor ever so much more loudly for attention.

Our eyes, however, will never be exclusively on the past. Like motorists, we keep one eye on the rearview mirror for the purpose of guiding our progress. The contemporary scene is ever present in our reflections, and historical texts are made to yield morals, cautionary observations, and inspiration for present-day psychologists. Some rearview mirrors bear the inscription that objects seen in the mirror are closer than they appear. I would claim that the same applies to the figures seen in this book.

I also believe that there is a broader audience for a book such as this among people who are interested in the history of science and of ideas or who, like me, are simply fascinated by the human mind and its operations. I do not presuppose on the part of readers prior familiarity with the authors discussed, with the issues singled out for examination in their writings, or with contemporary treatment of those issues. The book is intended as a first introduction to historical reflections on contemporary psychology. It is self-contained—in all but one sense. The qualification is prompted by the hope that readers, at least sometimes, will succumb to the temptation to turn to the writers themselves for a fuller understanding of the matters raised. To encourage this I attach to each chapter an indication of the most relevant passages in the author I have been discussing. Occasionally I add one or two particularly pertinent secondary sources, but in general I ignore such sources, which by their sheer bulk and number all too easily overwhelm beginners and obscure their view of the originals.

The book has its immediate origin in an undergraduate course that I have been giving at McGill University for just under a decade. Its roots go back much further. Even during the 1950s as a young high-school teacher in the outskirts of Dublin, I rode my bicycle the five miles into town to buy each issue of the Penguin series on the philosophers as it appeared: Berkeley, Kant, Leibniz, and so on. Each cost the equivalent of about 50 cents. As I became less straightened for funds, I began a life-long collection of the original writings of these authors, often but not always in cheap editions or second hand. Over the years I have come to see them as colleagues who puzzled over the same issues as we do. Very often something I was doing myself or something that a friend was working on was the key to understanding an important historical line of thought. Sometimes it was the other way about. A historical insight was the key to a contemporary puzzle. For me there has been a dialectic between the contemporary and the historical to which I want now to give a more definite shape. The large secondary literature on each of the writers we will encounter is, nearly always, written by scholars whose basic interests are remote from those of present-day experimental psychologists. There is also a place for a study of the historical figures as seen through the eyes of a contemporary experimentalist/theorist.

Not that I will offer unusual or novel interpretations of historical figures. Nothing could be further from my mind. With one exception, I will propose the standard interpretation of each author, precisely because it was that understanding that had an impact on theories of the human mind. Any originality there may be in the book is in the contact made with the experimental psychology of our own day and in the manner of evaluating a historical text. The one exception is in the chapter on gestalt psychology, because I believe that an essential element in the seminal work of the founder of gestalt psychology, Christian von Ehrenfels, has been overlooked.

I chose the authors, and I chose the issues to study in their writings. It is inevitable that there should be a subjective element in the choice. I have written only of figures that I felt I had come to know well enough to be able to relate them to contemporary work. And yet I hope that historians of ideas as well as contemporary psychologists who go through the book will agree on the importance of each of the figures chosen and each of the issues raised in their work. Disagreement is more likely to focus on omissions, and often I might well agree. I want it to be perfectly clear at the outset, however, that I am not attempting to write a comprehensive textbook on the history of psychology or a comprehensive history of any of the figures or movements I write about. Choice of a writer or issue indicates that I thought them illuminating for contemporary psychology; omission of a writer or issue does not mean I thought them unimportant. Limits were placed by the fact that the course was a single semester one: two lectures a week for twelve or thirteen weeks. There were also the limitations of my knowledge.

The book ends with two rather different, though contemporaneous, movements that began in the early years of this century: the behaviorist movement of John B. Watson and the gestalt movement of Max Wertheimer. After them it is more difficult to claim that some figure or movement is historical. Later figures seem rather to be part of the contemporary scene.

The book exclusively covers psychology in what is called the "West." It neglects Muslim thinkers who were influential on the development of medieval theories of the mind. These Muslim thinkers include in their number the Sufi mystics, but alas I did not feel I knew enough to say anything insightful about them. The same applies to the whole world of Buddhism, of which there are several forms. These movements did not greatly influence the development of contemporary Western psychology, which is not to say that the study of Sufi or Buddhist theories of the mind would be unrewarding for Western psychologists.

We have, then, 25 reflections on Western writers. There is a danger that so many lectures on as many great thinkers will be fragmentary and disjointed. I hope to have avoided the danger by concentrating on a few psychological themes. In fact, I seldom move beyond the theory of cognition and high-level perception. It might be, then, that a charge of narrowness of coverage, rather than disjointedness, would be more in place. This narrowness is to some extent justified by the fact that the academic subject of psychology was far narrower in earlier times than it is today. Perhaps the only major subject in traditional psychology that I have omitted is the theory of the will. Still, I find that I have more than enough to deal with in perception and cognition. Again in the interests of continuity, as well as comprehensibility, I have drastically restricted the number of technical terms, and those I do introduce continue to be used throughout. I define each as I go along, and as an aid for students, I collect the definitions, sometimes in slightly expanded form, at the end of the book in the Glossary.

The book derives further unity from the fact that in the early chapters four major themes are identified: Plato's problems of learning and truth, Aristotle's principled delimitation of cognition, and St. Augustine's problem about the mind's access to idealizations. These are explained in the proper places. One idea of the book is to trace the treatment of these themes across the ages to the present time—not that each author will be studied for his treatment of all four, but that in each author one or more of the themes will be raised. Sometimes the task will be to see how an author offers an interesting new approach to a theme; sometimes it will be to study how an author has evaded a theme or failed to see it. Another recurrent theme from Hobbes on is the effects of deciding to do psychology on the model of some other science: kinematics, mechanics, chemistry, biology, or computer science.

The reader will find that my own views of perception, learning, and cognition influence how I read a text and how I evaluate its contribution. I have written extensively on practically all the issues that come up for discussion, but I do not expect the reader to have read what I and my collaborators have written. I scarcely refer to those sources. Instead, I have attempted the difficult task of writing each evaluation so that an intelligent reader who has not read another line I or any commentator has written may be able to understand the evaluation and see some of the reasons for it. Indeed, I hope that in going through these reflections, readers will come to appreciate (even if they do not accept) a perhaps different idea of what the core problems of psychology are and how to go about solving them. At any rate, such an idea runs through the book, so much so that I have been urged by my friends and collaborators, Marie La Palme Reyes and Gonzalo Reyes, to add a final chapter bringing together the theory that has guided evaluations throughout and presenting that theory in more graspable form. This is a daring departure in a book of historical reflections. Nevertheless, I have added a final chapter along the lines they suggest. It balances the first chapter, which is a general Introduction, and to mark that fact I have called it, fancifully, an "Extroduction."

Acknowledgments

My first word of gratitude goes to my graduate student Geert-Jan Boude-wijnse, who has three times been my teaching assistant for the course Modern Psychology in Historical Perspective. He it was who persuaded me to write up my lectures in their present form. The immediate stimulus was a severe threat to my health in the fall of 1992. In the end the threat was groundless, but Geert-Jan seemed to urge the evangelical counsel: work while it is still day, for the night cometh when no man can work. He and I together made a special study of the origins of the gestalt movement in psychology, a study whose fruits are presented in the appropriate chapter.

I owe a debt to all my teaching assistants over the years, especially Leslie McPherson, who was the first to teach this material with me and was an enthusiastic supporter of the importance of developing a new approach to the history of psychology. Also to all the students who took the course and showed by their questions or puzzlement where I had not made myself clear. Many passages, otherwise unacknowledged, were provoked by the silent protests of confused students. These students also wrote term papers on some of the topics covered in the chapters. I also learned from these papers.

My wife, the acutest of critics, took part of the course one year and read substantial portions of the text, pencil in hand. Others who read portions and commented include Marie La Palme Reyes and Gonzalo E. Reyes, James O. Ramsay, and George A. Ferguson. My indebtedness to these friends is continually mounting in more ways than I can list. They encouraged my belief in the interest of the ideas presented in the text.

They also persuaded me to adopt toward contemporary psychology a more conciliatory tone than I was inclined to.

Several publishers to whom I submitted portions of the manuscript suggested that to be in tune with the content of courses in the history of psychology I should drastically reduce, if not eliminate entirely, discussions of philosophical writings on psychology. My reaction was firm and immediate: if there is an imbalance, it is in the standard courses on the history of psychology, not in my book. On the other hand, I received encouragement from the senior editors of several publishing houses: Angela von der Lippe of Harvard University Press, Julia Hough of Cambridge University Press, and senior editors of Oxford University Press and of Basil Blackwood. I am grateful to them for the interest they took in a manuscript that they had no intention of recommending to their houses. In the end it was Harry Stanton of the MIT Press who made me the first firm offer to publish. I accepted immediately. I did so the more readily for the fact that Harry Stanton had published two earlier books of mine, *Names for Things* and *A Border Dispute,* and I had very much enjoyed working with him and his wife, Betty.

All of the material in this book is new in the sense that it is published here for the first time. Portions of the chapter on Hobbes, however, appeared in an article called "Ideals and psychology," published in *Canadian Psychology,* 1990. Portions of the chapter on Brentano appeared in the article "The rejection of Brentano and cognitive psychology," published in *The Journal for the Theory of Social Behavior,* 1993. Portions of the chapter on Freud appeared in a review article of Paul Roazen's *Meeting Freud in His Family* that I wrote for the *Literary Review of Canada,* December 1994. I am grateful to the editors of those periodicals for permission to use the material that had appeared in their pages. Several people read the piece on Freud for me: Richard Koestner, Norman White, David Zuroff, and others. Not everyone who read it was as laudatory of it as I would have wished; I learned a good deal from discussions about what people thought amiss.

Over the years I have had the extraordinary good fortune of having Judi Young as my secretary. She types up the first version of all my manuscripts. She is patient, wise (having to work for several professors all with fair-sized egos), accurate, and able to read my handwriting. As I write these words, I ask myself if there is anything else that I ought to say about her. Nothing comes to mind, except that she is invariably charming and good humored. Nothing I write seems to say precisely what I would like to say: I can only hope that Judi realizes how much I appreciate her and how grateful I am to her. She made the preparation of this manuscript appear like child's play; she also ensured that it was a pleasure.

Over the time of the preparation of this manuscript I have had the financial support of yearly individual grants from NSERC (National Research Council for Engineering and Science); with Gonzalo E. Reyes, a collaborative research grant from FCAR (the Quebec organization covering, more or less, the same research areas as NSERC); and with Gonzalo E. Reyes, Brendan Gillon, and Michael Makkai, an NSERC interdisciplinary collaborative research grant. This financial support has meant that we could tackle projects that might otherwise have daunted us. It also meant that we had the collaboration of a gifted group of postdocs, notably: Houman Zolfaghari, Richard Squire, and Marie La Palme Reyes. Some of the money was used to support graduate students: Dean Sharpe, David Nicolas, Geert-Jan Boudewijnse, who contributed more to the book than is elsewhere acknowledged. I wish, then, to record my gratitude to these funding bodies.

For some years I have had a close connection with Polish psychologists. When the manuscript was ready, I gave a copy to Prof. Ida Kurcz, professor of cognitive psychology in Warsaw University and in the Polish Academy of Sciences. She liked it and asked if she might send it to Dr. M. Zagrodski with a view to having it translated into Polish. Dr. Zagrodski had previously translated my *Border Dispute* into Polish and seen the translation through the press. I naturally agreed and was delighted to hear in due course that, funds permitting, Dr. Zagrodski would arrange for a translation being made and published. This was encouraging at a time when I still did not have an English publisher. The Polish move also encouraged English publishers to look more carefully at the text, if only to see what had taken the Poles' fancy.

Through the Rearview Mirror

1

Introduction: Three Very General Observations on Psychology and Its History

There is a view, fostered it seems by folklore in departments of psychology, that psychology proper began in 1879 when Wilhelm Wundt opened the first laboratory for psychological experiment. There were forerunners, to be sure, and psychology students generally have some impression about them. If they have taken courses in philosophy, they may know some of them reasonably well. I sometimes sense a certain impatience with these forerunners, however, and some psychologists seem to regard them in much the same way that modern chemists regard alchemists, who are the chemists' forerunners. Chemists demarcate the difference between the marginal forerunners and the serious ones by calling the one alchemists and the other early chemists. I also sense that some psychologists employ the word "philosopher" to speak about Wundt's forerunners with something like the force and flavor that attaches to the word "alchemist." Now Wundt was a philosopher; the only chair he ever held was in philosophy. But then he was a prominent contributor to physiology, and he was a serious experimenter in psychology. Much is forgiven him because he is a transitional figure, from philosophy to psychology, and some latitude must be allowed to those who effect such transitions. After all, the story goes, he is the father of psychology.

This widely held view strikes me as a serious distortion of fact. It is easy to discover this by comparing Aristotle's psychology (in *De anima*) with his physics (in the *Physics*). The *Physics* contains much that is of philosophical interest, but its physics has almost all been scrapped. With good reason, because its theories of space, of time, of the motions of physical bodies, and of their basic constituents is simply wrong. The same cannot be said of his *De anima*. I venture to say that it is still the most important book for any psychologist to read, not just for its place in the history of ideas but for the relevance of its teachings on perception and cognition to contemporary work in those areas.

A word of warning! Reading Aristotle is like chewing rocks, neither pleasant nor easy. His polished works all perished, and only his lecture notes survive—not a distinguished form of literary composition. Something of the interest of the notes on psychology will emerge, I hope, when we come to Aristotle. I hope to suggest their depth and importance, whether or not in the end you accept them.

For present purposes, though, all we need is the comparison with the *Physics*. It gives the lie to the almost automatic claim that psychology is a new discipline whereas physics is an old one. Psychology as a serious, systematic discipline is almost 2,000 years older than physics. In comparison, modern chemistry is a fledgling, merely 200 years old. Incidentally, the word "psychology" was coined only at the end of the eighteenth century. Earlier generations called the discipline by its object of study: "on the soul," "on the mind," or simply "on human understanding."

One may protest that physics and chemistry have made more spectacular advances than psychology, and while these things are difficult to assess, I would be inclined to agree. If the protest is true, however, it may well indicate a moral. Psychology is not an easy subject. If it were, perhaps the progress over 2,000 years would have been more substantial. It should not surprise us, then, to find that it is as difficult as anything in physics. Even in these historical exercises we should be prepared to use our conceptual powers to their utmost.

Another protest is sure to surface. The psychology of the ancients was not experimental or systematically observational, whereas contemporary psychology is both. This protest too is justified, but it does not mark as deep a divide as one might think. People have been observing psychological phenomena of all sorts since the beginning of human experience: children learning to talk, perceptual illusions, feats of memory and failures of memory, struggles to solve problems, differences in personality, behavior disorders and mental illnesses. Doubtless in all these areas and others, experiment, systematic observation and measurement aided by statistical techniques, can bring increased precision and deepen understanding. At the same time it is possible to reach profoundly interesting positions in psychology on the basis of everyday experience and observation. As a matter of fact, Aristotle fared better in his psychology based on everyday experience than in his physics based on everyday experience. Perhaps the difference is that we have access to the intuitions of the objects of study in psychology but not to those (if there are any) of the objects of study in physics. The topic of intuition will recur.

Whatever the explanation, before the days of experiment and statistics, thinkers of genius were able to write psychology that still repays reading. And there were many such. Almost every great figure in Western thought until well after the Scientific Revolution, say until 1650, wrote on psychology. Sometimes the motivation was the relevance of psychology to medicine, law, theology, or pedagogy; sometimes it seems to have been the intrinsic interest of the subject. I have sometimes wondered whether the psychology that prevails in a society does not characterize that society in its most fundamental aspects. Surely the predominant view or views of what a human being is are the core of a civilization, and psychology is one of the key contributors to and constituents of those views. An illuminating example is the American Declaration of Independence and the view of human nature that inspired its most influential phrases.

Before going further, we should try to understand the conception of psychology that entitles Plato and Aristotle as well as professors in modern psychology departments to the title "psychologist." The central phenomena have always been human knowledge and beliefs and human desires as guided by knowledge and beliefs. For convenience I will refer to all these as beliefs and desires, and I will say a word of explanation about them presently. First, I want to stress their centrality. Whether or not some other aspect of human functioning was considered "psychological" depended on the intimacy of its relation to beliefs and desires. This ruled out breathing and ruled in perception, because our perceptual systems are one of the main sources of beliefs. It ruled in memory and imagination, because memory stores beliefs and decisions, and imagination displays them and their possibilities for the realization of desires. It ruled in hunger, thirst, the needs for warmth, shelter, security, and love, and all those drives that we embrace under the word "motivation," because these are the moving forces behind desires. It ruled in emotion as an intimate accompaniment of belief and desire, indeed as influencing drives or as constituting a drive in its own right.

I should immediately add that psychology was rarely concerned about why people held one belief and not another or why they chose one course of action rather than another. It was deeply concerned about the form that beliefs took and how they made contact with the extramental world. It was also concerned about how the various components interact: whether, for example, the content of belief is given in perceptual experience; whether perception and cognition are of a piece or whether their theories are distinct; whether there are innate beliefs and desires; the nature of learning. To make the point more vivid, psychology was more concerned with the apparatus of the mind than with the particular uses to which the apparatus is put—just as an anatomist is concerned about the skeletal and muscular structures of the body and how they function together, rather than about the particular purposes to which they are put, such as walking to work or playing tennis.

Psychologists, as psychologists, have not attempted to justify desires as ethical or beliefs as veridical. These matters were dealt with in ethics and in what came to be called, not so very long ago, "epistemology." Psychologists considered it the job of psychology to explain the presence in the human mind of an ethical intuition and, among other things relevant to the truth of beliefs, of a logical intuition.

Most of the psychologists we will meet were also metaphysicians; that is, they studied being and its fundamental divisions. For example, they asked themselves whether change is real and whether to explain it one had to posit cause as a reality, cause as something more that the regular and close succession (or constant conjunction, to use Hume's phrase) of perceptual phenomena. Metaphysics and psychology constrain each other. If I as a metaphysician claim that there is causality over and above constant perceptual conjunction, I must surely claim that I can somehow detect such causality. How otherwise could I argue for the reality of cause? But then I must in my psychology make provision for knowledge that goes beyond the purely perceptual. On the other hand, if my psychology rules out any such knowledge, I must also, to be consistent, renounce any right to claim that causality of the sort we are discussing is real. My purpose in giving this illustration is not to argue for any metaphysical or psychological position but simply to bring out the interdependence of the two disciplines. Interdependence, however, is not identity. None of the figures we study identifies psychology with metaphysics, with the exception of Bishop Berkeley (and perhaps Hume). Notoriously, Berkeley identified reality with perception. To distinguish psychology and metaphysics is the rule rather than the exception.

The reasons for studying the history of psychology are probably as varied as the people who study it. One reason that seems to have escaped attention derives from the relation between psychology and metaphysics. Whether they know it or not, students of perception and cognition adopt some metaphysical position. Usually it is the metaphysics that prevails at the time they are working. They adopt it, for the most part, inadvertently, by a sort of intellectual osmosis. It is not by chance that behaviorism, which neglected, or at least downplayed, beliefs and desires in the ordinary understanding of those words, flourished at the same time as logical positivism, which regarded all metaphysics as airy nonsense. One of the benefits of studying the history of psychology is that it introduces a variety of psychologies, each in conjunction with a compatible metaphysics. This exercise provides, in a relatively painless manner, perspectives on the metaphysical positions that are implicit in the psychology of the day. It renders us more sensitive to the metaphysical implications of our own psychological positions.

The history of psychology also shows us where certain psychological positions lead. We owe it to the genius and honesty of David Hume that if we insisted on perceptual proof for every belief, as he did, we would have to give up the belief that we exist when we are asleep. Obviously, we cannot have perceptual confirmation of our own existence during periods of unconsciousness. David Hume asked, What can we believe if we believe only what our perceptual systems tell us? He had the courage not to shy away from the answer: that we lose the right to believe in the sort of personal identity that we all assume. The significance of this is that if we do not accept the conclusion, we must change the psychology. There has to be a compatibility between the metaphysics and the psychology. It is fair to say that in Hume psychology has priority over metaphysics. He, more than anyone else I know, worked out the consequences. It seems to me that many psychologists today adopt Hume's psychology while refusing to adopt his metaphysics. It might be that the resulting theory is coherent, but its coherence needs a defense that is responsive to Hume's arguments and concerns. All of this constitutes a reason to study Hume, who in this context is merely a particular illustration motivating a much more general claim.

Whatever the usefulness of studying the history of psychology might be, it must be conceded that students of physics or chemistry today are seldom required to study the history of their subjects. Why, one may ask, should things be different in psychology? I cannot speak for physics or chemistry, although some of my physicist and chemist friends lament the absence of a historical dimension in the education of their students. Be that as it may, psychology students are in urgent need of the history of their subject. I will offer just a single example. The prevailing modern psychological theory of concepts represents concepts as a set of features *abstracted* from the perceptual array. Forming the concept of a dog, for example, is understood as abstracting from perceptual presentations of dogs those features that are common to dogs. To form the concept of an animal is to abstract those features that are common to animals. Animal features are thought to be a proper subset of dog features because dogs, being animals, should possess all animal features, but since not all animals are dogs, some dog features must be dropped to form the concept of an animal, namely those dog features that do not belong to all animals. This position has much that is wrong with it, as we will see, and it ran into serious difficulties. These difficulties are not the point here. The point is that the theory showed insensitivity to a tradition, going back at least to Plato, that discusses what a concept is and how it is formed. In particular, one of the first pieces that St. Thomas Aquinas wrote, *De ente et essentia,* refuted the modern theory in anticipation. To stick with our example, Aquinas held that the set of properties in virtue of which we claim that Freddie, say, is a dog are exactly the same as those in virtue of which we claim he is an animal. It matters not, for the moment, that the properties Aquinas envisaged as entering into concepts are not immediately given in perception. The point is that animal properties are not a proper subset of dog properties. Those in virtue of which a creature is an animal are a perceptual system, a locomotive system, a digestive system, and so on. Those in virtue of which it is a dog are a canine perceptual system, a canine locomotive system, a canine digestive system, and so on. To find out what makes a creature a dog, we repeat everything we mentioned for animal, but we describe each in a more specific manner. In support of this Aquinas noted that a proper part of a dog cannot be predicated of a dog: we cannot correctly say, "A dog is a head." We can, however, correctly say, "A dog is an animal." Aquinas concluded that animal cannot denote a proper part of dog. This makes obvious difficulties for the whole modern account of abstraction.

We will come back to this theme. All I want to indicate here is that the history of psychology helps to make people aware of the presuppositions of their research practices and of their theories. Being aware of them and of some alternatives engenders greater rationality, greater control. The history of psychology also ought to alert people to some foreseeable pitfalls and blind alleys. But apart from all this, there is the simple depth and value of the psychological insights that observers of genius have extracted. The writings we will look at are not museum pieces; they are important for what they can contribute to present-day understanding of the mind.

To sum up, I claim (1) that psychology is among the oldest of the sciences with a rich history to which many scholars of extraordinary ability have contributed, (2) that across this tradition, beliefs and belief-informed desires have been at the core and other human capacities were considered psychological if they were intimately related to our apparatus for forming beliefs and desires, our apparatus for representing them, and our apparatus for acting upon them, (3) that we can expect to benefit from a knowledge of the history of psychology in that it can throw light on the presuppositions of present research practices and the theories that have been erected with their aid. History offers us a range of alternatives for consideration. We can reasonably hope that a knowledge of history should deepen our theorizing and guide us away from pursuing what history has shown to be blind alleys.

2

Plato on Learning

Biographical Note

Plato (428–347 B.C.) was an Athenian of noble family who was a member of what we would nowadays call the Socrates seminar. At the age of 40 he founded a school called "The Academy"—from which the words "academy," "academic," and "academe" come. Plato directed this school until his death and numbered Aristotle among his students. The Academy lasted some 900 years (longer than the University of Paris). He left in the form of dialogues one of the largest and most influential bodies of philosophical writings that survives from the ancient world.

The word "learning" is used to cover a wide and complex range of phenomena. We say that we learned English, learned our way around a new city, learned to cycle a bicycle, and learned that Mozart wrote 41 symphonies. The sort of learning that we are studying in this chapter is of the type exemplified by the last item. It is sometimes called "learning-that" to distinguish it from "learning-how," which has to do with skills. At any rate, the learning that concerns us here is of the type that results in new items of knowledge, in new beliefs, or in changes to old beliefs, and thus has an intimate relation with action.

Learning is a theme in many of Plato's dialogues, but here we will look at just one, the *Meno*. Its special importance is that it proposes a problem for any theory of learning. The force of the problem is that learning is either impossible or useless, which would imply that there is no learning of the type in question.

It is important to understand the role of such problems in theory construction. On the face of things, they usually take the form of demonstrating that a seemingly innocent position leads to contradiction. If the problem is deep and well constructed, it cannot be brushed aside. It challenges the theory builder to dig deeper, to reexamine suppositions, to reformulate questions, to get around the seeming contradiction—or to give in. It matters little whether the proposer of the problem believes that the contradiction is real; what matters is that the problem challenges and sets new standards for theory building. Plato's problem of learning should be familiar to every psychologist.

The general setting is a question that Meno puts to Socrates, the question "Is virtue something that can be taught? Or does it come by practice?" Socrates observes that in order to answer, they should first inquire into what virtue is. Various definitions are proposed and each in turn is shown to be unsatisfactory because examples are produced to show that the proposal is either too broad or too narrow; it either accepts as virtuous, actions that are obviously not virtuous or it rejects actions that are obviously virtuous, at least by the lights of the participants in the discussion. The participants thus find themselves in the curious position of seeming not to know what virtue is because they fail to define it, while at the same time knowing what it is well enough to think up clearly recognizable examples of virtue and vice. In the end they wonder whether virtue is not a gift of the gods that some people have by "divine dispensation." For what it is worth, this strikes me as a ploy for bringing the discussion to an end. Fortunately, our interest in the dialogue lies elsewhere.

At one juncture, when they have exhausted their ideas for a definition of virtue, Socrates says that he simply does not know what virtue is but that he is prepared to carry out "a joint investigation and inquiry into what it is." At this Meno returns,

But how will you look for something when you don't in the least know what it is? How on earth are you going to set up something you don't know as the object of your search? To put it another way, even if you come right up against it, how will you know that what you have found is the thing you didn't know? (*Meno*, 80d)

This gives Socrates the opportunity to state the problem of learning.

I know what you mean. Do you realize that what you are bringing up is the trick argument that a man cannot try to discover either what he knows or what he does not know? He would not seek what he knows, for since he knows it there is no need of the inquiry, nor what he does not know, for in that case he does not even know what he is looking for. (*Meno,* 80e)

Although it arises in the attempt to say what virtue is, the form of the problem is perfectly general. It is instructive to test the problem of knowledge in far simpler contexts, like attempting to say what a chair is. People are ready to volunteer definitions, but others are equally ready to point to counterexamples. There is the curious combination of ignorance, at least when a definition is required, and knowledge, as displayed in the choice of counterexamples.

Does the problem apply in the domain of observation and experiment? Well, take a seemingly simple phenomenon. Suppose the chain keeps coming off your bicycle. You examine it and notice that the chain looks loose. Perhaps you experiment by removing one link and discover that the trouble disappears. Do you now know what caused the chain to come off? By no means. All you have done, probably, is to prevent the troublesome factor(s) from operating. There surely is no law that loose chains come off. Frequently you go along quite well with a loose chain and then it comes off. Notice, however, that you had to know that the looseness of the chain might be relevant. Otherwise, there would be nothing to prevent you from experimenting with such possible factors as the color of the bicycle or the direction you were cycling in. In all probability, serious inquirers would study irregularities in the chain, in the wheels over which it ran, in the alignment of these wheels to one another, in the mechanism for changing gears and its operation. How do people know that these are the likely sources of trouble? Experience! One can almost hear the reply. But that is no answer, since we are studying how experience leads to knowledge.

Whatever Plato thought, none of this is meant to show that learning is impossible. It is meant to show that there are no easy ways out of the problem. Appeals to experience simply miss the point. If there is learning, and I believe there is, experience surely plays a part. But how? That is what the problem invites us to specify, and in so doing, to deepen our understanding of learning. The reader should be warned that philosophers of science generally find the process of scientific discovery utterly mysterious. So mysterious that Karl Popper, in *The Logic of Scientific*

Discovery (1959), concluded that science progresses by falsifying hypotheses. Scientists propose hypotheses that they can never prove, he felt, but that they can sometimes disprove. That was the best he felt he could do with the problem of inquiry. Popper's idea is familiar to psychologists as that of rejecting the null hypothesis. In the example before us, we might feel entitled to reject the null hypothesis that the looseness of the chain had nothing to do with the trouble. We would then deem it highly probable that the looseness had something to do with it—a useful piece of information but hardly enough to satisfy a scientist.

One may feel that scientific discovery is especially obscure, so let us change our attention to more elemental forms of learning. W. V. O. Quine (1960) devised a celebrated modern version of the problem featuring a linguist learning a word (seemingly) for rabbit in a quite unfamiliar language. To bring some freshness, here is another example. My wife and I once fostered a nine-year-old Korean boy named Pyung-wa who came to Montreal for heart surgery. He knew not a word of English at the outset, nor we a word of Korean. One morning my wife made scrambled eggs which drew from Pyung-wa an expression that sounded to us like "joa." For some reason we took it to be a word in Korean, rather than an exclamation like our "Wow!" Let that pass, and join us in wondering what the word meant. We daringly decided, on no very adequate grounds, that it had something to do with scrambled eggs, rather than, say, Orion's Belt or Montreal. But what? Did "joa" mean scrambled eggs or eggs; did it mean food or hot food; did it mean plate of food or plate of scrambled eggs or portion of scrambled eggs; did it mean hot, yellow, tasty, nasty, good? Did it mean physical object on a plate or physical object of just that shape? One needs little imagination to continue the possibilities indefinitely. Quine, however, shows that matters might be worse than the examples hitherto given suggest, for we might wonder whether by "joa" this boy meant a time slice of scrambled egg or an undetached portion of scrambled egg. The lesson is that since the possibilities to test are infinitely or at least indefinitely numerous, along these lines we could not find out in our lifetime what "joa" meant.

Why not consult a Korean who knew English? No reason whatever not to, but that merely sends one back a step to how this Korean learned what "joa" meant (and what the proffered English equivalent meant).

For that matter, how did Pyung-wa learn what it meant? Socrates would say that either he knew what it meant, and so did not have to learn it, or he could not have learned it in the time available. No use impatiently exclaiming that he learned it and there's an end of it. For that simply leaves the problem of how he learned it untouched. Until one has wrestled with the problem, one has not even taken the first step in the construction of a worthwhile theory of learning.

Notice that Popper's strategy is not helpful. If we were to propose possible interpretations without an idea of which was likely to be correct, we could not be confident of striking on the right one before the end of the universe. And even if we were lucky enough to strike upon it in our lifetime, Socrates would demand to know how we would recognize it as being correct. Of course, this is exactly what Popper would say, but this answer is unsatisfactory on the reasonable assumption that, however we explain it, Pyung-wa had managed to *learn* the meaning of the word.

Plato's own solution when he wrote the *Meno* was that we do not learn such items of information at the time we come to be able to employ them; we recollect them. He suggests that the soul picked up such items prior to its union with the body, items that lie inaccessible until they are elicited by suitable experience. People who read this today often replace the soul's existence prior to union with the body with the process of evolution. Noam Chomsky is well known for proposing that there are genetically communicated constraints controlling the learning of a language. Something of the sort seems inevitable, but stating it thus is utterly inadequate. Chomsky and his coworkers have attempted to be quite specific about the form of the constraints.

First, let us look at Plato's own reason for adopting this position, which he puts in the mouth of Socrates. Plato's reason is the contrast between the inability to define virtue and the ability to give counterexamples to proffered definitions. The interlocutors seemed both to know and not to know what virtue is. It seemed that what guided the successful choice of counterexamples and led to their recognition as such was an idea of virtue that was not directly accessible to consciousness. What was more natural than to propose that the knowledge that Socrates and Meno sought existed in the mind and that they were merely attempting to recall it? This is the famous theory of learning as recollection or reminiscence.

To strengthen this line of solution, Plato has Socrates draw out from an uneducated slave boy the solution to a problem in geometry: find a line whose square is eight square units. Socrates draws diagrams in the sand and leads the slave boy to the conclusion that the answer is the line joining the center points of two adjacent sides of a square on a line that is four units long. The details of the exercise, though interesting in many ways, need not detain us. The point was that the slave boy could see that the solution was necessarily correct. Where, then, did he acquire the mathematical and logical knowledge that enabled him to see that? Not from teachers, because slaves had no teachers. The moral we are to draw is that it was lying dormant in his mind waiting to be elicited by suitable experience.

There are inadequacies with this solution, and they led Plato to abandon it, at least as a comprehensive explanation. One obvious one is how to explain how the soul learned the knowledge in a previous existence. He has no suggestion for how the soul in isolation from the body could have learned what it could not learn with the body's assistance. The statement of this problem did not confine the difficulty to an embodied soul. What about genes? The same problem applies. All that evolution offers in this connection is random drift in the genes coupled with natural selection. That merely states that creatures in whom the genes had created the necessary preconditions for reminiscence would have a survival advantage over creatures not so endowed. It seems reasonable that creatures who could learn a language would have an advantage, but no light whatever is thrown on how they came to be that way. The appeal to random genetic drift indicates a failure to explain. We say a process is random when a certain sort of insight fails.

Another well-known problem relates to the selection of the appropriate item of information from a sea of supposedly stored items. It is difficult to say how many items an adult might know, and not only because we are not sure what to count as one item. For what it is worth, some authors estimate than an educated adult knows about 100,000 words. Suppose that we set the number of items of information for an adult at a conservative 50,000, and suppose that they existed from infancy in the adult's mind, as the theory of reminiscence requires. How does the adult know which item to recall on a particular occasion? How could my wife and

I know which item to recall as the rule for interpreting "joa" in the mouth of Pyung-wa? I am making the simplifying assumption that "joa" in Korean has an equivalent in English, but that does not help substantially. There are still too many possibilities.

I have spent a large part of my adult life puzzling about how children learn the meanings of the words they pick up in their mother tongue. I am not attracted by Quine's main line of a solution, which denies the existence of meanings. Nor am I attracted by the approach of present-day Platonists (here Jerry Fodor 1975 is often mentioned), as they deny that concepts can be learned. Yet in all my work I feel the presence of Plato in the wings, countering my tentative theories with the problem of inquiry. In working through the issues, what is surprising is the amount of unlearned structure that must be posited. There is no simple way around the problem. This has been the experience of others who have accepted the challenge of giving a precise account of word learning. Today there is a new spirit among workers on cognitive development that in general tendency, if not in detail, shows sensitivity to the concerns of the *Meno*.

In this chapter I introduced the problem of inquiry. Briefly put, it is this: there is no need to learn what one already knows, and there is no use trying to learn what one does not know, because even if one were to chance upon what one was looking for, one would not be in a position to recognize it as the object of one's search. I brought out the force of the problem by considering the learning of a single word in a foreign language. I showed that appeals to genetics to solve the problem, while probably justified, are woefully inadequate. I ended by saying that contemporary theories of cognitive development go a long way to vindicate the core of Plato's insight.

Bibliographical Note

Plato (1961). *The Collected Dialogues of Plato.* Edited by E. Hamilton and H. Cairns. Princeton: Princeton University Press. The most convenient source for Plato's work. The main dialogue for this chapter is the *Meno*.

Popper, K. R. (1968). *The Logic of Scientific Discovery.* 2nd ed. New York: Basic Books.

3

Plato on Truth and Knowledge

A recurring theme in many of Plato's dialogues is knowledge and truth (see, for example, the *Phaedo, Republic, Phaedrus,* and *Theaetetus,* which some scholars believe were written in that order). The connection between knowledge and truth is not hard to find. If I am justified in claiming that I know who directed a certain movie, then it must be that my belief in the matter is true. If I suspect the possibility that my belief is erroneous, I should not claim that I know who directed the movie, only that I believe it was so and so. Plato was much concerned with the contrast between knowledge and belief. I will emphasize what they have in common. While knowledge has a special link with truth, it makes perfect sense to ask of any belief whether it is true. Both cognitive states can be evaluated for truth.

One of the things that most impressed Plato about truths is their permanence. He firmly believed that sentences like "2 + 2 = 4" are not only true, but that they are eternally true. The same applies to "Dogs are animals"; if this sentence is true now, it is true forever. It will not change truth values if dogs become extinct. "Dinosaurs are animals" is no less true despite the fact that dinosaurs are extinct.

While Plato was mainly occupied with what we might call necessary truths, he also realized that there are humbler truths. Take the following sentence:

(1)   Charles de Gaulle was born in France.

It expresses no scientific law, and yet it will always be true that Charles de Gaulle was born in France, even if historical records to prove it are destroyed. It would then be impossible for people to ascertain where he was born, but it will nonetheless be true that he was born in France.

The puzzle is, since our perceptual systems present objects (like Charles de Gaulle and France) as fleeting and changeable, what explains the unchanging nature of truths that involve these things? De Gaulle was born and died; France in its modern form dates only from the end of the first world war. The truth about de Gaulle's birthplace will outlast them both.

Perceptual properties are especially changeable and fleeting. A dog's color, weight, characteristic sounds, and characteristic movements change appreciably as it progresses from puppyhood to old age. They cease altogether when the dog dies and is buried. The appearance of even mountains changes daily, depending on where they are viewed from, weather conditions, and cloud cover. They disappear altogether on a dark night.

Plato seems fully justified in contrasting the changeability of the perceptual array with the unchanging character of truth. We must remember that many of our own cognitive states express truths that were true before we were born and that will remain true after our death. This incommensurability of truth and the objects that ground it deserves a name of its own. I like to call it "the problem of truth" to distinguish it from the problem of inquiry.

It is important to avoid being tripped up in this connection by sentences with indexicals in them. Sentences like (2) depend for their truth value on who is speaking and when.

(2)   I was in Montreal yesterday.

They achieve a permanent truth value only when the indexical expressions are given particular interpretations, as in (3):

(3)   Emma Thompson was in Montreal on 20 December 1993.

Then the sentence is as permanent in truth value as any. Permanent truth, in this context, is not to be confused with deep or important truth.

When I expound the problem of truth, it is not uncommon for alert students to say that truths depend on sentences to express them. This is meant to lop off some of the permanence; the idea being that if there were no speakers of English, there would be no one to express sentences (1) or (3). In modern psychology many people believe that English sentences translate sentences in a language of thought, so they would concede that even if English speakers were all to perish, the same truth could be expressed in the language of thought. In any case they would allow that the same truth could be expressed in Chinese, Swahili, or any other natural language. And so they would allow that the truth in question would perdure until the extinction of the human race.

This line of thought seems muddled to me, since it confuses tokens of English sentences with their types. Tokens have physical existence, whereas types are abstract objects, that is, objects that exercise no causal activity and are not themselves affected by the causal activity of other things. Plato might have been prepared to concede that if there were no English speakers, there would be no tokens of English sentences. Yet he would have protested that his claim was based on types and was unaffected by the arrival and disappearance of English speakers. The matter is subtle, but fortunately it need not hold us up. In a conciliatory mood, let us suppose that "Charles de Gaulle was born in France" remains true only until the death of the last human being. We can still generate the problem, pointing to the incommensurability of transient things with the curtailed permanence of the truths concerning them. The problem loses little of its force.

What has this problem to do with psychology? After all, it is a metaphysical question to ask what gives to truth whatever permanence it has. And Plato's interests seem to have been mainly metaphysical. Indeed, he proposes (in the *Phaedo*) a metaphysical doctrine of eternal and immutable ideas to handle the permanence of truth. He believed that the objects one found in the world were imperfect copies of perfect and immutable ideas, where ideas are understood to be abstract objects, some of which serve as perfect prototypes for the objects of perceptual experience and all of which can give rise to knowledge (as opposed to opinion). The immutability of the ideas accounted for the immutability of truth.

Plato, however, is also sensitive to the psychological implications of his metaphysical theory. In the closing pages of book V of the *Republic* (p. 476 to the end), he distinguishes two psychological states to match the metaphysical distinction: knowledge, which pertains to the immutable forms, and opinion, which pertains to their copies in the world of ordinary experience. In any case the problem can be transposed into a psychological version.

The Problem of Truth—Psychological Version

Since the perceptual experience of human beings is of a world whose objects are temporary and changing, how can human beings relating to such objects grasp truths that they recognize as permanent?

This, it seems to me, is the deepest problem that a psychologist has to face. I am tempted to call it *the fundamental contradiction of psychology*—to use an expression suggested by my mathematician friends Gonzalo Reyes and Bill Lawvere.[1] Whatever the terminology, one can hardly overestimate the importance of the problem. To ignore it is to miss the main problem of cognition, and thus in some sense to miss the very heart of psychology. It is strange, then, to have to confess that I have never seen this problem mentioned, much less discussed, in contemporary psychological literature. I have seen a fine article by Walt Weimer (1973) on the problem of inquiry, but nothing on the deeper problem of truth— not even in the better manuals of the history of psychology. It makes no sense at all to dismiss the problem on the grounds that its author was a philosopher. One might as fairly dismiss all of Descartes's mathematical work on the grounds that he too was a philosopher.

Plato's own way of dealing with the problem was to downgrade perception and its objects and upgrade the eternal ideas. His famous analogy of the prisoners in the cave (in the *Republic,* book VII) has them at first looking the wrong way. They are facing the shadows of the ideas, not the ideas themselves. The way to set things to rights is to have them look the other way, but that is not at first a pleasant experience.

When one was freed from his fetters and compelled to stand up suddenly and turn his head around and walk and to lift eyes to the light, and in doing all this felt pain and, because of the dazzle and glitter of the light, was unable to discern objects whose shadows he formerly saw, what do you suppose would be his answer if someone told him that what he had seen before was all a cheat and an illusion, but that now, being nearer to reality and turned toward more real things, he saw more truly? . . . Do you not think that he would be at a loss and that he would regard what he formerly saw as more real than the things now pointed out to him? (*Republic,* book VII, 515c–d)

Obviously, the analogy is fanciful. For all that, it is highly illuminating about what goes on in science. Physicists, it is well known, spend prodigious amounts of time working on idealized, mathematical models of the phenomena that interest them. Their greatest achievements seem to take the form of mathematical abstractions. Although the point of departure may be a system of particles in motion in classical mechanics, the product is Hamilton's equations in the form of partial differential equations, and although the point of departure may be measurements of particles moving in a force field, the product is Schrödinger's equation. It is as though physicists must turn their backs on phenomena and turn to idealizations. Mathematics applies to physical systems only under idealizations: treating the mass of a body as a force acting through a geometrical point, treating the path of a projectile as a geometrical line, and so on. Plato writes as though mature scientists would not return to the phenomena, as though they would fasten their gaze exclusively on the idealizations and their mathematical description. This, of course, is not what happens. Mathematical treatment of the data suggests theories, and to choose among them, scientists must return to experiment and measurement. There is an iterative process of going from phenomena to idealization and back again.

Take another example. Crick and Watson were not experimenting or even directly studying experimental data when they discovered the double-helix structure of DNA. They were, naturally, immersed in the relevant findings, but at the moment of their discovery they were, in Watson's phrase, "fiddling with molecular models" (1968, 55). They were attempting to build an idealized model of reality. An indication of that fact is that the model they constructed was not a copy of any actual string of DNA but a model that rendered perspicuous the chemical language in which DNA is expressed and the principles by which the two helixes combine. When the main insight came, then, they had turned away from the phenomena and toward the abstract structure.

For many years one often heard the complaint, frequently from experimental psychologists, that the field was amassing a huge amount of data that did not seem to fall into anything like a theory of mind. To many it seemed that psychology lacked a unifying theory. The theories we had developed related to isolated pockets of data collected in experiments on the memorization of nonsense syllables, the memorization of English words, the perception of written English words, masking effects in perceptual experiments, and what have you.

With the advent of computer modeling, all that appeared to change, and psychologists tackled larger bodies of data. The Turing machine itself is a mathematical idealization of an effective procedure, including, it seems reasonable to add, an effective mental procedure. At any rate, it can reasonably be regarded as idealizing the class of formally correct proofs, and therefore merits the serious attention of psychologists interested in human reasoning. Nevertheless, computers do not interpret their symbols into the world outside the computer as we interpret our symbols into the world outside us. It follows that computers do not model the psychological ability that underlies the problem of truth: the ability to interpret a physical and changeable entity (say a token of a sentence) into a nonchanging and permanent truth. In some sense computers know nothing of truth, since they do not interpret their own states. They are, as the phrase has it, symbol crunchers and not semantic engines. It follows that they are not the appropriate idealization to help us with the problem of truth, though they are appropriate for other psychological purposes.

While Plato may have overstressed the value of abstractions, he certainly seems justified in drawing attention to their place in science. In the *Theaetetus* the bulk of the discussion goes to establishing that perception on its own is just not enough. Among the arguments offered is that we sometimes know past and future events, even at a time when there is no possibility of perceiving them. At one point Socrates puts the point dramatically: if perceiving were knowing, then perceiving utterances in a language that was unfamiliar would be the same as knowing what was said—which is clearly nonsense. The example helps to bring out the main point. One perceives fleeting strings of sounds; what they express may be permanent truths (or permanent falsehoods). Whatever one thinks of Plato's metaphysics, and there is surely something wrong with it, whatever one thinks of his theory of perception and its role in our mental lives, and it too is scarcely sustainable, nevertheless the problem to which he draws attention is of lasting and fundamental importance. For it surely is a fundamental property of the human mind that it can interpret a fleeting sentence as a nonfleeting, permanent truth.

Plato's problem of inquiry and his problem of truth will recur continually as we see one thinker after another attempting to grapple with them. It will be enough for now to have grasped them.

This chapter introduced two technical terms that we will need to carry with us, so I here begin the process of tying down certain terms.

Abstract object   These are objects that, exercising no causal activity and being unaffected by the causal activity of other things, are eternal and immutable. An obvious example is the number 3, or any number.

Platonic ideas   Plato proposed that some abstract objects, serve as the perfect prototypes of the objects we experience in perception. Knowledge, as opposed to mere opinion, is of these ideas, and they account for the immutability of truth. These abstract objects can be taken as corresponding to Platonic ideas. Platonic ideas must be distinguished from the ideas we have in our minds, but more of these at another time.

Bibliographical Note

Plato (1961). *The Collected Dialogues of Plato*. Edited by E. Hamilton and H. Cairns. Princeton: Princeton University Press. The main Platonic dialogues that formed the basis for the reflections of this chapter were the *Phaedo, Republic, Phaedrus,* and *Theaetetus*.

4

Aristotle on Knowledge and Understanding

Biographical Note

Aristotle (384–322 B.C.), son of the Macedonian king's physician, was born in Stagira (and hence is often called the Stagirite). He spent 20 years as a student in Plato's Academy, beginning when he was 17 and continuing until Plato's death in 347 B.C. The next few years seem to have been devoted to biological studies at Assos, where among other things he experimented on the foraging capacities of bees. In 342 B.C. he became the tutor of Alexander the Great. About 335 B.C. he opened in Athens a new school, which was housed in a gymnasium called the Lyceum. He and his followers were known as Peripatetics, from Aristotle's habit of walking as he taught. All that survives of Aristotle's writings are his lecture notes, not an attractive form of composition. His main work on psychology is *De anima* (On the mind).

Aristotle often learned the interesting problems from Plato, but he often did not accept Plato's approach to them, much less Plato's solutions. Aristotle's genius is mainly in laying down fruitful approaches to problems rather than in solving them. This is true of his handling of the problem of inquiry and the problem of truth.

In the *Meno* Socrates leads a slave boy to make a geometrical discovery and concludes that the slave boy must have known the solution all along, that he was merely recollecting it. At least that is the story that Plato tells. Aristotle could not accept the idea that there is no learning, that all the knowledge people ever have is innate. He did not have a solution for the problem of inquiry, but he was nevertheless convinced that there must be one. So, casting about for an approach that might lead to one, his attention was drawn to the diagram that Socrates drew in the sand. Here, he felt, was an important clue.

To recapture his insight, just imagine that you have to prove Pythagoras' theorem (in any right-angle triangle the square on the hypotenuse is equal in area to the sum of the squares on the other two sides). And suppose that you are not allowed to draw any figures for study or to imagine any. You see at once that the task is hopeless. Now, I understand that the theorems and proofs of Euclidean geometry can all be stated in general terms, without the use of any diagrams. Alfred Tarski, the great logician, used to give a course demonstrating this (personal communication from Gonzalo Reyes, who attended such a course). In some way, then, one can "do" Euclidean geometry without images of particular figures. It took a whole term, however, for Tarski to prove the first theorem of book 1 of *The Elements of Euclid*. In some way, the exclusion of particular examples (of particular points, lines, triangles, and so forth) runs counter to the natural functioning of the human mind. While in strict logic one can formulate the proofs without particular instances, one craves for particulars. In all probability, no theorems of geometry would be discovered without them.

Whatever the case with geometry, it is clear that no advance can be made in biology or physics without studying particulars. If the object is to understand the nature of bees, one must study some. Convinced of this, Aristotle laid down as a postulate that the mind is incapable of thinking without thinking of particulars. That is the force of "image" in the following passage: "No one can learn or understand anything in the absence of perception, and when the mind is actively aware of anything it is necessarily aware of it along with an image" (*De anima,* 431b, 6). Aristotle uses the word "perception" (I use that word instead of "sense," which is what the Oxford translation gives) to cover visual imagination as well as vision, hearing, and the other external perceptual systems. I am not sure whether Aristotle's postulate is inescapable. If we include under the rubric of "perception" all manner of symbols (including words) and all manner of diagrams, perhaps it is. At any rate, Aristotle's insistence on perceptual input seems preferable to Plato's disdain for it.

Is perception the answer, then? It cannot be the whole answer, although it is a crucial part of it. Aristotle learned too much from Plato to attempt to finesse the problem of truth with perception alone. He goes on to ask whether cognition is really of a piece with perception, as so many contemporary psychologists believe. Contemporary orthodoxy sees cognition merely as extended information processing: the supposed information being in the form of stimulation of perceptual organs at one level, being in the form of percepts at another level, and becoming cognitive upon further and perhaps deeper processing. Aristotle, in anticipation, will have none of this. He sharply delimits cognition from all other psychological states. Indeed, he has a criterion for judging whether a psychological state or activity is cognitive (*De anima*, 429b, 27).

Aristotle's criterion of cognition   Those mental states and events are cognitive in which "the alternative of true and false applies."

Since there can be no question of true and false at the level of stimulation of perceptual organs, this criterion separates such stimulation from cognition. For the rest, the criterion must be understood in the context of Aristotle's theory of perception, of which more in the next chapter. Suffice it for the present to say that Aristotle believed that the perceptual systems could not be mistaken in apprehending their primary objects. Cognitive states, however, all involve predication and thus have the property of being true or false.

Let us examine this more closely. Aristotle is well aware of a possible objection and asks us to consider the sun, which we "imagine to be a foot in diameter though we are convinced that it is larger than the inhabited part of the earth" (*De anima*, 428b, 3–4). Perception, then, can be misleading. But do the alternatives of true and false apply at the perceptual level? To examine this further I will replace the sun with the Müller-Lyer illusion (figure 4.1), largely for the sake of a familiar diagram. Certainly, the visual system presents the top line as shorter than the bottom one. Length of lines, however, is not the primary object of vision (which is

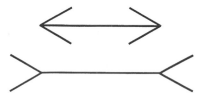

Figure 4.1
The Müller-Lyer illusion

color); in Aristotle's terminology length is a concomitant property, about which error is possible. Note in passing that the illusion is seen only when the visual system is working properly. If it failed to present the top line as shorter it would (for mysterious reasons) be malfunctioning. To return to our theme, we should distinguish between illusion and falsity. Aristotle's point is that falsity enters only if we judge that reality is as it appears to be, if we judge that the top line is shorter.

To make the point more forcefully, consider the Irish sentence in (1):

(1)   Tá sneachta bán.

The perception of (1) does not on its own suggest any truth or falsehood. Add syntactic information: "Tá" is (one form of) the copula in the present tense; "sneachta" is a mass noun; "bán" is an adjective predicated of "sneachta." One still has nothing (except, of course, the linguistic analysis of the sentence) that can be evaluated for truth. It is only when the words are given their proper interpretation that the notions of true and false have purchase. In fact, the sentence says that snow is white. It is true just in case snow has the property of being white.

One way to make Aristotle's point is to say that one can ask of percepts on their own whether they are well formed. Questions of truth arise only after percepts have been interpreted and a judgment formed. Put this way, Aristotle's criterion of the cognitive is clearly a forerunner of Noam Chomsky's autonomy thesis (see Chomsky, 1957, chap. 8). Chomsky maintains that we have an intuition of the grammaticality of a string of words that is independent of the interpretation of the string. We can read Aristotle as saying that we have an intuition of perceptibility that is independent of interpretation.

Aristotle's criterion for cognition is of capital importance for psychology. It implies that any line of research that neglects interpretation is not cognitive. It follows, for example, that physiological psychology cannot capture the core of cognition. From the perspective of physiological psychology the interpretation of cognitive states is invisible. From that perspective the most to be hoped for is the physical factors in the environment that caused some brain state or event and their effects in the brain. But the physical cause of my coming to know through vision that Freddie (the dog) is in the room is not the animal that bears the name

"Freddie." The physical cause in question is the configuration of electrons in a certain part of Freddie's exterior. But Freddie is still Freddie even if he is given a haircut and almost all those electrons are removed. Besides Freddie is mostly made up of interior parts, which are invisible. Clearly the physical cause of my perceptual knowledge is not the object of my judgment that Freddie is in the room.

Aristotle's criterion also raises problems for those in computer modeling who claim to be studying cognition. If Aristotle is right, they should ask themselves if they are modeling cognition at all. Whatever the answer to the more general question of whether in principle it is possible for a computer to interpret its symbols as human beings interpret theirs, there is broad agreement that at present computers do not do so. Grant this and grant the validity of Aristotle's criterion, and it follows that whatever they are doing, computer people are not modeling cognitive states or events. This is not for a moment to suggest that their work is irrelevant for psychology as a whole, because there are all sorts of psychological states and events that are not cognitive.

Is Aristotle's criterion for cognition correct? This is not the place to attempt to settle the matter definitively. As we continue our journey through these historical reflections, we will see several reasons for thinking that Aristotle was right. Suffice it for the moment to have drawn attention to the criterion and to have indicated its potential significance. [See the postscript to this chapter. For an explanation, see the preface.]

Aristotle's criterion of the cognitive seems very natural in a student of Plato's who was familiar with the problem of truth. What could be more natural than to assign those states and events that express truths to one of nature's special compartments? Yet the question of how the passage from perception to cognition proper is effected returns with renewed force. To emphasize perception as the main source of knowledge, as Aristotle does, is to invite the query about how to bridge the gap between the two.

First, a brief but necessary word on what happens to Plato's immutable forms in Aristotle's hands. Plato, remember, postulated that the dogs one sees running in the street are imperfect copies of an immutable and perfect prototype. This doctrine gave rise to many problems, some of which were known to Plato and some of which were added by Aristotle in book A of the *Metaphysics*. Aristotle scrapped the Platonic prototypes and argued that what makes something a dog is its possessing the structure of a dog, a structure that is realized in each dog and in nothing else. Aristotle called such a structure a "substantial form." In other words, the substantial form or structure of a dog is whole and entire in each and every dog. It includes a heart, a liver, kidneys, lungs, and whatever else makes up a dog. These are causally interacting parts. In turn, a part—the heart, for example—may consist of causally interacting subcomponents. A part, then, may itself be a structure, a substructure of the whole. The only existence that an overall substantial form has is in the dogs that realize it and, most important for psychologists, in the minds that succeed in understanding it. For, according to Aristotle, to understand the substantial form of dogs is to succeed in representing it in the appropriate manner in one's mind. This psychological intuition is as simple and sound as can be. We commonly say when we understand some structure, say that of a clothes dryer, that we have it in our heads. Having situated the substantial form of a dog in a real dog and in the mind that comprehends it, Aristotle felt that there was no need for immutable prototypes of the sort that Plato believed in. The substantial form's immutability arises from the biological fact that one generation of dogs transmits it whole and unchanged to the next. This was long before the days when there was talk of genetic drift.

It was also before the realization that species, as well as individuals, become extinct. Aristotle would have to say that the substantial form of dinosaurs has ceased to exist, since there are no more dinosaurs and since (as I suppose) no human mind contains an adequate representation of the substantial form of dinosaurs. Perhaps it is unfair to reproach Aristotle for not solving a problem of which he could not have been aware. At the same time, one must recognize that the point constitutes a difficulty for his theory.

The central problem of cognition, as Aristotle saw it, is that the essential information for a substantial form is not given in perception. What our perceptual systems put us in touch with is perceptual properties, or accidents: a dog's color, texture, shape, sounds, movements, smell, and so forth. The dog's substantial form is a system of causally interacting organs: heart, pancreas, lungs, tendons, muscles. How do we go from accidents to the substantial form in which the accidents reside?

In answer Aristotle specifies an operation that takes perceptual data (accidents) as input and, when successful, yields substantial forms (intelligible structures) as output. Although Aristotle did not coin the term, this operator came to be called by his followers "the active intellect." Its job is to construct substantial forms upon suitable perceptual input and feed them to the passive intellect (Aristotle's own term), where they are understood.

And in fact mind as we have described it is what it is by virtue of becoming all things [passive intellect], while there is another which is what it is by virtue of making all things [active intellect]: this is a sort of positive state like light; for in a sense light makes potential colors into actual colors. (*De anima*, 430a, 15.) [See the definition of *passive intellect* in the Glossary.]

Having characterized its input and output, Aristotle had little to say about the nature of the active intellect. His genius was to lay out the problem in clear form, challenging his successors to fill out the theory. I believe he did his job exactly right, and that succeeding generations have not succeeded in doing theirs. They have not given a fuller and deeper theory of the active intellect. Part of the difficulty one senses in reading some medieval Aristotelians is that they felt that it was enough to name the active intellect. A deeper difficulty was a loss of the problem of truth with the arrival of medieval nominalism. Indeed, the success of nominalism was due in large measure to the dismissal of substantial forms, and with it the dismissal of the task of describing the active intellect. One reason for the success of nominalism seems to have been a growing realization that the particular system of physics and biology that Aristotle taught seriously jeopardized the task of discovering substantial forms of the type Aristotle posited. Together with an appreciation of the difficulty of discovering substantial forms grew a skepticism about the need to do so. Perhaps nominalists thought that control of nature based on perceptual appearances was enough. For all that, it seems to me, Plato's problem of truth remains in full vigor even for nominalists. Accidents are changeable, and truth is not. More than that, however, we simply do manage to go beyond appearances and comprehend underlying structure. The whole history of science proclaims this fact. The challenge Aristotle set us stands as defiant as ever, whether or not we recognize its existence.

Aristotle did add a little on the active intellect. In one especially obscure passage he wrote,

> Mind in this sense of it is separable, impassible, unmixed, since it is in its essential nature activity (for always the active is superior to the passive factors, the originating force to the matter which it forms). . . . When mind is set free from its present conditions it appears as just what it is and nothing more: this alone is immortal and eternal . . . and without it nothing thinks. (*De anima*, 429a, 18–24)

This passage will be read in different ways by commentators of different stamps. This much seems clear from his words: that the active intellect survives the corruption of the body, even if nothing else does. It follows that Aristotle sees the active intellect as being in some sense independent of matter, as immaterial. This marks him as a dualist, but of which type it is not easy to say. [See the definition of *matter* in the Glossary.]

Plato's and Aristotle's dualism will have an immense impact on Western thought through the Christian claim that human beings survive their own death. It would be a mistake, however, to emphasize the dualism here, because it is not essential in understanding the problem of truth or in grasping the core of Aristotle's approach to it. For that is precisely what the active intellect amounts to: it is a challenge to describe a psychological operator that creates mental representations of substantial forms upon suitable input of perceptual properties (accidents). If we do not like Aristotle's dualistic characterization of the active intellect, we are obliged to develop our own. Indeed, whether or not we like it, the duty remains because it simply is not enough to say that the operator in question is immaterial. We should be attempting to say how various perceptual arrays constrain its operation and whether there are also some top-down processes as well as bottom-up ones. But this is not the place to attempt a solution to what is surely the central problem of psychology, a solution powerful enough to handle the fundamental contradiction of psychology.

We need to tie down certain technical expressions that keep occurring in the translations of Aristotle introduced in this chapter and that will recur in the chapters to follow. To collect them here is a good way to summarize the content of the chapter.

Substance   A substance is an individual, such as a dog, a person, or a rock. *Substance* emphasizes what remains constant throughout the existence of the individual. The most immediate answer to the question "What is an individual?" is the substantive (or common noun) that has a special relation to the individual's substance.

Accident   Accidents are (mostly) variable attributes of substances. For example, a dog may be sitting at one time and not at another. So, to be sitting is an accident. Accidents do not exist on their own; they are individuated by the substances to which they belong. [For example, many things can be sitting. We individuate the present case of sitting (distinguish it from other cases of sitting) by the particular substance to which it pertains, in this case the particular dog in front of me.] An accident is typically described with a predicable (a verb or adjective) [for example, "black," "sitting"].

Substantial form   A substantial form is the basic structure or organization in a substance. It determines the substance to be of some particular type: a dog, a person, or a stone. It is the basic source of intelligibility in a substance. Accidents are secondary determinations of a substance.

Matter   Matter itself is a structureless constituent of a physical substance, but it is capable of being structured by a substantial form. Being formless, matter in itself is unintelligible. Matter is the principle of individuation (a point, perhaps, that becomes fully clear only with Thomas Aquinas). Matter accounts for the possibility of there being many individuals in a single species. Substantial form is a principle of sameness across the members of a species; matter is a principle of difference, of individuation. [An example may clarify this. Suppose that I have two small black poodles and, as a joke, named them both Freddie. Let us further suppose that they were identical in all respects, so that even I could not tell them apart. Does that mean that there would be only one dog Freddie? Obviously not. Although they have the same substantial form, they have different matter. We can summarize this by saying that matter individuates the substantial forms.]

Active intellect   Although this term does not occur in Aristotle, it is traditionally used in expositions of Aristotle's psychology. The active intellect is the intellect in its function of accepting perceptual information (describing accidents) as input and discovering the substantial form beneath the accidents. The output of the active intellect is a mental representation of the substantial form, without the matter. Since this representation is true of all the members of the relevant species, it is a *universal*.

Passive intellect   The passive intellect is the intellect in its function of grasping and understanding mental representations of substantial forms. It is a mistake to think of the active and passive intellects as two distinct intellects; rather, they are distinct functions of a single intellect.

Postscript

Is Aristotle's criterion for cognition correct? This is not the place to attempt to settle the matter definitively. In my opinion, it is correct, but I do not believe that it serves to distinguish perception from cognition. In fact, I see visual perception as yielding sentences in a language of vision, sentences that are interpreted into visual gestalts and their visual properties. At the same time, I believe that Aristotle is right to distinguish between perception and cognition proper. Perception places us in touch with what Aristotle called "accidents," the superficial and (mostly) variable properties of objects. Cognition proper is mainly concerned with getting beneath the superficial to structure, which comprises interacting components, for example, the different components in an animal's body. This will all become clearer as we continue our journey. The main point for the moment is to have drawn attention to Aristotle's criterion and to have indicated its potential significance.

Bibliographical Note

Aristotle (1941). *Basic Works of Aristotle*. Edited by R. McKeon. New York: Random House. The main text for this chapter is Aristotle's *De anima*. It has become standard, when referring to Aristotle's texts, to use the page number, column letter, and line number of the Bekker edition of the Greek text of Aristotle's work.

5

Aristotle on Perception: Three Questions

Aristotle held some views on the perceptual systems that appeal more for their neatness than for their soundness. He held that there was just one proper object for each perceptual system: for vision it is color (which for Aristotle includes shades in the black-white dimension), for hearing it is sound, for taste it is flavor, and so on. Indeed, the test of whether some perceptual attribute is the proper object of a perceptual system is that no other system has access to that attribute. Otherwise, the attribute is a common perceptible, in the sense that it is accessible to two or more systems. Among the common perceptibles are movement, rest, number, shape, and magnitude.

The special property of the proper objects is that there can be no error in regard to them: "Each perceptual system has one kind of object which it discerns, and never errs in reporting" (*De anima*, 418a, 15). It is not easy to see what he meant by this, but perhaps a few words can be added in clarification.

That you love the taste of garlic while I detest it would not count against Aristotle's claim. We both agree that we are experiencing a particular taste, the taste of garlic, and disagree only in our appreciation of it. Neither would it disturb his claim to find that someone mistook a bird call for a human whistle. The relevant quotation extends what we have just seen.

Each perceptual system has one kind of object which it discerns, and never errs in reporting that what is before it is color or sound (though it may err as to what it is that is colored or where that is, or what that is that is sounding or where that is). (*De anima*, 418a, 15–17)

It is not clear whether color blindness, which was discovered only in the early nineteenth century by John Dalton, is a counterexample. A color-blind person correctly registers the presence of color and errs about the particular shade. There are more devastating counterexamples. People who hallucinate that they are hearing voices are, as the saying goes, "hearing things," that is, hearing things that are not there. Their hearing seems to fall short of infallibility in reporting "that what is before it is sound."

Aristotle's view of what happens during perception is more interesting. For him, to perceive is to "receive the perceptible forms of things without the matter" (*De anima*, 424a, 17). Recall that an Aristotelian substance is a substantial form individuated by matter. [A substantial form is the pattern of properties that makes an individual a dog, a person, or a rock. "To individuate" means to distinguish *this* dog, person, or rock from others; we can do so by noting that while the substantial form is the *same*, it exists in *different* instances of matter.] Accidents, like color, reveal their status because the substance can survive changes in accidents but not a change in substantial form. When a dog dies, its substantial form is no more; the organic structure has been so seriously disrupted that we no longer have a dog but only the corpse left behind by a dog. Aristotle's conception, then, is that in the visual perception of a sweater (say) the visual system adopts the color of the sweater, but not the sweater's matter or its substantial form. The visual system does not become a sweater, but if the sweater is red, the visual system quite literally becomes red.

What has the power of perception is potentially like what the perceived object is actually; that is, while at the beginning of the process of its being acted upon the two interacting factors are dissimilar, at the end the one acted upon is assimilated to the other and is identical [the Greek word is *similar*] in quality with it. (*De anima*, 418a, 3–5)

When a quality resembles its perceptual representation, we say (in a terminology developed much later) that we are dealing with a *primary quality* of the object; otherwise the quality is called *secondary*. [For example, the size of an object is experienced as size; so size is a primary quality. However, the frequencies of the light reflected by an object are not experienced as frequencies, but as colors; so color is a secondary quality.] These seventeenth-century terms were introduced in pursuit of what I believe to be a tragic mistake. We will meet them again. For the moment it is sufficient to note that a quality is considered primary if mental representations share the quality they represent. With this in mind, it seems that for Aristotle all proper objects of perception are primary qualities. This inspires confidence that our perceptual systems faithfully report the perceptual properties of the objects that surround us. Faithfulness is guaranteed by the fact that perceptual systems report properties by assuming them themselves. It now appears that this aspect of Aristotle's theory is wrong; that in the language of the seventeenth century, there are no primary qualities, only secondary ones. This does not mean that the perceptual systems are untrustworthy; it only means that they do not report qualities in the way in which Aristotle thought. To see this, note that the English words "blue" and "red" denote colors, but these words do not themselves have the colors they denote. In fact, those words in spoken form have no color whatsoever—a fact that does not take from their usefulness and trustworthiness.

In the second chapter of book 3 of *De anima* Aristotle asks a question that no one before him seems to have asked: How are we aware that we are seeing or hearing? Does the eye see that it is seeing; the ear hear that it is hearing? Aristotle is of the opinion that they do. This immediately raises the question What is the color of the process of vision; what is the sound of the process of hearing? Remember that the proper object of seeing is color and that of hearing is sound. No color, no seeing; no sound, no hearing. Here is where his doctrine of primary qualities comes to the rescue. In seeing a red sweater the visual system becomes red, so in this instance the color of the visual process is red—or so Aristotle thought.

If, however, there are no primary qualities, the theory is in trouble. Indeed, it is preposterous to hold that the process of perceiving a red sweater is itself red. It is equally preposterous to hold that the process of vision is itself one of the objects of vision. We need a different answer to this extraordinarily interesting question. Let us leave it aside for a moment until we have wrestled with another question of this chapter of *De anima*.

How, Aristotle asks, do we manage to tell that the quality of being white is different from that of being sweet? At first this looks like a dull question until one notices that it is vision that detects whiteness and taste that detects sweetness. So the question is about how vision and taste communicate with one another so as to notice that their objects are different. Commentators sometimes illustrate Aristotle's argument by having us imagine a blind man and a sighted man who has no sense of taste. The blind man can tell which things are sweet but not which are white; the sighted man can tell which are white but not which are sweet. If they can communicate with one another, they will be able together to tell which things are both white and sweet and which are one but not the other. For, having tasted something sweet, the blind man can hand what he has just tasted to the sighted man and ask him to place it in one pile if it is white and in another if it is not. Success depends on the ability to communicate.

Return to vision and taste. We can only tell which things are white and sweet and which are one but not the other if we can compare the messages of each. To change the metaphor, if vision speaks Chinese and taste speaks Swahili, unless someone can translate to a common language, there will be no comparing messages. This is Aristotle's point.

Therefore discrimination between white and sweet cannot be effected by two agencies that remain separate; both the qualities discriminated must be present to something that is one and single. (*De anima*, 426b, 17–18)

The easiest way to conceptualize what Aristotle has in mind, what he calls the "common perceptual system" (often misleadingly called "common sense"), is as a language of thought. This would be a language into which all the perceptual systems are compiled (to borrow a word from the computer people). This language would be the central exchange that Aristotle has in mind. Aristotle did not so conceptualize the common perceptual system, or the sense that is common, but I believe that to do so is a legitimate development of his thought. Later Aristotelians, notably William of Ockham, will posit the existence of a full-fledged language of the mind. It is not contrary to the spirit of either Aristotle or William of Ockham to identify this language of mind with the sense that is common.

In the contemporary scene Jerry Fodor (1975) has argued that there must be a language of thought. Many have judged his proposal to be a novel and rather daring idea. It upset Wittgensteinians particularly, because a language of thought would be a private language, and hence it would be impossible for any person to check his or her use of it against another person's. Besides, it seems as if Wittgenstein had disposed of the whole idea in the opening pages of *Philosophical Investigations.* There he comments on St. Augustine's suggestion that we learn our mother tongue with the aid of a language supplied by nature, an innate and therefore truly natural language. If you read Wittgenstein closely, however, you will find that he merely rules out Augustine's view as ludicrous; he does not offer any substantial argument against it.

Whatever the reason, Fodor's argument has not found much favor with philosophers of mind. Part of the reason may have been that it may have been taken as a novelty; whereas if my conceptualization is correct, it is almost as old as philosophy. In any event, Aristotle's arguments for it seem to me completely convincing. It is reassuring, then, to be able to report that psychologists who work on language learning and language processing generally accept the notion of a language of thought. In fact, they see the language of thought as the central component in what Noam Chomsky calls "Universal Grammar," that is, the set of innate constraints that guide the learning of natural languages and thus control their structures. Of course, the language of thought cannot be the whole story, because there are many different natural languages, whereas, the belief is, there is only one language of thought. If there were nothing more to Universal Grammar than the language of thought, there would be only one natural language. In other words, the diversity among natural languages cannot be explained by appeal to a completely uniform language of thought. The constraints of Universal Grammar, then, must be not so tight as to limit the class of natural languages to one yet tight enough to rule out infinitely many logically possible languages. Most important, they must be tight enough to guarantee the intertranslatability of all natural languages. To bring about such intertranslatability is one of the main functions ascribed to the language of thought.

I believe that the issue of the language of thought will not be properly understood until it is seen in the context of Aristotle's question about how we can tell which things are white and sweet. In this connection it is instructive to advert to the new work on deaf children learning a sign language as their native language. Ursula Bellugi and her coworkers have demonstrated that American Sign Language is a straightforward language on an equal footing with English or Greek. And Laura Petitto and her coworkers have produced substantial evidence that the course of learning a sign language by children of deaf parents is strikingly similar to the learning of spoken languages. It seems then that Universal Grammar is not in any special way tied to audition. It is, as it were, above modality, which is exactly what Aristotle claimed for the sense that is common. It too is above the modalities of the external senses. The findings for sign languages, then, strike me as support for my conceptualization of Aristotle's theory and for situating Universal Grammar in the sense that is common.

It is now time to return to the question I temporarily laid aside: How do we know that we are seeing or hearing? We saw that Aristotle's answer in *De anima* runs into trouble if there are no primary qualities. Fortunately, he offers another answer in a more minor work, *De somno et vigilio* (On sleeping and waking).

Every perceptual system has something peculiar, and also something common; peculiar as, e.g., seeing is to the system of sight, hearing to the auditory system, and so on with the other systems severally; while all are accompanied by a *common* power, in virtue whereof a person perceives that he sees or hears; for, assuredly, it is not by the special system of sight that one sees that he sees; and it is not by mere taste, or sight or both together that one discerns, and has the faculty of discerning, that sweet things are different from white things, but by a faculty connected in common with all the organs of perception. (*De somno et vigilio*, 455a, 13–20)

While there are obscure elements in this passage, I read it as claiming that it is because of the common perceptual system that we are aware that we are seeing or hearing. In view of the fate of the supposed primary qualities, this is a far more satisfactory position than that of *De anima*.

How are we to conceptualize the operation of common perception [or rather the common perceptual system]? One way to look at it is that each perceptual system communicates to the common system in a language of its own. The common system notes the language and is thus informed as to which system is operative, vision or audition. Messages in these input languages are compiled into the language of common perception. This is the main reason that there is communication across systems. But this is not enough. Remember the blind man and the sighted man who between them succeeded in discovering which things were both white and sweet and which were one and not the other. They had to be able to say to each other, "You say *this* is sweet, and I can see that *this* is white." Yet how can the common perception know that the *this* of vision picks out the same object as the *this* of taste? This is a puzzling matter, but by relying on a suggestion given to me by Marie La Palme Reyes and Gonzalo Reyes, I think we can begin to glimpse at least part of the answer.

What could the word *this* pick out at the perceptual level that is the object of both visual attention and gustatory attention? The suggestion is that the [common] perceptual system posits a perceptual object, collapsing over the modalities of vision, audition, taste, and so on, much as at the conceptual level we for some purposes collapse across the categories [or kinds] WIFE, MOTHER, and WOMAN to arrive at a single individual of the kind PERSON. [See the definition of *kind* in the Glossary.] To collapse in this way is to ignore differences and treat them as a unity. The idea is that the perceptual system as a whole can sometimes ignore the differences peculiar to vision or taste and treat something as a common perceptual object. To anticipate, William of Ockham claims that the language of the mind has demonstratives (as well as terms in other syntactic categories). It is just such a demonstrative that is needed to bridge the attentive processes of two or more systems of external perception.

We seem to be particularly good at coordinating perceptual modalities and come into the world well prepared to do this. Mendelson and Marshall (1976), for example, found that within a few hours of birth infants will orient their eyes in the direction of a voice that comes from one side. It is as if they want to *see* the object that is producing the sound, as if they want to have a single object for vision and audition. There are many infant studies yielding similar results. The ability remains in vigor throughout life. Witness the fact that at the movies we have the powerful illusion that the heroine is a single object that we both see and hear. In reality, however, what we see is an image on the screen and what we hear comes from speakers on either side of the screen. There is no object that we both see and hear, yet we have a powerful illusion that there is.

The final question I draw attention to is in some ways the most profound in Aristotle's treatment of perception. When he has completed the review

of the literature and turned to his own theory of psychology proper, the
first question he asks is,

Why do we not perceive the perceptual systems themselves as well as the external
objects of perception, or why without the stimulation of external objects do they
not produce perception, seeing that they contain in themselves fire, earth, and all
the other elements that are the direct or indirect objects of perception? (*De anima,*
417a, 3–5)

Another way to put the same question is, Why do we not perceive images
on the retina or their projections to the visual cortex? Why, for that matter, do we not perceive the retina and other parts of the eye, since they
are visible. Aristotle appears to have no answer. He just throws out the
question, seemingly content to leave it as a challenge to his students. Of
course, it conveys a subtle observation that we could all too easily miss.
Perception certainly involves stages of processing and perceptual representations at various levels, but these are not what we perceive. Rather,
by means of them we perceive external objects.

It is all too easy to say that what perceptual systems attend to are the
objects that set perceptual processes in motion. But this merely repeats
the original problem in a more troublesome form. Since events at the
retina set in train events at later levels of neurological processing, why
are we not aware of events at the retina? On the other hand, if we are
looking out the window at trees being swayed by the wind, why do we
not perceive the wind, since it is the wind that sets up the motion that
we perceive. This is a problem that will recur, so we need a name for it.
Let us call it "the intentionality problem." It is, as we will see, one of
the most enduring problems in psychology and, if badly handled, one of
the most treacherous.

I said that Aristotle's genius was to pose questions in forms that are useful
to science. In this chapter we have seen three: (1) How can we tell that
we are seeing rather than hearing or touching? (2) How can we tell which
things are both white and sweet and which are one without being the
other? (3) Why do we not perceive our perceptual organs and perceptual
representations, rather than the perceptual objects that we do perceive?
Aristotle does not have satisfactory answers to any of the three questions;
for the third he has no answer at all. We are indebted to him for the

questions and for his suggestions about how to think of them. They are hard questions that still await an answer, but there is no escaping them, because they are fundamental to the theory of perception.

In line with my aim to tie down special terms, I here add three:

Sense that is common   The sense that is common is an inner perceptual system. It deals not with information coming directly from the environment but with the outputs of the external perceptual systems. It has two special functions: (a) to coordinate the information coming from different external perceptual systems, (b) to register which external system is the source of some item of information.

Intentionality   Etymologically, the word "intentionality" means to strain toward. It was frequently employed in the Middle Ages to register the fact that in perception and cognition we are not aware of internal representations of the objects perceived or thought about; we are aware of those objects themselves. The metaphor is meant to suggest that the mind ignores mental representations of objects and "strains toward" the objects themselves.

Kind   [A kind is a way of referring to, or grouping, individuals that allows one to individuate the members of the kind (distinguish them as individuals), to trace their identity over changes, and in principle to count them. Prototypical examples are the so-called *natural* kinds, such as DOG, ANIMAL, and in general the things referred to by count nouns. Kinds allow us to interpret expressions such as "two . . . ," "some, but not every . . . ," "this is the same . . . as that," etc. What I will call the Fundamental Postulate says that there is no reference without the support of a kind. To understand this, assume that I point to a mannequin in a shop window and say, "I like that." What do I mean? Without further clues you cannot know whether I am referring to the mannequin itself, its clothes, the way that it has been placed in the window, etc. However, if I say I like that MANNEQUIN, or I like those CLOTHES, then I am able to convey my meaning by first getting the reference right (these two words refer to kinds). Some people have argued that examples discussed by biologists (e.g., S. J. Gould) showing that there is no way of deciding whether some siamese-twin sisters are actually one person or two implies that kinds are not required for reference. But kinds are needed even to ask the question of what it is that we are dealing with (siamese twins) that could be one person, or maybe two, or maybe neither.]

Bibliographical Note

Aristotle (1941). *Basic Works of Aristotle*. Edited by R. McKeon. New York: Random House. The main Aristotelian texts for this chapter were *De anima* and *De somno et vigilio* (On sleeping and waking).

Fodor, J. A. (1975). *The Language of Thought*. New York: Thomas Y. Crowell.

6

The Book of Genesis and Psychology

I have looked through the various textbooks on the history of psychology on my shelves and in none do I find any discussion of the Bible. Once in a while the Bible is mentioned, but in some such context as the reception of Darwinism. There seems to be no attention to the Bible as a document of psychological import in its own right. This is surprising because surely no other book has so influenced Western thought about what human beings are, their fundamental make up, their ability to gain knowledge, their needs, their sense of justice, and their beliefs about mental health.

Each of the reflections in this book is incomplete in its coverage of the topic it addresses. Nowhere am I more painfully aware of the limitations than in dealing with the Old and New Testaments. For instance, in discussing the Old Testament I confine myself to the opening pages of Genesis. Better, however, an incomplete coverage than no coverage at all.

The special feature of the opening of Genesis is that there is just one God who created everything—at least as Christian Europe read, "In the beginning when God created the heavens and the earth . . . ." Other Middle Eastern creation stories had two gods at the source of everything. For instance, in the Babylonian epic *Enuma Elish* there is a male god Apsu and a female god Tiamat, who eventually war and the heavens and earth are constructed out of Tiamat's dead carcass. Apsu thus did not create everything. Other creation stories such as the Middle Eastern *Gilgamesh* or the Greek and Roman creation myths also had at least two source deities. Only Genesis, it seems, has one (see Sarna 1970).

A particularly important alternative to the Genesis account of creation is associated with the name of Mani, who was born in southern Babylonia

in A.D. 216. He founded a religion that bears his name, "Manichaeism."
He seems to be the origin for Europe of the belief that the world as we
know it emanates from two creative sources: a good creator, identified
with light, and an evil creator, identified with darkness. It is not for nothing that we have the expression "the powers of darkness" and that in
Star Wars the evil force is called "the dark side." St. Augustine at one
time was an adherent of Manichaeism and only with difficulty, and perhaps never completely, escaped its influence. The attraction of Manichaeism is that it provides a ready explanation for the presence of evil in the
world. Mani can attribute evil to Darkness, whereas Jews must in some
sense attribute it to God, who created everything. Implicitly, Genesis says
that the struggle between good and evil is part of the divine plan.

In the present context the importance of Manichaeism is that it admits
the possibility of a fundamental incoherence at the heart of things. Human beings for the Manichaeans are composite, their souls being captured light and the matter of their bodies being trapped darkness. There
is, then, no reason to believe that the true descriptions of human nature
form a coherent theory. In some profound sense there is no reason to
believe in the intelligibility of any creature, since matter could be a source
of incoherence and incomprehensibility at the core of things. Notice that
Aristotelian matter, being completely unintelligible, does not function in
this way. Precisely because it is unintelligible, we can form no true descriptions of it that could give rise to inconsistent true descriptions of a
physical body. Manichaean matter is not completely unintelligible, and
so it can give rise to inconsistent but true descriptions of a physical body.

Manichaeism was perhaps the central ingredient of the Gnosticism
with which Christianity was forced to contend in the early centuries of
its existence. Manichaeism resurfaced over most of Europe in the eleventh
and twelfth centuries as "Catharism" or "Albigensianism." It is especially
important to us because this is just at the dawn of the modern period,
at the time when the first European universities were founded. The way
orthodox Christianity dealt with Albigensianism was brutal but, appar-
ently, effective. It sacked the Albigensian strongholds and burned their
inhabitants at the stake. Thus, stamped in blood on the European mind
emerging in the High Middle Ages are a rejection of Manichaeistic dual-

ism and the incoherence it entailed and a reaffirmation of the monotheism of Genesis (see Brenon 1991).[1]

The second strain in Genesis that is important to us relates directly to psychology.

Then God said, "Let us make humankind in our image, according to our likeness. . . . So God created humankind in his image, in the image of God he created them; male and female he created them." (Genesis, 1:26–27)

A little later when Noah saves human beings and all living creatures from the flood, the same observation is repeated: "Whoever sheds the blood of a human, by a human shall that person's blood be shed; for in his own image God made humankind" (Genesis, 9:6).

Interestingly, Genesis has Adam manifest his likeness to the Creator, who has just been described as the maker of everything, not by having Adam make something like a shoe or a hat, but by naming the beasts.

So out of the ground the Lord God formed every animal of the field and every bird of the air, and brought them to the man to see what he would call them; and whatever the man called every living creature, that was its name. (Genesis, 2:19)

What is so special about naming beasts that it could serve to show the divine likeness in Adam? First, I should be clear about the type of name involved. In Genesis 3:20, Adam is portrayed as giving a proper name to his wife, Eve. To name the animals, however, was to assign common nouns that pick out the species to which each belongs: "crocodile," "giraffe," "elephant," and so on. My question then becomes, What is special about giving names to species? I have very little idea of the theory that guided the author(s) of Genesis, but here is one way, arising from my own work, to make sense of the text.

The extraordinary thing about species, or kinds as I like to call them, is that they are abstract entities. One can see a sheep or a dog; one cannot see the kind to which it belongs. The kind DOG comprises all the dogs that ever were, are, and will be. It is fixed once and for all and does not change as old dogs die and young ones are born. That is why we can use the same word to speak of dogs long since dead and dogs not yet born, as well as of dogs that are alive at present. The importance of these kinds in our conceptual lives cannot be overstressed, because it is the kinds that give us individuals and handle their identity. For example, the kind DOG specifies what is to count as an individual dog, say Freddie: the whole dog, including all its invisible interior parts but not the collar it is wearing or any mud that may be on its paws. Yet a dog is not to be identified with the set of its molecules or with the set of its parts. For example, if Freddie is a grown dog, the set of molecules that forms his body was never born, but Freddie was. It follows that Freddie is not identical with the set of his molecules. All the fundamental work of individuating and handling identity is done by kinds. Without them there is no grasping of any truth. While I do not know the guiding intuition, the author(s) of Genesis must have sensed that there is something special about individuals and kinds, and I agree.

A large part of science is to discover what kinds of things there are and the structures or forms associated with them. The structure for dogs specifies what it is to be a dog; that for iron specifies what it is to be an atom of iron. Genesis does not say that Adam managed to learn the internal structure of the animals in any of the kinds he named. But it gave enormous support to the faith that the human mind is capable of doing so, at least in principle.

To see that this is so, think of the general picture guiding the narrative in the opening chapters of Genesis. There is a single God with the power and the intelligence to create everything that exists. Because he is unique, there is no intelligence except his at work in creation. The implication is that true descriptions of any creature will form a coherent set. There is no source of incoherence in reality. It follows that the structure for any kind of creature is at the very least intelligible. That is, nature is intelligible. Now the same Creator that made all the creatures also made human beings. Human beings in some special way were created in the image of the Creator. That this image resides principally in their intelligence is signaled by the fact that they could name the kinds of creatures; not just perceptually distinguish among kinds, but recognize that associated with each perceptual type is an abstract object, a kind. It follows from all this that there is a basic compatibility between the intelligibility of creatures and the intelligence of human beings. After all, the same God created nature with its intelligibility and the human mind with its intelligence, and human intelligence was created so as to be able to grasp the intelligibility of creatures. Genesis does not say whether the job of grasping the structure of any kind will be easy or difficult. It merely guaranteed a basic compatibility between the structures and the human mind. Still, it offers an approach, if not an answer, to Plato's problem of inquiry, because it suggests that the mind has the right sort of structures for attaining truth.

Experience has shown that the underlying structures have mostly been very recondite. It has been an enormous struggle for physics, chemistry, biology, and other sciences to reach their present levels. Often progress has involved daring idealizations; always it has involved going beyond the evidence. Where did the confidence come from that the effort was worthwhile, that nature is intelligible, and that the human mind is capable of grasping the intelligibility? Albert Einstein (1956) has something interesting to say in response. The following excerpt is from a letter to Maurice Solovine, an old friend of his university days in Zurich, to whom he wrote in a totally unbuttoned manner.

I have no better expression than "religious" for this confidence in the intelligible nature of reality, an intelligibility that is at least to some extent accessible to human intelligence. Where such confidence is lacking, science degenerates into stupid empiricism. I don't give a damn whether the clergy manage to turn this to account. No matter, without it you get nowhere. (Einstein, 1956, 102, letter of 1 January 1951)

Einstein seems not to have accepted Genesis's guarantee, since he felt there was no valid way to go beyond the "miracle" of human intelligence. But millions of people in the Western world did, and it seems to have bolstered their confidence.

There are a few other points that I should cull for psychology from the first chapters of Genesis. One is that the whole human race descends from a single couple, Adam and Eve. This intimates that all their descendants, also being human, share the image of the Creator. It also suggests that in the most profound manner all human beings are equal, since all are descended from the same couple and since all share the divine image. Certainly there are moments in the Old Testament that attribute special status to the seed of Abraham. But there are other moments, the opening of Genesis among them, that emphasize the common humanity of the whole human race. Here is another, from Isaiah:

I am coming to gather all nations and tongues; and they shall come and see my glory. . . . I will send survivors to the nations, . . . to the coastlands far away that have not heard of my fame or seen my glory. . . . And I will also take some of them as priests and Levites, says the Lord. (Isaiah, 66:18–21)

Naturally, it is this thread, not the one that emphasizes the special status of Jews, that takes deepest root in Christian Europe. It is echoed in the American Declaration of Independence, which declares that all men were created equal.

The divine likeness is not confined to an intelligence that can reasonably aspire to understand nature. It is an intelligence endowed with moral insight. This is conveyed by the fact that alone among creatures, a moral charge is laid upon humans: eat not the fruit of the tree of knowledge. The story tells that nevertheless they ate it, and that God was angry with them and punished them: Eve, by giving her a sexual urge that would lead to painful childbirth; Adam, by cursing the ground from which he would have to wrest a living. The presupposition is that Adam and Eve were not following any law of nature, however hidden, in eating the forbidden fruit; that, in the most common understanding of the expression, they could have done otherwise. In Hobbes and Spinoza we see this belief wither, to be replaced by the belief that the notion of free will rests solely on the failure to grasp the tangled and often hidden set of causes that determine our decisions. But Genesis is on the other side, bolstering the belief that human decisions are not always the result of hidden determinants, that they are sometimes and at least to some extent free. This is a claim of fundamental importance to psychology.

Because all human beings are descended from Adam and Eve and therefore participate in the divine image, they all have a moral sense. Unless I am mistaken, Genesis promotes the opinion that basic moral insight is genetically communicated, not socially imposed as Freud, Piaget, Kohlberg and a great many modern psychologists would have us believe. After all, sensitivity to the moral dimension is part of the divine image, according to Genesis, and is handed on genetically. I believe that Genesis tells us something more than this. It tells a story to account for the fact that one's moral sensibilities cannot be grounded in parental approval, legal codes, or any sort of averaging over experience, because we can always ask whether the injunctions of parents are just, whether the law is just, whether the average pattern of behavior is just, which would not be possible if justice were what parents approved of, what the law says, or what most people do. Genesis says that Adam and Eve were created in a state of perfect justice: at peace with each other, in harmony with the rest of creation, and in harmony with the Creator. The picture is that they retained an appreciation of perfect justice, even after the fall, and that this access to ideal justice is handed on to their descendants as part of the divine image, as a reflection of the state they once experienced. This is the founding legend for the Western understanding of morality. It too is echoed in the Declaration of Independence, because, as we will see, it is principally in moral sensibility that Jefferson believed all humans to be equal. Thus, at least in the domain of morality, Genesis has a solution for the problem of how we have access to ideals that transcend experience: the relevant sources of information are genetically given. I will presently identify the problem of how the mind has access to idealizations as St. Augustine's problem.

We have by no means exhausted the psychological import of the opening pages of Genesis, much less of the Old Testament. We saw, nonetheless, the import for science of belief in a single Creator, and for psychology of belief that humankind is made in the image and likeness of the Creator. This signals the intelligibility of creation and its compatibility with human intelligence. We also saw the founding legends for belief in the equality of all human beings and for belief in the genetic, as opposed to social, origins of the ideal of justice. We also saw in Genesis the founding legend for belief in free will.

Bibliographical Note

Brenon, A. (1991). *Le vrai visage du Catharisme*. Editions Loubatières.
Sarna, N. M. (1970). *Understanding Genesis: The Heritage of Biblical Israel*. New York: Schocken.

7

The Impact of Christianity on Psychology

Although Christianity became a different religion from Judaism, it did so only gradually, and it did not set aside its Jewish roots. Jesus is reported as saying, "Do not think that I have come to abolish the law or the prophets [the Jewish religion]; I have come not to abolish but to fulfill." (Matthew, 5:17). This extract is from the Sermon on the Mount, whose main message can be interpreted (not without opposition) as a call to interiorize the spirit of Judaism rather than to observe the law mechanically. One result of this stance is that Christianity retains the Jewish Bible and with it the book of Genesis. Through Christianity, Genesis had an impact on Western thought that it would scarcely have had otherwise. Christendom, as the ensemble of Christian countries came to be called, thus absorbed the lessons of Genesis: the singleness of the Creator guaranteeing the coherence of true descriptions of any creature; guaranteeing too the compatibility of human intelligence with these creatures—their commensurability, so to speak—from the standpoint of knowledge. [If there were many creators, it is possible that the product of one creator might not understand the product of another creator.]

Often in the New Testament ideas that already exist in the Old appear with fresh emphasis and vigor. This happens particularly in the account of creation in the prologue to St. John's Gospel.

In the beginning was the Word (*logos*), and the Word was with God, and the Word was God. He was in the beginning with God. All things came into being through him, and without him not one thing came into being. What has come into being in him was life, and the life was the light of all people. The light shines in the darkness, and the darkness did not overcome it. (John, 1:1–5)

This passage deliberately echoes the opening of Genesis, whose first words are also "In the beginning."

The English has "Word" where the original has *logos,* the Greek word that gives us "logic" and the ending "-ology" as in "psychology," "geology," and so on. It is meant to be understood as something like theory: theory of the *ge* (earth) in "geology"; theory of the *psychē* (soul, mind) in psychology. John, then, portrays the Creator's intelligence as theory personified. It is this theory that guided creation: "All things came into being through him, and without him not one thing came into being." The Albigensians could read this passage, indeed the whole prologue, as describing the action of the good creator, the light, and yet leave room for the work of the evil creator, the darkness. Orthodox Christians read it as describing the creative action of a single God, guided by his divine intelligence. They saw the prologue as echoing Genesis and emphasizing the intelligibility of creation, since every aspect of it reflects the Creator's intelligence.

Moreover, divine intelligence is not merely reflected in nature, and human intelligence is not merely in the image of divine intelligence. Divine intelligence is still operative today. It illuminates human minds at the present time in their quest for knowledge and justice. A little later than the passage cited we read, "The true light, which enlightens everyone, was coming into the world" (John, 1:9). This will give rise to the doctrine of divine illumination in St. Augustine and, in transposed form, in Descartes. It is the claim that the solution to Plato's problem of inquiry and problem of truth is divine intervention. This is not, of course, so very different from Plato's own solution at the end of the *Meno,* where knowledge of virtue is claimed to be a gift of the gods.

St. John's Gospel, then, gives even greater assurance than Genesis that the natures of things are intelligible and that the human mind, created in the image of this intelligence and participating in its light, is able to discover these intelligible natures.

The personification of divine intelligence as the Word is part of what leads to the Christian doctrine of God as a Trinity of persons, a doctrine that comes to be filled out and crystallized in the early centuries of Christianity. It is the belief that while there is but one God, that one God is a community of three divine persons: the Father, the Son, and the Holy Spirit. This has implications for the theory of social cognition.

One clear psychological implication is that if human beings are made in the image and likeness of God, they are made in the image and likeness of a community of persons; not just in the image of a solitary and isolated Creator, as Genesis might be read as suggesting. A human intelligence, then, is essentially a social intelligence. This is a more dramatic claim than Aristotle's aseptic remark in the *Politics* (1253a, 1) that "man is by nature a political animal." Now, obviously human beings depend on a couple of human beings (parents) for their very existence; on long continued support for their growth to maturity; on traditions of technology for food, clothing, and shelter; on political organizations for justice and defense. Christianity, however, is claiming that in its very constitution human intelligence is more profoundly social than these observations suggest. It claims that the divine image in humans is a social one. To begin to see something of what is involved, observe that infants come with a social instinct that leads them to learn a language, itself an essentially social business. To do so infants must assume the posture of seeking to join a speech community, of mastering its linguistic conventions, of meaning by expressions what the community means. This in turn involves regarding other persons as beings with intentions that they express in language to other human beings, as beings with social intentions.

This is only part of what Ray Jackendoff (1992) postulates as "the faculty of social cognition," with which nature endows every person. He sees that faculty as subtending children's interpretations of certain objects as persons who are social agents with socially ratified roles, obligations, and commitments; with socially recognized rights and possessions. Like languages, social structures vary, and children must learn which ones obtain in their locality. Nevertheless, they come well prepared for such learning. All this fits well with the traditional Christian doctrine that human beings, created in the image of a community of divine persons, are essentially social. Thus Christianity offers a partial answer to Plato's problem of learning, at least in the domain of social cognition. Again it is a genetic answer.

The prologue of St. John was read as portraying divine intelligence, not as something isolated and aloof, but as communicating with the

Creator and also with creation. It was inevitable that the prologue should be read by Christian Platonists as presenting the Word (*logos*) as the seat of the intelligible structures for the various kinds; as communicating to creatures their intelligibility. So the Word is the source of the structures in creatures, and if the Word enlightens the minds of everyone, there is hope of success in attempts to grasp these structures. All of this has to be seen in a social context. Just as Christians receive their religion from a historical community, explore it with the aid of their contemporaries, and hand it on to their children, so too in the secular domain, people must seek to extend the knowledge that their forebears handed on to them, with the aid of their contemporaries, while accepting the obligation of handing on their insights to posterity. Knowledge was not viewed in medieval universities exclusively as technologies but, to an important degree, as an end in itself. Just to know nature was good in itself, because it was to appreciate the handiwork of the Creator. Like St. Albert the Great in the thirteenth century, many of the medievals who seriously applied themselves to the sciences of nature were primarily theologians. Far from believing that science and religious faith are incompatible, they believed that they are mutually enhancing. Not that debates were always conducted in an even-handed manner, as the condemnation of Aristotle and Aquinas in 1277 by the Archbishop of Paris attests. Such events, though far-reaching, were about how to settle disagreements, not about the need to reach agreement. I am not aware that any medieval theologian denounced science. They all, as far as I know, subscribed to the fundamental principle that science and faith are, indeed must be, compatible. In the 1400s there was a growing skepticism about the likelihood of success in endeavors to understand the world, whether natural or supernatural, and there was a reaching for simplicity. But there was no suggestion of a fundamental opposition of religion and science. Scientists had to fear the sin of pride and appreciate the modesty of their achievements. No one insisted on this more than Cardinal Nicholas of Cusa, who wrote a celebrated book called *Learned Ignorance* in that century, but he himself was a scientist and mathematician to whom the idea of fundamental incompatibility was alien.

Implicit in the New Testament is a view of mental health that has relevance for an important area of human cognition, namely knowledge of how to conduct our lives. There is, of course, the philosophical discipline of ethics that seeks, among other things, to discover principles that lead to moral behavior. The Sermon on the Mount (Matthew, 5) makes scant contact with this discipline but exalts the poor in spirit, the meek, those who hunger and thirst after justice, the merciful, the pure in heart, the peacemakers, those persecuted for the sake of righteousness, and those reviled for their religious beliefs. Matthew's list has nothing to do with Aristotle's guidelines in the *Nicomachean Ethics*.

The set of beatitudes, indeed the whole New Testament, claims to describe how a social being ought to live. The theory can be summed up simply. From the lawyer who questioned him about how to gain eternal life, Jesus elicited the response: "You shall love the Lord your God with all your heart, and with all your soul, and with all your strength, and with all your mind; and your neighbor as yourself" (Luke, 10:27; echoing Deuteronomy, 6:5). Jesus approved. The perfection of Christian life, its health, is love: love of God and of one's fellow human beings for God's sake. The beatitudes spell out what these two loves entail—far more than mere justice. The Spanish mystic and poet John of the Cross, in the beginning of one of his poems, puts it in a way that is comprehensible to students: "At eventide they will examine thee in love." The complement of this doctrine is that selfishness, the opposite of love, is mental illness. This is the traditional Christian view of mental health and mental illness. Interestingly, the mentally healthy are not preoccupied with their own health. The main thing, it seemed, was to be properly oriented—the rest followed.

One should point out that the sort of mental illness in question here is the sort that might be called neurosis, if one is permitted a broad and somewhat dated classification of mental illnesses into neuroses and psychoses. By "psychoses" I mean for present purposes those disorders that one might reasonably hope to cure one day with chemicals: schizophrenia, certain forms of depression, Alzheimer's disease, and so forth. The disorders that I include under the term "neuroses" at least admit questions of morality. One is deemed to have some measure of responsibility for the related behavior disorders: aggression, sexual misbehavior, substance abuse, and so forth. It is only to the extent that there is voluntary control that the commandment of love is applicable.

Traditional Christian teaching recognized that deviant behavior may not be so fully under an agent's control that it can be righted by an act of the agent's will. If my behavior is deviant, part of the responsibility may lie with me in that I failed to take due account of my own welfare and that of others, and in consequence built up evil habits. But my misdoings may also be the result of damage done to me by parents, teachers, employers, or others who have had an influence on me. When we inquire into the origin of the harmful treatment that I received, a similar division is found. My parents may have been partly responsible for the harm they did to me, but they in turn may have been to some extent bruised by the treatment they received at the hands of those who had influence over them. Carry this back to the origins of the human race and we have one of the basic intuitions underlying the Christian doctrine of original sin (the eating of the forbidden fruit by Adam and Eve). It is, at least in part, a psychological claim that all human beings are psychologically damaged by the treatment they have received at the hands of damaged people. The extent that an individual's damage is not of his or her own doing is the extent to which it is attributable to original sin.

There are other, more theological, construals of original sin, but there is also the psychological one just given. It amounts to the claim that one is born into and grows up in an imperfect society, and one inevitably shares the imperfection. The damage cannot be set right completely. In particular, the doctrine of original sin stands in opposition to ideologies, like Communism, that promise a complete cure when some great victory is won, some great injustice set to right. Human beings in their present state are incapable of realizing the sort of perfect society of which their genetic sense of justice gives them a glimpse.

The New Testament, like the Old Testament, rejects a fundamental opposition between good and evil. It therefore provides some guidance about the greatest problem for the theory of social cognition and indeed one of the greatest for our understanding of nature as a whole: the problem of evil. Instead of a fundamental opposition between good and evil, Genesis (implicitly) opts for a dialectical opposition between the two, which means that evil is to be turned to advantage. Growth in moral understanding and growth in moral stature are to be achieved by each somewhat warped individual in the company of other warped individuals. As W. H. Auden says, "You shall love your crooked neighbor with your crooked heart."

Traditionally, an ability to cope with hatred, illness, tragedy, and death is the hallmark of personal maturity and of well-grounded mental health. Jesus did not seek out such evils, but he was not deflected from his path by them. The whole New Testament is essentially the story of a supremely good man who was brought down by interest groups who could not abide his goodness and its influence. Jesus is portrayed as accepting a death that he both foresaw and foretold. Since this man was also the Word, this was the greatest evil in the history of the world, but, Christians claimed, it brought about the greatest good, the redemption of the whole human race. This is a story that Christians not only read in their sacred book but also reenact in the drama of the liturgical year. This is a message that is deeply rooted in the European mind, in European architecture, in the sacred emblems of Europe, in European art. It colored people's whole attitude toward life. Not of course that all Christians lived solely by the gospels, but that all were touched by the ideals they expressed, some very deeply indeed.

At the end of the nineteenth century Nietzsche proposed an ideal of a very different superman, one who imposes himself on people and history by sheer force of character and will. This was in conscious opposition to the teachings of Jesus, which Nietzsche found weak-kneed and wimpish. While Nietzsche had an impact on certain Fascist leaders, over the centuries it is the suffering figure of the Gospels that has been the dominant image. He is weak where Nietzsche's superman is strong; instead of crushing his enemies, he succumbs to them. He died unknown in a remote part of the world. He exemplifies in his person the dialectical turning of evil to good.

The triumph of Jesus is marked by an empty tomb, which signaled his victory over death. He promised life everlasting to his faithful followers. Now life after death, especially before the resurrection of the body, is a concept that had no firm foothold in the Jewish mind, although for a time before Jesus it was beginning to gain adherents. In the time of Jesus the Pharisees and Sadducees were locked in dispute on this very issue; the Pharisees holding to a belief in the resurrection of the body, the Sadducees rejecting it. Jesus's own teaching, his empty tomb, and the epistles of St. Paul come down on the side of the Pharisees and of resurrection. What about the period immediately after death when the body is subject to corruption? Gradually the belief grew among Christians that people survive the death of their body. This gave powerful impetus to a doctrine that Christians found ready to hand in the work of certain philosophers, notably Plato: the doctrine of psychological dualism. In the *Phaedo* Socrates, on the point of drinking the hemlock, looks forward to a more perfect life in another world in the company of the spirits of those who have passed over. Plato held that a human being is a composite of a material body and nonmaterial soul. Christianity adopted this dualism, although not always precisely in its Platonic form. Such dualism offered some support for the claim that a person survives death: when the material part disintegrates, the nonmaterial part continues on.

Dualism has certainly had religious support in Christendom, but in its origin and in its essence it is a psychological theory. At the very least, it claims that there are some operations of the human intellect and will that no purely material structure could perform. As a theory, it must stand or fall on psychological evidence. Dualism continued almost unchallenged in the Western World until the time of Hobbes, in the seventeenth century. Thereafter it came increasingly under attack from writers whose thought was deeply influenced by advances in physics. While these things are difficult to assess, I believe that the majority of writers on psychology, so many of them Christian clergymen, held one or another form of dualism until the time of Darwin. Darwin argued for the evolution of all species, including human beings, by the operation of purely physical forces on purely physical stuff. No place in his scheme for a nonmaterial component in human nature! Not much support either for the belief than humans are in the image and likeness of God!

But we are getting ahead of ourselves. Returning to the pre-Darwinian era, we find Christianity repeating with renewed imagery and vigor the main messages of Genesis. We saw in the Christian doctrine of the Trinity support for the psychological view that the human mind is essentially and profoundly social. We saw encouragement for the study of natural science not solely for purposes of controlling nature but also out of reverence for the Word (*logos*), who is encountered, indirectly, in "the book of nature." We saw the traditional Christian view of mental health as love and of mental disorder as selfishness. We saw the conceptually and psychologically important doctrine that evil can be faced and turned to good. This was referred to as the dialectic of good and evil. This is only the most extreme example of the dialectical relations ubiquitous in nature and, naturally, in the way the mind operates. This is not the place to go into such relations, beyond noting that Plato's paradox of truth is really a dialectic of permanence and change. Finally, we saw the impetus toward psychological dualism given by the Christian claim that people survive the death of their bodies.

Bibliographical Note

Jackendoff, R. S. (1992). *Languages of the Mind: Essays on Mental Representation.* Cambridge: MIT Press.

8

St. Augustine of Hippo: Christian Platonist

Biographical Note

Augustine (A.D. 354–430) was born at Tagaste in North Africa to a pagan father and Christian mother (St. Monica) some 30 years after Constantine the
Great had legitimized Christianity for the Roman Empire. Augustine grew up a
pagan and as a young man embraced Manichaeism. To complete his studies of
rhetoric, he spent several years in Milan, in northern Italy. At this time he lived
with a concubine with whom he had a son, Adeodatus, who to the father's
immense sorrow died at the age of 12. In Milan he came under the influence
of St. Ambrose, was converted to Christianity, and began a life of evangelical
rigor in the society of like-minded Christians whom he gathered around him.
He received holy orders and, on returning to Africa, was elected bishop of
Hippo. As he was dying the Vandals were laying siege to Hippo. His psychological writings are scattered throughout the immense corpus of his (mainly)
theological writings. One of the most concentrated in psychological content
is his *Confessions,* which some claim to be the first autobiography. His
writing, like Plato's, often has a moving quality that is rare in a theologian or
philosopher.

It would not be unreasonable to maintain that, apart from the Bible,
Augustine of Hippo is the writer who has most profoundly influenced
Western thought over the longest period of time. His influence was not
seriously challenged before the end of the twelfth century; it was still
clearly dominant in the High Middle Ages; in the fourteenth century it
dwindled somewhat with the advent of Nominalism; it regained its dominant position again in the sixteenth and seventeenth centuries at the hands
of Puritan reformers, John Calvin (a Protestant), and Cornelius Jansen
(Catholic Bishop of Ypres), whose *Augustinus* inspired the movement

known as Jansenism. Although all Augustine's writings are mainly theological, he was fascinated by psychology, and even his most theological
speculations, for example *The Trinity,* are suffused with his psychological
theories. He is, then, the most influential writer on psychology until
modern times.

Augustine is a Christian Platonist. In him we find most of the great
Platonic teachings in Christianized form. Augustine was by no means the
first church father to "baptize" Plato (more accurately, the neo-Platonism
that was available in Latin, since for most of his life he knew but little
Greek), but he was the most thorough. For 1,000 years, until in the Renaissance Marsilio Ficino translated Plato's dialogues into Latin, what
the West knew of Plato was mainly what they read of him in Augustine.

In Augustine's hands the Platonic forms are replaced by ideas in the
mind of the Creator. For Augustine, what all dogs have in common is
that they are corporal realizations of the divine idea of a dog, the concept
that guided the creation of dogs. [See the definition of *Platonic ideas* in
the Glossary.] Interestingly, Augustine was open to the idea that God did
not stock the world with ready-made plants and animals. In his great
commentary on Genesis, *De Genesi ad Litteram* (translated in 1872),
he suggests that instead God planted seeds (*rationes seminales*) from
which plants and animals developed, perhaps over a very lengthy period.
St. Augustine was not what is nowadays called a "creation scientist." His
evolution, however, should not be mistaken for an evolution of species,
because in Augustine's theory, there is no development of one species
from another.

One advantage of Augustine's move is that the divine idea of a dog is
not itself a dog. Plato believed that the source idea of a dog is a prototypical dog, and that the dogs one sees in the street are but poor copies.
Augustine saw nothing inferior in the dogs that people have in their
homes. From the standpoint of someone interested in natural science,
Augustine's position is healthier than Plato's. It encourages one to study
perceptually available dogs if one wants to learn about their nature. [See
the definition of *nature* in the Glossary.] Augustine can also give an attractive account of what it is to participate in the nature of a dog: it is
to be a corporal instantiation of the divine idea of a dog. To understand
his meaning, it helps to think of an engineer in Detroit designing a new

automobile. From his blue print thousands of automobiles are produced, each instantiating the blue print in material fashion.

In this picture the reason for the immutability of truths about dogs is obvious. It is the immutability of God himself that grounds the immutability of the divine idea of a dog and hence the immutable truth of propositions describing the nature of dogs and their properties. For Augustine, as for Plato, there was a problem in explaining how truths relating to one dog and not others (such as being sick one day) can all attach to the single source idea of the species. Augustine had something relevant to say about how divine ideas reflect both multiplicity as well as commonality, but I will not go into it.

For Augustine, the problems of learning and truth take the following form: given perceptual contact with fleeting and changeable objects, how can human beings, themselves changeable in innumerable ways, discover the immutable natures of things? To understand Augustine's answer, we must look at his theory of perception. But first, it bears repetition that for Augustine, like Aristotle and unlike Plato, the immutable natures of species are present, albeit in corporeal and therefore mutable form, in the creatures to which one has perceptual access. The problem is, how do we discover them and recognize their immutability, given the nature of our experience?

Augustine did not have the same disdain as Plato for the perceptual systems. He was up to date for his time on the role of the nerves and brain in perception as understood by contemporary anatomists. Besides, in *The Trinity* he says, "But far be it from us to doubt the truth of those things that we have perceived through the senses of the body" (bk. 15, chap. 12). After all, our perceptual systems were fashioned by a wise Creator who wished us to employ them in pursuit of knowledge and in guiding our lives. At the same time, he is as aware as Plato of the fleeting quality of every perceptual presentation: "We agree fully . . . that everything with which the bodily sense comes into contact cannot remain in the same condition for even an instant of time, but passes away and disappears" (Second Letter, trans. 1872). For all that, perception affords access to immutable truth. But how? To bring out the extent of the problem he employs an example that through Descartes becomes well known in our own time. In *On the Immortality of the Soul* he asks us to think of a piece of wax whose perceptible properties, color, texture, shape, may all change, leaving nevertheless the same piece of wax. The contrast he is making is between change in accidental properties without change in substance. Substantial change is also possible, as for example when the wax is burned, but Augustine wants us to concentrate on cases of substance constancy in the presence of change in accidents. The relevance is that "everything that the bodily sense comes into contact with" is an accident and changeable, and therefore a poor index to the unchanging substance. How, then, can we gain any knowledge of substance or of substantial form?

Augustine was faced with two problems where Plato had only one. The first was isolated by Aristotle: how can we gain knowledge of a substantial form when all we have direct access to is accidental, perceptual properties? The second is Plato's: from changeable objects how can we grasp unchanging truths about their nature? Part of Augustine's greatness is his refusal to shy away from either problem, for example by denying that perception is a source of truth. On the contrary, in *The Trinity* (bk. 12, chap. 11) he speaks about "knowledge (*scientia*) that is derived from experience with changeable things." The word "knowledge" betokens truth. He holds firm to both ends of the contradiction.

To these problems Augustine adds a third, which we may fairly call "Augustine's problem," since in it he isolates a particular problem relating to our knowledge of permanent truth. In the chapter just cited from *The Trinity* he distinguishes between knowledge (*scientia*) of changeable things and wisdom (*sapientia*) regarding unchangeable things. Among the objects of wisdom he mentions the natural numbers and geometrical objects, such as points, lines, and plane figures. Together with these objects he mentions certain systems of rules, all of which he takes to be immutable: the computation rules for numbers, the rules of geometric inference, the rules of logic more generally, and the ethical rules for the proper conduct of one's life. For Augustine, what distinguishes the objects and rules that relate to wisdom is that they are not known through experience of changeable things. Unlike John Stuart Mill and like Gottlob Frege, both of the nineteenth century, Augustine refuses to base the principle of contradiction, say, on any sort of induction over experience of the physical environment or on psychological abhorrence of cognitive dissonance. Augustine takes such a principle to be a truth that we bring to experience; not something derived from it. He also takes it to be other than a mere operative principle of the human mind, a kind of blind compulsion. Rather, the principle of contradiction is a truth grounded in the unity and coherence of divine truth, a truth, moreover, that is naturally grasped as such by the human mind. Augustine's problem is a genuine one, and for its profundity it deserves to be placed alongside Plato's problems and Aristotle's problem. Any psychology worthy of the name must have some approach to all three.

The scope of Augustine's problem bears some elaboration. Many people might readily concede that fundamental truths like the principle of contradiction are not derived from perceptual experience. They might even concede that the numbers and their properties are not known through such experience. They are likely to be surprised, however, by the claim that geometrical objects and their properties are not perceptible. After all, geometry books are full of geometrical drawings, and mathematics teachers cover blackboards with them. But this is to miss an important point. The objects of geometry are all idealizations over direct perceptual experience. A geometrical point can be regarded as the limit of the process of drawing dots with decreasing diameters—a geometrical point has no diameter. A geometric line can similarly be seen as the limit of drawing physical lines thinner and thinner—a geometrical line has no thickness. And so on for other geometrical objects. Augustine was fully aware of this:

I have seen lines drawn by architects and they are sometimes as fine as the thread spun by spiders. But these principles [basic constituents] are different. They are not images of things which the eye of the body has reported to me. We know them simply by recognizing them within ourselves without reference to any material object. (*Confessions*, bk. X, chap. 12)

As we will see, this is a fact that escaped Thomas Hobbes, who had no use for such idealizations. Nevertheless, well nigh the whole mathematical community is on Augustine's side and thus admits, at least implicitly, the validity of Augustine's problem in the area of geometry, which is not to say that the mathematical community would accept Augustine's solution.

With this understanding of ideals as embracing principles of reasoning and rules for correctly operating, as well as geometrical and other idealizations, we can formulate Augustine's problem:

Augustine's problem   Since ideals are not fully realized in the objects or actions that one experiences, how can we explain the mind's access to them?

Augustine has a single strategy for dealing with all three problems: divine truth communicates to each soul a stock of concepts and rules, some to be elicited only in connection with suitable perceptual experience, some that are independent of such experience. Augustine comes down firmly on the side of unlearned ideas in the human mind. In this he agrees with Plato. In the most basic sense, then, the mind does not construct concepts to represent the natures of creatures that are presented perceptually. Instead, preexisting concepts are elicited from the mind's unlearned stock. Augustine's solution to Aristotle's problem is not at all Aristotelian (on this point and much else, see O'Daly 1987, 206, n. 122, from whose masterly account of Augustine's psychology I have benefited greatly). Aristotle endows the mind with an active intellect whose function is to construct in the mind a concept appropriate for some set of perceptual experiences. Augustine attributes no such power to the human mind. So how is the appropriate concept elicited?

The answer is direct divine illumination of the human mind. This is not a sort of divine imposition or invasion but the operation of uncreated enlightenment in accordance with the human mind's own nature. "But who is our teacher but the truth that never changes? Even when we learn from created things, which are subject to change, we are led to the truth that does not change" (*Confessions,* bk. XI, chap. 8). It is because the human mind is bathed in divine light that the human mind can grasp immutable truths and know them to be immutable. "The light of men is the light of minds. The light of minds is above minds and surpasses all minds" (*Lectures on the Gospel of St. John,* tractate 3, para. 4, trans. in 1872). The human mind sees truth in the light of eternal and immutable truth. This is the solution to Plato's problem.

It is divine illumination, too, that engenders wisdom and guides its use—a position that thus solves Augustine's own problem. The objects and rules of wisdom are communicated to the soul by the Creator, and their operation there is guided by divine illumination.

The beauty of truth and wisdom . . . does not pass with time, and does not move with space. . . . It does not depend on the senses of the body. . . . It is eternal for all. . . . Without, it advises; within, it teaches. For this reason it is clear that the beauty of truth and wisdom is, without doubt, superior to our minds, which become wise only through this beauty and which make judgments, not about it but through it, on other things. (*On freedom of the will,* bk. 11, chap. 14)

With divine illumination the mind's access to truth is infallible. Not that one always grasps the truth in some area of concern, but that when one does grasp it, one knows.

But in the intuitions of the intellect it is not deceived. For either it understands, and then it possesses truth; or if it does not possess truth it fails to understand. (*De Genesi ad Litteram,* bk. XII, chap. 25)

The honest intuition of comprehending something is the result of divine illumination. When the intuition of comprehension fails, and Augustine frequently laments its failures in his own studies, the illumination is inadequate, and the best to be hoped for is probability.

Augustine, not surprisingly, is a psychological dualist. He held that the human mind in its intellectual capacity is nonmaterial. His main line of argument is that the knower must be commensurate with the known. Human knowers know corporeal beings, like dogs and stones. They also know nonmaterial things, like natural numbers and geometrical objects. These latter things, as we have seen, have no corporeal existence. It follows, Augustine argues, that the human mind must be noncorporeal, to be at the same ontological level as these noncorporeal, mathematical objects. The human mind can also know God, who is non corporeal, and this too argues for noncorporeal status of the mind (see *De Quantitate Animae*). There is no problem for Augustine in a noncorporeal being knowing corporeal beings. The noncorporeal is ontologically superior to the corporeal; the superior can grasp the inferior, but not the other way round. That the human mind should be able to know God is more of a problem. It is solved, in that the human mind's knowledge of God is finite, whereas God is infinite—imperfect knowledge of a perfect being. This redresses the balance somewhat. For the rest, the human mind's powers are elevated by grace, to permit a less imperfect, though still far from perfect, knowledge of infinite perfection. But here we leave psychology for theology.

Further, Augustine was what is called a substance dualist; that is, he believed that body and soul (with mind pertaining to soul) are separate entities. In *De Moribus Ecclesiae* (1.52, trans. in 1872) he gives his celebrated definition of a human being as "a rational soul using a body." This, as we have seen, means a noncorporeal soul using a corporeal body. In all dualist psychologies there is a problem in explaining how the corporeal can affect the noncorporeal. Augustine, as we have seen, solves it by positing divine illumination.

The mind being itself noncorporeal is most commensurate with itself. It follows that it understands itself with greater success than it understands anything else. This indicates how Augustine believed psychology should be studied. If you want to understand the minds of others, begin with your own: "For when does a mind know another mind if it does not know itself?" (*The Trinity,* bk. IX, chap. 3). The idea seems to be that we know what it is to perceive, remember, imagine, understand, desire, judge, and decide through awareness of these operations in ourselves. Implicitly, this is in opposition to the stance of contemporary psychology, so burned by the exaggerated claims of the introspectionists that it is uneasy about attending to the operations of one's own mind.

In self-awareness Augustine finds certainties that have a distinctly Cartesian ring. Where Descartes says "Cogito, ergo sum" (I think, therefore I am), Augustine says "Si enim fallor, sum" (Even if I am deceived, I am). Augustine adds, "I will to be happy . . . , and I know that I know this; I do not will to be deceived, and I know I do not will this" (*The Trinity,* bk. XV, chap. 12). Elsewhere he observes that his intellect is capable of grasping that vision is not hearing, nor hearing vision. This is not the place to explore the full implications of his views on self-awareness. It must suffice to draw attention to them and to indicate that the most light on the possibilities for such a study is perhaps cast by the descriptive psychology of Franz Brentano at the end of the nineteenth century.

We will come across much of what we have just seen in Augustine again when we come to Descartes. Descartes often strikes me as Augustine through a distorting mirror: the elements are the same, but they look different. We find in Descartes a similar substance dualism; we find unlearned ideas; we find divine illumination in a greatly altered form; we find very similar moves to combat skepticism; we find even the example of a piece of wax surviving the change of all its perceptible properties; we find similar attention to the psychological import of mathematical knowledge; we find deep sensitivity to the Platonic problems of learning and truth. What we do not find is the same confidence in the human mind, nor do we find the enraptured religious thought. There are 1,200 years between the two men, and so much has happened in the interval.

Bibliographical Note

Augustine (ca. 397/1961). *Confessions*. Translated by R. S. Pine-Coffin. London: Cox and Wyman.

O'Daly, G. (1987). *Augustine's Philosophy of Mind*. Berkeley: University of California Press. A scholarly account of St. Augustine's psychology.

9

St. Thomas Aquinas on Individuals and Concepts

Biographical Note

Thomas Aquinas was born in 1224 in southern Italy to a noble family. He went to a school of the Benedictines in Montecassino at the age of 5. He took an M.A. degree from Naples and, to his family's dismay, entered the newly founded order of begging friars, the Dominicans. He studied theology at Paris and, under St. Albert the Great, at Cologne. He taught mainly in Paris. He died in 1274. Aquinas, whose philosophical work was mainly inspired by the (newly rediscovered) work of Aristotle, is one of the great systematic thinkers of Europe. His psychology is to be found mainly in his *De anima* (On the soul, trans. in 1951), in his commentary on Aristotle's *De anima*, and in questions 75–90 of the first part of his most celebrated treatise *Summa theologica* (Handbook of theology). His analysis of concepts, which is the focus of the present chapter, is perhaps best set out in the short article *De ente et essentia* (On being and essence), which appears to be the first piece he wrote for a general readership. Unless otherwise identified, references in this chapter are to this work.

In leaving St. Augustine and moving on to St. Thomas Aquinas we leap 800 years and pass over at least two delightful figures, Boetius in the sixth century and St. Anselm in the eleventh. We pass over the breakdown of the Roman Empire and the absorption of the invading peoples, and place ourselves squarely in the High Middle Ages. This is the period of the building of magnificent cathedrals and monasteries, many of them still in use. It is the period in which universities were first established in the West, most of them still surviving. In fact, it is the beginning of the Renaissance. It saw the rebirth in the West of science and mathematics, resulting from the discovery of Greek and Arabic works in those areas. It is also the period of recovery, in translation, of the corpus of Aristotle's work as we know it today. The intermediaries were the Arabs, who furnished commentaries of their own on Aristotle, among them a particularly important one by Averroës (Ibn-Rushd). Aquinas, who like many medieval authors was fond of nicknames, frequently referred to Aristotle as "the philosopher" and to Averroës as "the commentator."

It proved to be difficult to integrate Aristotle with Christian theology. Aquinas had the handicap of not knowing Greek. He was fortunate, however, to have the best translator of the day, William of Moerbeke, among his fellow Dominicans. Aquinas's efforts disturbed conservative theologians, whose opposition led in 1277 (shortly after Aquinas's death) to the condemnation of a great many of his positions by the Archbishop of Paris, Etienne Tempier. Some would see this event as being as momentous in its day as the condemnation of Galileo by Pope Urban VIII in 1633. Tempier's condemnation came after the end of Thomas's career. Let us turn back now to its beginning.

Thomas Aquinas discovered in Aristotle a system of terms whose importance was obvious but whose meanings in relation to one another were not easily specified. Among these were "genus," "species," "essence," and "being." *De ente et essentia,* among other things, tackles this system. This involved solving several problems still of vital interest. Among them we will look particularly at how he conceives the relations among individuals, their accidents (which include their perceptual properties), and the hierarchy of categories in which they belong. This looks back to Plato's problems of learning and truth; it also looks forward to such empirical approaches as that of John Stuart Mill, which is still alive in almost all the current psychological work on word learning and concept formation. It looks forward to them, I believe, by undermining them in anticipation. It is high time people heard the news.

To make things concrete and familiar, think of a dog whose name is "Freddie." "Freddie" names a certain individual who is a dog, and hence an animal. We are familiar with the idea that the animals form a taxonomy in which "animal" is the generic term, with "dog," "cat," etc., being specific terms. The problem is, how are the concepts of dog and animal related to one another and to Freddie? The standard answer favored by most psychologists today is given in terms of perceptual features. It is

Table 9.1
The number of perceptual features needed to distinguish a concept at various
levels

Level	No. of perceptual features
Freddie	1,000
Dog	100
Animal	10

that a concept is the set of perceptual features that decide category membership. The concept of dog is the set of those features that are characteristic of all dogs and decide whether or not a certain creature is a dog; the concept of animal is the set of those perceptual features that are characteristic of all animals and decide whether or not a creature is an animal. The concept of Freddie is the set of such features that are characteristic of all presentations of Freddie across the range of his existence, from puppyhood to death. One might, if in a truculent mood, say that there are no perceptual features attaching to Freddie in the stillness of the night and conclude therefrom that the set that characterizes him across all circumstances is the null set, but let this humor pass until we come to David Hume.

Freddie has perceptual features that not all dogs have; dogs have features that not all animals have. In the interests of vividness, let us fancifully put numbers on the features at the different levels, as in table 9.1. There have to be more features associated with the concept of Freddie than with the concept of dog, because Freddie has some features that not all dogs have; likewise there have to be more features associated with the concept of dog than with that of animal. That is really all that I wish to convey by the array of numbers.

The first thing to ask, since it looks like the simplest, is, What might the 10 features for animals be? Soon the impression of simplicity vanishes. While every animal has some color(s), there is no color that is common to them all. Neither is there any shape, sound, weight, style of movement, smell, or feel common to all animals. By going through the entire set of perceptual modalities, we find that we have to assign the null set of features to the concept of animal. By a parallel argument we have to assign the null set to the concept of plant too. We then have it that the concept of animal = $\varnothing$ = the concept of plant, which by transitivity of identity gives us that the concept of animal = the concept of plant. The conclusion that "animal" and "plant" are assigned the same concept is disastrous.

There are various ways for radical empiricists to attempt to avoid this disaster. [See the definition of *radical empiricist* in the Glossary.] Some escape routes, suggested by Wittgenstein and Vygotsky, involve being flexible in the choice of features at a level; at present in the realm of computers and artificial intelligence the idea is to assign weights to features, so that a concept is modeled as a weighted subset of perceptual features.

All of this Thomas would have found interesting, but not in connection with concept formation. He would have said that these efforts are aimed at the problem of how we perceive that some creature is a dog, rather than at what it is to be a dog; at how we recognize Freddie, rather than at what it is to be Freddie (or rather, an individual of the kind DOG). The distinction is completely reasonable and obvious. If I tell you that the lady with the pink dress is Margaret Thatcher, you can use that information to determine who Mrs. Thatcher is. You do not, however, imagine that wearing pink dresses is constitutive of what it is to be Mrs. Thatcher, that she would cease to be Mrs. Thatcher if she wore a dress of some other color. By a parallel argument, then, we must distinguish the means that may serve to tell which things are dogs from what it is to be a dog. With this in mind we can easily grasp Thomas's general point. It is that what it is to be an animal cannot be just a part of what it is to be a dog (as the standard approach would have us believe), although the example he uses is "man" rather than "dog."

Whatever is included in the species is included in an indeterminate manner in the genus. If indeed animal were not *all* that man is, but only part of it, "animal" could not be predicated of a man. For no integral part of a whole can be predicated of that whole. (§ 8)

The point can be put this way, again in connection with Freddie. We say of him "This dog is an animal." Now take any proper part of Freddie, like the head: we cannot correctly say "This dog is a head." It follows that by anticipation Thomas has ruled out the idea that the concept of animal is a proper part of the concept of dog.

What, then, is the relation between the concepts of dog and animal? And how do these relate to the individual Freddie? This brings us to the principal message (for us) of *De ente et essentia.*

The nature of the species is indeterminate with respect to an individual [in the species] just as the nature of a genus is with respect to a species. Thus, just as a genus, when predicated of a species, embraces in its meaning, albeit indistinctly, *all* that is determinate in a species, so too a species, when predicated of an individual, must signify the *entire* essence of that individual, albeit indistinctly. (§ 14.) [See the definition of *essence* in the Glossary.]

Just as the concept of animal is not a proper part of the concept of dog, so the concept of dog is not a proper part of that of Freddie. All of Freddie is dog, Aquinas is telling us, and all of him is animal.

We can understand better what Aquinas has in mind if we listen to biologists. There is great uncertainty about how to set up taxonomies, especially about which items of information to use in reaching classificatory decisions, but the following picture, which in outline was familiar to Thomas, is accurate enough for our purposes. It is that what makes an individual an animal is having a digestive system, having a locomotive system, having a reproductive system, etc. I have been told that the list for many biologists contains eleven items. On the other hand, what makes the individual a dog is having a canine digestive system, having a canine locomotive system, having a canine reproductive system, etc. The point is that all items in the animal list appear again in the dog list. This is completely different from the standard psychological schema.

You might suspect that the way a digestive system is specified to be a canine one is by adding items of information. In one way this is, of course, true, but it misses Thomas's main point. Take the digestive system. The entire system, not just part of it, must be characterized at both the generic and specific levels. This is easier to see if we return to Freddie. Freddie as a whole is a dog and also an animal. The hair is both dog hair and animal hair; the shape is both a canine shape and an animal one; the tail is a dog tail and an animal one. To change the presentation, the expressions "dog" and "animal" do not divide up the perceptual information. It's not that the front of Freddie is a dog and the back an animal. Similarly, it's not that part of his digestive system is canine and part animal. It is all canine, and it is all animal.

Exactly parallel considerations apply to the relation between the individual Freddie and the species to which he belongs, DOG.

To take a different tack, one of the main points at issue here is that the essential structure of dogs, or for that matter of animals, is not given directly in perception. It has to be comprehended through the action of the active intellect, working from perceptual information but going far beyond it. Here Thomas parts company with Augustine. Thomas thought that the human mind, like other created agencies, has within it natural powers to achieve its goal. In its ordinary action, then, the human mind does not require direct divine illumination, he taught. Any divine illumination is indirect; it is built into the human mind, which, after all, is created in the image and likeness of the divine mind. On this point Thomas is quite clear, and he ruffled conservative sensibilities.

Thomas did hold onto another idea that he found in Augustine: to say that all dogs instantiate the same substantial form is to say that they all instantiate the same idea in the divine mind. Thomas was not excessively sanguine about our ability to comprehend these ideas. He felt that we generally get the genus right, but not the finer detail. "In perceptual objects we do not even know the essential differences" (§ 31).

In this Thomas is implicitly distinguishing the divine idea of DOG from any concept that we may have formed of the species. This enabled him to be relaxed about our efforts to comprehend the substantial forms of creatures that are embraced under our everyday words: "dog," "cat," and so forth. He is able to say, "The noun 'man' signifies the essence of a man" (§ 15), even if we are unable to spell out what that essence is. For Thomas, by the way, the word "essence" denotes substance, but in relation to existence; it denotes substance as limiting existence to be of a particular sort but also as what is brought into being by the addition of existence. The essence of man, then, exists in every man. The immutability of the essence, and hence the permanence of the truths about man's nature, are grounded in the permanence of the divine ideas. Thomas's solution to Plato's problem of truth, then, is along the same lines as that of Augustine. Our words for kinds and properties of kinds denote the relevant ideas in the mind of the Creator, and this explains the permanence of the truths our words express.

Let us return to the gap that Thomas finds between perception and cognition proper. He is putting flesh on the bare bones of the Aristotelian idea that the concepts we form in connection with perception are not given immediately in the perceptual array. Nor are they extracted directly from the perceptual array. Nor are they imposed on the mind from the outside, as many psychologists have assumed. They are constructed by the mind in collaboration with the perceptual system and thus in collaboration with the objects themselves.

In token of the distinctness of perception and cognition, notice that we can hold a perceptual object constant and vary the concept that is correctly applied to it; we can also hold a concept constant and vary dramatically the perceptual objects to which it applies. For example, we can correctly apply to the perceptual figure of Freddie the concepts of dog, poodle, male poodle, quadruped, mammal, pal, nuisance, animal, etc.; the concept of animal is correctly applied to the perceptual presentations of a dog, a snake, a fish, a bird, an ant, a lobster, etc. In the light of Aquinas's analysis we see that such switches of concept and object are switches not in the choice of perceptual features but in the manner in which the whole object is conceptualized in one case and in the manner in which the concept is instantiated in the other. It follows that when Thomas says, as he frequently does, that the mind *abstracts* the substantial form from perception, he means nothing like what modern psychologists mean by the word "abstraction." It would be far closer to his way of seeing things to say that the mind constructs mental representations of substances on the basis of perceptual presentations.

There is, however, a danger in replacing "abstract" with "construct." The exchange might suggest that the mind has no access to the real structures of things, but only to its own constructions. This is closer to Kant than to Thomas, who insists that the mind's constructions are not *what* people know but that *by which* they know. He is particularly sure footed in the matter of intentionality, never mistaking a stage in the processing of information about to an object for the object known. For Thomas, an attentive reader of Genesis and St. John's Gospel, the mind was designed to grasp reality, not just representations of reality. It is not, then, limited to mere mental constructions.

It is instructive to note that the ordinary word that Thomas uses for what the intellect constructs is *species intelligibilis,* which means intelligible outline or sketch. For example, when you walk in the snow, you leave a *species* (outline) of your boot in the snow. Not, however, a *species intelligibilis*; for a *species* to be *intelligibilis,* it has to convey the intelligibility of that of which it is the impression. That is exactly what a blueprint attempts to do. Just as the blueprint of (say) a clothes drier represents the structure of the device in a purely conceptual or intelligible manner, abstracting altogether from perceptual properties, so the intelligible outline represents the substantial structure of an object, abstracting altogether from perceptual properties.

This brings us to a third theme in *De ente et essentia.* Thomas observes that we can, without contradiction, conceive that any existing creature might cease to exist, or that to be is not an essential property of any creature (§ 26). The substantial forms or structures of the objects we discover in the environment are neutral with respect to existence. Freddie exists, but nothing in his substantial form requires that he should. This led Thomas to make a distinction between essence and existence, a distinction that we do not find in Aristotle. The distinction has import for psychology that is not easily overrated.

One of the reasons the distinction was important to Thomas was that it made room for causality and change. Aristotle in his metaphysics conceptualized substances as substantial forms individuated by matter. Now forms are structures considered in isolation from matter, which means that they are inert. The structure of a dishwasher apart from the matter in which it might be instantiated will wash no dishes. Matter too, for Aristotle, is inert. This reveals a profound inadequacy in Aristotle's theory, for there is no reason to believe that if two inert principles (matter and form) are combined, the combination will be anything but inert. The result is that although Aristotle wrote important chapters on four different types of causality (or explanation), his basic metaphysics makes no provision for causal operations that effect change. Thomas remedies this by positing existence as something dynamic. This is going to need unfolding.

Probably the simplest way to conceptualize Thomas's theory of existence is as energy. For him, to exist is to have causal energy. Essence, on the other hand, he construes as a limitation of energy: a dog's essence determines his energy to be of a certain type. This is very reminiscent of the physicists' view that all matter is energy (or mass-energy, as they would say) and the energy congeals into various basic patterns that are limitations of energy: photons, electrons, protons, neutrons, and so forth, each with its particular mass, electrical charge, spin, and so forth. For Thomas, there is a dialectical relation between existence and essence: existence is energy without which a particular essence would not exist in the world; essence, on the other hand, is a specification, and hence determination, of energy.

The way this relates to psychology is as follows. The mind receives perceptual data from the environment, for which the active intellect endeavors to construct an appropriate conceptual representation. A real substance, however, is a system of causally interacting parts. The reason the mind is able to detect such causally significant structures is that it grasps the existence or energy of physical objects. It is precisely because it can go beyond form or structure to energy that the mind can discover structure. But the mind has no concept of energy; it treats energy as an unanalyzed primitive. This is very much in keeping with how physicists see mass-energy.

Aquinas, then, would accept David Hume's conclusion that causality is not directly given in perception. He would not have accepted Hume's conclusion that all there is to causality is a certain regularity in the occurrence of perceptual patterns. He would not, I believed, have rejected the idea that certain perceptual sequences create a perceptual impression of causality—the cognoscenti will think of Albert Michotte's work in this connection (for a brief account of Michotte's work, see the chapter on Hume). Aquinas, however, sees the mind as going beyond appearances to reality, and the reality that underlies appearances is a causally dynamic one. More interesting still is his insistence that causality eludes not only our immediate perceptual powers but even our conceptual powers as well. Concepts, being inert, must represent structure in an inert manner. Nevertheless, the mind is aware of causality, *for we know more than we can conceptualize.*

For Aristotle, the main business of the mind is to form and comprehend concepts of the types of object that are presented perceptually. For Thomas, the mind's main business is to grasp reality, to register existence, and the main guarantee of existence is perception. Aristotle took perception, which Plato had downplayed, and restored it to a place of honor. Thomas went further still, grounding our sensitivity to reality in perception. Not that we can know only what we can directly perceive, but that our grasp of reality is surest when it is based on perception. The reason is that perception starts out as the causal effects produced in our perceptual organs by causally active, and therefore real, objects. There is a healthy empiricism in Thomas, surpassing even that of Aristotle.

In view of his emphasis on existence, it will come as no surprise that, for Thomas, the supreme act of mind is judgment, because judgment is a decision about reality, about what exists, or as one might say, about truth and falsity. In judgment, the mind decides whether a certain representation of reality is faithful to reality or not. For this to happen, the representation must be already interpreted as a possible situation; judgment itself is a decision as to whether the actual situation corresponds to the (possible) described one. Judgment is a neglected subject in present-day philosophy of mind. In present-day psychology there is plenty of research on the judgments people make in various circumstances and on factors that affect judgment. I know of no work by a psychologist on what judgment is or on where it fits into a general theory of psychology. If Thomas is right about judgment, present-day psychology is missing a core element of its subject.

Thomas Aquinas usually agrees with Aristotle but also goes beyond him. I did not repeat what we have already seen in Aristotle, preferring to concentrate on what he adds to Aristotle. We saw three main points. First, the concept of a genus is not a proper subset of the items that feature in the concept of one of its species. Both concepts contain the same items; they vary in degree of specificity. Second, concepts are not abstracted directly from the perceptual array. They are more constructed than abstracted. Yet all this does not undermine their veracity. Third, the human mind registers existence. Existence and essence are dialectically related, mutually determining each other. Existence for Thomas is an act, something dynamic. It is sensitivity to this dynamism that yields knowledge of structures consisting of causally interacting components. The mind forms concepts of such structures; it has no concept of existence, which it treats as a primitive. The mind, then, knows more than it can conceptualize. Judgment reflects sensitivity to existence as distinct from structure.

Here we ought to tie down two more terms that we will frequently need again.

Essence   The most basic meaning of "essence" is substance, which is, remember, substantial form individuated by matter. But "essence" denotes substance in opposition to existence, whereas "substance" denotes the same thing in opposition to accidents. Essence limits existence and makes it one sort rather than another. Because "essence" denotes substance, it developed a secondary meaning: what is indispensable or, as we say, essential.

Concept   A concept is a mental representation of structural relations in isolation from any perceptual properties that may be associated with them. When the structure to be represented is a substantial form, the related concept is an *intelligible outline,* which we construed as a blueprint.

Bibliographical Note

Aquinas, T. (ca. 1252/1949). *On Being and Essence.* Translated by Armand Maurer. Toronto: Pontifical Institute of Mediaeval Studies. A translation of *De ente et essentia.*

10

St. Thomas Aquinas and Dualism

We have already seen that Plato, Aristotle (obscurely), and Augustine were dualists. Augustine's version of dualism, as that of Plato, is substance dualism: in each person there are two distinct substances, a corporeal one and a noncorporeal one. St. Augustine's expression is "a rational soul using a [material] body." This seems to be captured in the common expression, "body and soul," which suggests something like a spirit lodged in a body. We even say in everyday speech, "I ate something to keep body and soul together." This reflects Augustine's idea accurately enough. The first Christian to dispute this position seems to have been Thomas Aquinas. We must try to understand his reasons for rejecting substance dualism. We must also try to understand the property dualism that he substituted for it, and his reasons for believing it to be true. One reason for a fairly full treatment of the topic is that it has almost vanished from contemporary books on psychology. Modern students of the subject ought to know what their antecedents held and why they held it.

Dualism is intimately connected with the Christian view that life goes on after death, but in itself dualism is a purely psychological position. In arguing for it, Thomas does not propose theological arguments, nor does he appeal to the authority of scripture. His reasons are all psychological: the operations of the intellect and will. They deserve to be considered as such, rather than as theological claims in disguise. Thomas was not the type who would try to slip something across.

One obvious problem with substance dualism is that it places a large gap between mind and body. It presents the soul as though it were a driver in a car. Invariably, the theoretician identifies himself with the driver, not the car. Naturally, drivers do not want scratches or dents on their car, but they don't feel them in the way they feel scratches and dents on their own bodies. The gap between drivers and cars seems to be far greater than that between people and their bodies.

Thomas went further. He made the obvious point that both Socrates's mind and Socrates's perceptual organs are parts of Socrates; parts, that is, of a single person, not parts of separate substances (*Summa theologica*, pt. 1, ques. 76, art. 1). He found the very suggestion of separate substances repugnant, because the definition of a human being, specifying the nature of each individual in the species, implicitly embraces both intellect and perception: a human being is a rational animal, and animals certainly perceive.

> There is no other substantial form in a person than the intellectual soul, which has the power to perform functions of perception and nutrition, and all other inferior functions. It alone accomplishes everything that inferior natures accomplish in other [creatures]. The same goes for the perceptual souls of animals and the nutritive souls of plants, and so in general for all higher level forms with respect to lower level ones. (*Summa theologica*, pt. 1, ques. 76, art. 4)

The reason for this is quite simple: every individual in a species has a soul, which is none other than the individual's substantial form or organization. Each individual has only one single overarching structure. In some individuals the structure is more complex than in others. Animals share a nutritive structure with plants, but the souls of animals are more complex, because in addition they make provision for perception, among other things. In a human being too, there is a single structure, called "intellectual" for its highest function but embracing also the perceptual and nutritive (and whatever other) functions. So far no biologist could be uneasy with Thomas's position, which is also Aristotle's. It is surely preferable to the two-substance theory of Augustine.

We should be clear what Thomas is saying. A human being has a pancreas, a liver, a central nervous system, and much more. Each of these components has an internal structure and all are coordinated in a single overarching structure, namely the human soul. It follows that the human soul is not distinct from the structure of the human pancreas or that of the human brain. These are all substructures of the human soul. It is quite contrary to Thomas's thinking to see the soul as distinct from the brain or the central nervous system or even the pancreas, for that matter. The only soul there is in a human being has to attend to biochemical secretions, hormones, blood circulation, and all the other bodily functions. This is an important part of what property dualism means.

So far there is no dualism in this presentation of Thomas's position. What makes him a dualist is his claim that the description given is incomplete; that there is more to a human being than the organization of bodily parts: brain, duodenum, liver, pancreas, etc.

The human soul is a form united to a body, but in such a manner that it is not completely comprehended by the body as though it were immersed in it, as other material forms are. The soul has capacities that surpass the powers of any [purely] material body. . . .

It has a capacity for understanding that resides in the passive intellect. Being united to a body it has the functions and powers that pertain to a body, such as nutrition and perception. (*Quaestiones disputatae de anima*, art. 2)

First the general approach. This he lays down in the section on human nature in the *Summa theologica*.

Each thing's nature is manifested by its operation. The operation peculiar (*propria*) to a human being is to understand In this humans surpass all animals, and so Aristotle in the [*Nicomachean*] *Ethics* (bk. X, chap. 7) finds in this operation the ultimate felicity of human beings, this being the operation special (*propria*) to human beings. The species for humans must be determined by that which is the source of this operation. (*Summa theologica*, pt. 1, ques. 76, art. 1)

While the idea is clear enough, one or two comments are in order. Thomas believes that among animals, humans alone are able to reason and understand, and thus humans alone have a nonmaterial component. He never offers any reason to believe this, and we will not pursue it, since whether or not (some) animals have a nonmaterial component is tangential to the claim that humans have such a component. For the rest, Thomas, like Aristotle, declares that the capacity to know is the supreme capacity in humans. Elsewhere he concedes that in ways the will is superior to the intellect, but for all that, the intellect is superior in the more basic sense that it discovers and presents to the will the good that the will desires (*Summa theologica*, pt. 1, ques. 82, arts. 3 and 4). The nature of the human intellect is to be discovered by studying the operations of the intellect, by studying what it can do.

I find two main arguments for dualism in the writings of Aquinas and a third line of thought that can be employed for the same purpose, since it is intended to show the superiority of humans to animals of other species. I begin with what seems to me the most cogent of the three, the one that he gives pride of place to in the *Summa theologica* and that he develops at greatest length in his *Quaestiones disputatae de anima.*

The proper objects of the human intellect are the substantial forms of the physical objects we find about us (*Summa theologica,* pt. 1, ques. 84, art. 7). This is what the mind is for—to understand the material world. While there are enormous difficulties in doing so, there is no principled limitation. There is nothing in the human mind, in particular there is nothing in the passive intellect (which is the mind precisely in its capacity to understand), that rules out any material object.

The passive intellect has to have the capacity [of comprehending] all that a human being can comprehend. Since it can receive all this, it must be separate from it. Anything that can receive other things, must in itself, be without them; just as the pupil [of the eye], which receives all colors, itself lacks color. A human being is made to understand the forms of all perceptible objects. It follows that the passive intellect on its own is denuded of the forms and natures of all perceptible objects. (*Quaestiones disputatae de anima,* ques. 2)

The analogy with the eye is oft repeated. It matters not the least to its effectiveness that the eye does not perceive all colors, only those of the visible spectrum. [Actually, if a color is not visible, it is uncertain whether to call it a color. We can understand the author's meaning by assuming that he refers to potential colors: colors that might be seen if the human eye could see the nonvisible parts of the spectrum.] Thomas can repeat his argument appealing not to all colors, just to all colors of the visible spectrum. His point is that the pupil of the eye must not itself be colored, since it has to transmit all visible colors. If the pupil were red, for example, like a piece of red stained glass, everything seen through it would look red, and other colors would be invisible.

With this understanding, let us turn to the mind. Thomas's line is that the mind is capable of expressing the substantial form of any physical object and hence cannot itself be the substantial form of any physical object. In passing, let us lay one possible line of objection to rest. Physicists tell us that in quantum mechanics it is impossible to know precisely both a particle's momentum and its position. It might seem, then, that there are some physical things that we cannot know. But this is not a counterexample. Physicists maintain that there simply is no such thing as a particle's precise position and momentum at a particular moment; there is no reality to it. Yet there is a problem of a sort. It is unclear what one might mean by "any physical object." Is a computer program, for instance, a physical object? Fortunately, this sort of problem need not worry us unduly, because the most important case is the human brain.

What about the brain? Thomas is saying implicitly that if the mind were the brain, it would not be able to understand itself, because what comprehends must be distinct from what is comprehended. The core of his argument can be put thus: either the mind is not identical with the brain and there is some possibility of understanding the brain, or the two are identical and there is no chance of understanding the brain. But neuropsychologists and others hope to understand the brain, and while the difficulties are horrendous, already substantial progress has been made. What are we to make of this?

The argument can be brought into sharper focus if one accepts that the brain (or the mind) has a language and if one attends to this language alone. Remember that Thomas believed that there is a mental language. I will not go into what he meant by that but simply use the idea of a mental language to make his argument for dualism more precise. Observe that if the mind and the brain are one, which is the position we are exploring, the mind's language is the brain's language. Imagine that neuropsychologists and neurologists are attempting to specify the brain's own internal language, which, in the scenario we are studying, has to be an interpreted language in which we can describe the world as we do. Can we specify the brain's language in the language of the brain? To see the type of problem involved, think of how one specifies a sentence like "Freddie is an animal." For syntax alone, one needs to be able to say that "Freddie" is a *proper name,* that it is a whole *noun phrase,* that it is the *subject of the sentence,* and so on. One puts each expression in the sentence in quotation marks and describes it in the appropriate syntactic terms. For semantics, on the other hand, one needs to say that "Freddie" refers to a certain individual in the kind DOG and that this individual has the property referred to by "is an animal." This would need to be spelt out in detail that need not concern us. One of the discoveries of the great logician Kurt Gödel is that it is possible to express the syntax of a language in the language itself. If, however, the system that the language describes is as powerful as arithmetic, it is not possible to express the semantics fully in the language. Since the human mind can handle arithmetic and much more, it follows (in our scenario) that the semantics of the brain's language—the rules for interpreting that language—cannot be fully expressed in the brain's language.[1]

There is, then, a deep point in Thomas's argument, but it is difficult to evaluate it. We simply do not know the extent of the limitation on expressing the semantics of the brain's language in that language. We must be content to leave it at that. Meanwhile, it seems only fair to add that once one adopts the neurological stance, attention fixes on neural structures and projections, neural transmitters, and neural activity—and semantics seems to disappear utterly. This suggests that the neurological stance is hampered less by a limitation in semantics than by a total blockage—at least at the present time. Whether this is a principled blockage is not easy to decide.

I leave to the reader to wonder about the implications for self-understanding if the mind is in some important sense nonmaterial. In that event, Thomas would say that the mind is not one of those objects that the mind is by nature designed to study. He does, nevertheless, hold that it does have some self-knowledge, given indirectly in its workings on physical objects. We will come back to the subject of self-awareness when we come to another great Aristotelian who, like Thomas Aquinas, was a Dominican, though only for a time, namely Franz Brentano.

Thomas's second argument for the nonmateriality of the human mind rests on the observation that it knows the substantial forms of objects under the guise of universals. This comes about, he claims, from the fact that the mind, in comprehending a substantial form, abstracts from the individuating circumstances. For Aquinas, the work of individuating natures is done by matter. What makes Freddie a different dog from Spot? In answer we cannot appeal to the substantial form DOG, because that, being what they share, makes them the same. Inspired by Aristotle, Thomas takes the individuating factor to be matter, an unanalyzed primitive in the system. But then the mind represents substantial forms as universals precisely because it leaves matter aside, and this suggests to Aquinas that the mental representations are nonmaterial. The way Thomas puts his case makes reference to bodily organs. Here he is arguing against the materialists.

> Much less can their case hold when we come to the rational mind, whose job is to understand and abstract intelligible outlines (*species*), not only as separate from matter but from all individuating material conditions—which is necessary for a knowledge of universals. But in this connection something can be added that is special to the rational mind. Not only does it receive intelligible outlines without matter and material conditions; in its own special operation no bodily organ can participate. (*Quaestiones disputatae de anima,* ques. 1, art. 1)

In his *Summa theologica* (part 1, ques. 75, art. 5) he gives the same argument with an illuminating addition. He says that if the mind were material, or operated through a bodily organ, it would at best know the substantial forms of other objects as particulars, not as universals—just as vision, which employs a bodily organ, presents shapes as particulars, not as universals. In effect, we can take him as saying that the brain is not the organ of the mind. It may house parts of the organs of the perceptual systems, but it is not the organ of the mind. Indeed, Thomas held that substantial forms have the status of universals only in minds, where precisely the absence of individuating conditions makes them applicable to many individuals.

This argument suffers from the fact that the whole Aristotelian theory of matter, as a metaphysical construct whose function is solely to individuate, has become suspect, and not, as we will see in the next chapter, solely for reasons deriving from modern physics. For all that, there is a deep intuition behind Thomas's argument, which I hope I may be permitted to put in my own way. If a human mind succeeds in forming an adequate mental representation of the biological structure of dogs, it has represented that structure as an abstract object. An abstract object is precisely one that is immutable, that stands outside the whole system of causal events in the universe. It is indeed difficult to see how a physical brain can make the right sort of contact with such an abstract object: thinking about it, referring to it, modeling it, and so on. But alas, it is also difficult to understand how a nonmaterial mind could do those things. Clearly, Thomas has his finger on a deeply mysterious property of the human mind. Unfortunately, it is not clear how the mystery is reduced by allowing a nonmaterial constituent in the mind.

The third argument for dualism derives from the fact that our minds present the structures of things as universals. This, as we just saw, Thomas takes as a token of the immateriality of the mind, which in turn means that the mind is sufficiently indeterminate in itself that it can represent the nature of any material thing. Seen from another angle, this property is also evidenced by the mind's infinite adaptability, although Thomas himself does not use this fact to argue for the mind's immateriality.

The intellectual soul, which comprehends universals, has an infinite capacity. That is why nature could not determine [for human beings] natural reactions, or fixed means either of defense or of shelter; as she does for other animals whose minds in their ability to apprehend and control are limited to certain particular things. In place of all these nature endows humans with reason, and with hands, which are organs par excellence. By means of these, humans can furnish themselves with an infinite variety of instruments for an infinity of purposes. (*Summa theologica*, part 1, ques. 76, art. 5, ad. 4)

Thomas is leery about completed infinities and here means, for example, that no matter how many instruments humans have already fashioned, they can fashion yet others (see *Summa theologica*, part 1, ques. 86, art. 2). With this minor point out of the way, we see in this passage a commonsense appeal to the special nature of humans: though they seem of all creatures the most helpless, they alone have discovered and continue to discover ingenious new ways of turning nature to their advantage. Other animals seem to be guided almost completely by instinct, supplemented by a limited and standard range of learned responses. While our knowledge of animal behavior has advanced to a level that Thomas could hardly have imagined, the broad point still stands. Indeed, the ingenuity of humans in observing other species is part of the infinite adaptability to which he draws attention.

All this Thomas seems to take as an indication that the human mind is free of the limitations that an exclusively material nature would impose. True, he had no inkling, of course, that automata would one day be devised that in principle, at least, are capable of employing finite and material means to accomplish infinitely many diverse adaptations. Yet it is not clear whether this counts for or against Thomas's argument. In some basic sense, automata have no purposes of their own, and so none of their varied responses are intended for their own benefit. In this they seem inferior to simple animals. Nevertheless, automata are material, and they are capable of infinitely diverse responses. It follows that of itself infinite diversity in responding does not establish immateriality.

The issues here are larger and more complex than I can hope to settle in a few sentences. Nevertheless, I may be permitted to say in favor of Thomas's way of viewing things that what is special about the human mind's adaptability is its insight into the nature of things and its grasp of their possibilities. It is not just that we comprehend the natures we discover, but that we can go beyond them, devising new structures, using nature's resources in ways that nature on its own does not. Automata, it seems reasonable to say, have no insights at all into the nature of things or into their possibilities. Moreover, the existence of these automata is itself a further proof of the sort of adaptability Thomas had in mind. Adaptability clearly marks humans as very different from automata— and indeed from other animals. I am not sure whether it can be made to count as an argument for immateriality.

One curious observation before ending. We do not seem to be limited to the logic we normally employ. An able writer like Italo Calvino discovered that our ordinary conceptions of a person take account of subaspects. There is the person as a whole, and there are the subaspects of family life, professional life, and so on. Italo Calvino delights us in his story of *The Nonexistent Knight* by confining the hero to a subaspect, namely the profession of knight, with no associated person as a whole and no other subaspects. Calvino and, in his wake, his readers have no trouble violating the ordinary rules. Other writers who violate ordinary rules include Robert Louis Stevenson, who has two distinct persons share a single physical body in *Dr. Jeckyll and Mr. Hyde*. We are somehow not limited to the ordinary rules of our own mind. These are striking examples of the adaptability Thomas had in mind.

Not everyone who has studied Thomas's writings has been convinced by his arguments for property dualism. Cardinal Cajetan, the great sixteenth-century Thomistic commentator and Dominican, felt that Thomas did not succeed in proving his case. Nevertheless, Thomas's arguments are profoundly interesting to a modern psychologist, particularly as they emphasize properties of mind that seem to have dropped from sight. To sum up, the arguments were three in number. (1) The human mind has the capacity in principle to comprehend the natures of all material things. (2) It represents these natures as universals, that is, in a nonmaterial manner. (3) The mind is not limited, as a material structure might be, in its insights into the possibilities of employing material things to advantage. This argument of infinite adaptability we will come across again in Descartes but there applied to the domain of language.

There are some more terms to tie down.

Universal   A universal is a representation that is true of many individuals. For Thomas, universals are always mental representations.

Abstract object   An abstract object is an immutable object, an object that is neither causally active nor affected by the causal activity of other things. Examples are numbers, computational rules, proofs, plans, and so forth.

Bibliographical Note

Two texts are most important for Aquinas's views on the nonmaterial nature of the human mind:

St. Thomas Aquinas, *Summa theologiae*, especially part 1, questions 75–79.

St. Thomas Aquinas, *Quaestiones disputatae de anima*, especially question 2.

11

Duns Scotus and William of Ockham: The Cusp of the Middle Ages

Biographical Notes

John Duns Scotus (1265–1308) seems to have been born in Berwickshire, Scotland. He joined the order founded by St. Francis of Assisi known as the Franciscans. He studied in Oxford and taught theology in Paris and in Cologne, where he died, aged 42. His nickname was the "Subtle Doctor."

William of Ockham (about 1285–1349) was born in the south of England, possibly Surrey, and he too joined the Franciscan order. He was delated to the Pope for heresy. Before his trial was completed, he sided with the Master General of the Franciscans in a dispute with the Pope and fled to the Emperor of Bavaria. For this he was excommunicated. He never held a university chair. He was reconciled with the Pope some time before his death. Many regard him as the ablest logician of the Middle Ages.

In this reflection we will look at two strains in Ockham's work that are of psychological import: (a) his response to Duns Scotus's handling of what is sometimes called the problem of the one and the many, together with the implications of that response for the theory of cognition, and (b) his theory of mental language. First the one and the many.

In the Aristotelianism that Duns Scotus inherited through Thomas Aquinas, each substance has its own nature, where "nature" means substance, but substance viewed as the source of activity. Freddie the dog was seen as having the nature peculiar to dogs; Spot the dog likewise. The job of the human mind is to discover this nature and represent it in a concept; that is, as a single mental expression specifying the nature of Freddie and equally that of Spot. To accomplish this, the mind has to extract the nature from its material and individuating circumstances. This extraction completed, the concept in the mind that successfully extracts it is already a universal, in the sense that it is true of many individual material creatures. As a concept in the mind, it is a universal; as realized in Freddie, it is a particular. Universals exist only in minds. Of course, for Aquinas they existed in the most fundamental manner in the mind of the Creator.

Duns Scotus was not happy with several details of this. One was the view that in the extramental world there is no such thing as a single nature common to Freddie and Spot. Against Thomas, he held, for example, that there exists in the extramental world a nature that is common to all dogs, although he conceded that this common nature is not universal. To be universal, it would need conceptual status, so that it could be predicated of many individuals.

The second, more troublesome, element for Duns Scotus was the idea that matter individuates the nature of Freddie from that of Spot. This doctrine invites the query, What individuates the matter in Freddie's body from that in Spot's? At this point Thomas cannot appeal to yet another layer of matter to individuate one lump of matter from another. In the Thomist system, there is no lower level of matter. Thomas's own view was that extramental matter is somehow sealed with quantities (*signata quantitate*), and that somehow the quantity attaching to Freddie's matter serves to individuate it from Spot's. I do not believe that sense can be made of this, and neither did Duns Scotus.

At this juncture Duns Scotus made a rather desperate move. He posited a special agent of individuation in each substance, distinct from its matter. He coined a rather awkward new word from the Latin for the demonstrative "this" (*haec*) to express his idea. He called the agent of individuation "thisness" (*haecceitas*). It had the function of "contracting" the common nature to a particular.

Commonality belongs to nature outside the mind and so does particularity. A nature of itself is common; it is particular only by means of something in an object that contracts it. A nature, however, is not of itself universal. I agree then that we must look for an explanation of universality outside of nature, but not of commonality. Granted commonality in the nature of an individual entity, we are obliged to seek [elsewhere] the explanation of its particularity, which something over and above nature must add to nature. (*Opus Oxoniense,* vol. 2, disp. 3, ques. 1, n. 10; trans. in 1964)

Duns Scotus had a psychology to match this ontology, but we will not go into it.

This is the position that confronted William of Ockham, a clear thinking man, and he did not like it. To begin, he decided that Duns Scotus was asking the wrong question, which was, Granted a common nature, how can we explain an individual of that nature? Duns Scotus was starting with commonality and worrying about how to explain particularity. Ockham turned this on its head. He felt that what we are most sure of is particulars, such as Freddie and Spot. The question he posed was this: granted particulars, what sense can we make of universals and common natures? (*Summa logicae,* bk. 1, chap. 15).

The way one important line of argument went was this. Take Freddie's nature; either it belongs to him alone, in which case it is not common, or it is common to many dogs, in which case it does not belong to Freddie in any special way. To grasp this more clearly, think of the Lincoln Memorial; either it belongs to Mr. Clinton, in which case it is not possessed in common by the American people, or it belongs to the American people as a whole, in which case it does not belong in any special way to Mr. Clinton. On the other hand Mr. Clinton's house in Arkansas belongs to him alone and is not the common property of the American people. When we return to the point Ockham is making, the result is conclusive. There cannot be any common natures of the sort that Duns Scotus claimed.

Our concepts in one sense are universal in that they can be properly predicated of many individuals. They are true of these individuals. Our concept of dog can be correctly predicated of both Freddie and Spot. But if we examine this concept in itself, rather than in the relation it bears to individual dogs, we see that it too is a particular concept, rather than a universal (*Summa logicae,* bk. 1, chap. 14).

So how do we form these concepts that in themselves are particulars but are predicable of many? We do it by studying individuals, by observing those characteristics in which they agree and those in which they disagree. In fact, species are known through their measure of agreement.

It does not follow that if Socrates and Plato agree more than Socrates and [a] donkey, there is some one thing in which they agree more. . . . Thus I say that

Socrates agrees more with Plato in virtue of his intellective soul; and similarly that he agrees with Plato more than with the donkey with respect to his whole being. Thus, if we are to be accurate we should not say that Socrates and Plato agree in some one thing which is their essence; we should say rather that they agree in several things, for they agree in their forms and in themselves taken as wholes. (*Summa logicae*, bk. 1, chap. 17)

It might at first glance appear that we have merely gone back to Aquinas, but it would be a mistake to think that. Notice in the last quotation that the notion of a humanity realized in two humans is firmly set aside. This line of Christian Platonism stemming from St. John's Gospel and proceeding through Augustine and Thomas Aquinas sees natures as realizations of concepts in the mind of the Creator, concepts that determine an essence for a species. Ockham opposed this tradition. He felt that such concepts would restrict the liberty of the Creator. For in the older view, if God wanted to create a human being, he would of necessity be guided by the supposed concept for human beings; if he wanted to create dogs, he would be constrained by the concept for dogs. Ockham rejected any such constraints on the divine will, claiming that God could do anything that did not violate the law of contradiction, such as creating a dog that was alive and not alive in the same respects at the same time. Yet in the absence of an essence there still could be a substantial form in each dog, for example. The forms of dogs are more similar to one another than the forms of a dog and a donkey. But there is no essence in which all dogs must agree. This is not unlike the notion of species that emerges with Darwin.

The resulting system is called "nominalism": what the members of a species have in common is not an essence or common nature but rather a name and a certain similarity among the members. There is no fixed set of properties that every member must possess, but there is something perhaps like Wittgenstein's family resemblance. It is also possible to think of an Ockhamistic species somewhat along the lines of Eleanor Rosch's idea of individuals clustering around a prototype and resembling the prototype to varying degrees. Rosch's species too lack an essence or common nature.

There is, however, a difference. As I understand it, Rosch's prototype is at the perceptual level, and distance from the prototype is to be measured in purely perceptual dimensions. Ockham, as I construe him, is not restricting similarity purely or even primarily to the perceptual level. He says, "Socrates agrees with Plato in virtue of his intellectual soul." The possession of such a soul was never thought to be given directly in perception. It follows that for Ockham a concept is not abstracted directly from the perceptual array.

Nevertheless, Ockham often talks in such a way as to invite the impression that the similarity that marks the species is closely related to perceptual properties.

> [A concept] is a kind of mental picture which as a thought-object has a being similar to that which the thing outside the mind has in real existence. What I mean is this: The intellect, seeing a thing outside the mind, forms in the mind a picture resembling it. . . . The case would be similar, analogously speaking, to the activity of an artist. . . . And in this way a universal is not the result of generation, but of abstraction, which is only a kind of mental picturing. (*Ordinatio,* disp. 11, ques. 8, *prima redactio;* cited in Böhner 1957, 41)

This must have jolted the orthodox Aristotelians. For them, since a concept is not given directly in perception, it has to be generated by the active intellect. Since for Ockham there is no nature, no essence, to be represented in a concept, it follows that the concept signifying dogs, for example, is little more than a term for a dog. Ockham, then, can be seen as alleviating the problem of learning. At least in his system we do not have to explain how the mind, on the basis of perceptual information, succeeds in learning the underlying nature. Whatever Ockham's precise intention, and I make no claim to special expertise in the area, the foregoing passage and many others like it could not have failed to lessen the gap posited by Plato and Aristotle between perception and cognition. In due course nominalism became fully explicit in the view that concepts are abstracted directly from perception, so that the similarities that constitute a species are all at the perceptual level. This we will see in the next chapter.

Ockham's influence was immense and long lasting. It is interesting, therefore, to inquire what other factors in the fourteenth century might have favored a move away from essence and toward a nominalism that more and more will stick close to the perceptual level? For one thing, it is a move in the direction of the psychology that is predominant today.

To my mind an important part of the answer is to be found in an essay by Annaliese Maier (1982, chap. 6), the great historian of medieval science. In it she describes the collapse in the fourteenth century of Aristotelian chemistry. Besides matter and form, needed for metaphysical purposes, Aristotle accepted the idea that every physical body was composed of some combination of the four elements: earth, water, air, and fire. Each element was itself a composite of matter and form, and the coordination of the matter and form of the elements with the matter and form of the substances of which the elements were constituents proved a major difficulty. Associated with the elements was a theory of qualities as the active factors in nature. We will not go into this further. We have seen enough to understand that this could not be made to work. As medieval scholars became more searching in their scientific work, they came more and more to appreciate the gap between the supposed Aristotelian natures and conceptual grasp of those natures.

Remember that Aristotle had described the mind as capable of discovering the natures of physical objects. Admittedly, Thomas Aquinas cautions against simple-minded optimism that natures are easy to discover. At the same time, he too described the mind as specially designed to discover the natures beneath the appearances of physical objects. What seems to have dawned on the scholars of the next century was that they had not grasped the nature of a single species and had very little prospect of doing so. In these circumstances it is understandable that an emphasis on appearance rather than underlying and invisible form was welcome. Ockham himself did not push appearance at the expense of underlying structure, but it is clear that this was the impact of his work. Besides, his influence was at first beneficial for science, for it was the Ockhamists who made the greatest contributions to science and mathematics and in so doing placed the scientific revolution in their debt. Note too that the advances of the seventeenth century were mainly in the area of physics (astronomy and dynamics) rather than in chemistry. The internal organization of animate and inanimate creatures proved a far tougher nut to crack.

In the long run Ockham's influence on psychology was not altogether healthy. It had the impact of making the mind's operations more superficial. There is less emphasis on the mind's creative and idealizing powers than in Aquinas. We will see this in the next chapter, when we study the nominalism of that other Englishman, Thomas Hobbes. With Ockham we see the dawn of the modern era, for truly between Duns Scotus and Ockham the Middle Ages passes over a cusp and present-day psychologists live on Ockham's side of it.

We must now move on to the second of our themes, Ockham's theory of a language of thought. We saw that one way, even if not Aristotle's own way, to conceptualize Aristotle's theory of an inner sense that is common to the external senses is as a language into which information from the external senses is compiled. We also saw in Augustine and Aquinas talk of an inner language of the heart or of the mind. In Ockham, however, who saw himself as an Aristotelian, this line of thought comes to full and explicit fruition. Ockham concluded that there is a language of the mind, in the fullest sense of the word "language."

A spoken term is a part of a proposition which has been uttered aloud. . . . The conceptual term is an intention or impression of the soul, which signifies or consignifies something naturally and is capable of being a part of a mental proposition. . . . Thus, these conceptual terms and the propositions composed of them are the mental words which, according to St. Augustine in chapter 15 of *De Trinitate*, belong to no language. They reside in the intellect alone and are incapable of being uttered aloud, although the spoken words, which are subordinated to them as signs, are uttered aloud. (*Summa logicae*, bk. 1, chap. 1)

As the passage makes clear, a term in the mental language is a conceptual term, that is, a concept. Moreover, Ockham wants us to take "term" and "language" literally:

In the case of spoken or written language, terms are either names, verbs, or other parts of speech; likewise, the intentions of the soul are either names, verbs, or other parts of speech (i.e., pronouns, adverbs, conjunctions, prepositions). (*Summa logicae*, bk. 1, chap. 3)

Elsewhere, in chapter 1, he says that while the significance of spoken or written words is a matter of convention, the significance of a conceptual or mental word is not. The reference of a mental word is not something that we have any power to alter.

There is in Ockham, then, a belief in what Leibniz later called a "characteristica universalis" (a conceptual language). The conceptual language helps to explain the intertranslatability of all natural languages. The conceptual language is also semantically perspicuous, capable of expressing in distinct and clear form meanings that are ambiguously expressed by some natural-language sentence (bk. 1, chap. 13).

This is, of course, an important psychological claim with consequences for the basic uniformity of the human mind across people despite differences in beliefs and preferences. Why, one may ask, does the idea of a full-fledged mental language first surface in the thought of William of Ockham? To answer, we need a little imaginative reconstruction. As a nominalist, Ockham held that what the members of a species have in common is principally a name. Now in English the name of the kind to which Freddie belongs is "dog"; in Latin it is "canis"; in German it is "hund"; in Irish it is "madra." In what sense, then, can we say that the members of the species have a name in common, seeing that different people call the species by different names? Ockham's answer is that the common name is first and foremost a unique term in the language of the mind. The terms of various spoken languages are subordinated to those of the language of the mind. Not that the English word "dog" first signifies the corresponding mental word, but that the mental word controls what the English word refers to.

I say that spoken words are subordinated to concepts or intentions of the soul not because in the strict sense of "signify" they always signify the concepts of the soul primarily and properly. The point is rather that spoken words are used to signify the very things that are signified by concepts of the mind, so that a concept primarily and naturally signifies something and a spoken word signifies the same thing secondarily. (*Summa logicae,* bk. 1, chap. 1)

Ockham's theory of a mental language not only develops an idea that is, I believe, implicit in Aristotle but also anticipates modern claims for a full-fledged language of thought, such as Fodor's (1975). Ockham's language of the mind serves the same functions as Fodor's language of thought: its grammatical categories limit the grammatical categories of natural spoken languages; it controls the interpretation of natural-language terms; it explains the intertranslatability of natural languages; it places the composition of thoughts on the same footing as the composition of sentences in spoken languages. Although Ockham does not say so, it is in keeping with his thought to say that the language of the mind guides the child's learning of a spoken language (that is, the language of mind is Universal Grammar) and helps to explain how we can talk about the things we see, hear, or otherwise experience perceptually. It is the language of intercommunication for the various information channels.

In this chapter we began with Duns Scotus's claim that there is a nature that is common to the members of a species and a special agent of individuation that "contracts" the nature and yields a particular, a "thisness." We saw Ockham's principled rejection of Duns Scotus's position and the nominalism with which he replaced it. Neither man gave an adequate account of the one and the many—not Duns Scotus starting from the commonality in a species, nor Ockham starting from particulars. The impact of Ockham's work for psychology was to remove the idea that the function of the mind is to discover natures beneath appearances. This in the long run led to emphasis on perception at the expense of cognition. The second line of thought we studied was Ockham's theory that there is a language of mind on a par with spoken languages, such as English. We saw something of the import of this theory for psychology.

There is one term to tie down:

Nature   The word *nature* means the same as *substance*, but nature is viewed as the source of activity.

To keep things straight, I should note the following:

Nature means substance as the source of activity.
Essence means substance as opposed to existence.
Substance itself is used in opposition to accidents.

Bibliographical Note

While there are some collections of extracts of Duns Scotus's works in English translation, I do not know of any that conveniently cover the issues in this chapter. William of Ockham fares better in this respect:

Ockham, W. of (1957). *Philosophical Writings*. Edited and translated by P. Boehner. London: Nelson.

Ockham, W. of (ca. 1349/1974–80). *Summa logicae*. Part 1, translated by M. J. Loux. Part 2, translated by A. J. Freddoso and H. Schuurman. Notre Dame: University of Notre Dame Press. Part 1 gives Ockham's theory of terms, and part 2 gives Ockham's theory of propositions.

12

Thomas Hobbes: Grandfather of Modern Psychology

Biographical Note

Thomas Hobbes (1588–1679), a vicar's son, was born in Wiltshire. At 14 he went to Magdalen College, Oxford, where he took a bachelor's degree. He then became tutor in the Earl of Devon's household, thus gaining opportunities for European travel. In Europe he discovered that Aristotelian philosophy had fallen into disrepute. There too he discovered Euclidean geometry and something of Kepler, Galileo, Descartes, and Gassendi's work. He wrote one of the seven sets of objections to Descartes's *Meditations,* to which Descartes replied. He visited Italy and met the elderly Galileo in 1636. Galileo seems to have encouraged him to attempt a psychology along the lines of Galileo's own kinematics. Hobbes is especially famous as a political theorist. His psychological writings are to be found in his *De homine* and *De corpore,* but especially in the early part of his most widely read book, *Leviathan.*

In moving directly to Thomas Hobbes, we miss many important psychologists, chief among them being the delightful, erudite, and in many ways profound Nicholas of Cusa (1401–1464), or Nikolaus von Kues, as his fellow Germans called him. He wrote an especially interesting book on psychology called *Idiota de mente* (An ignorant person's view of the mind). Nicholas, however, belongs to the Middle Ages, and we must hurry on to the dawn of the modern period, which we can identify with Thomas Hobbes, although in many ways Hobbes brings to flower the seed planted by William of Ockham. But we must not get ahead of ourselves.

Particularly during his third visit to the Continent (1634–1637), Hobbes sensed that physics had begun to move forward. The physics he learned about from Galileo is called "kinematics"—the theory of bodies in motion without reference to the cause of the motion. Hobbes felt that something new and important could be accomplished in psychology if it was seen as part of kinematics and studied with the same methods as kinematics. With this move, psychology for the first time comes to be studied on the model of something that is not psychology at all, in this case, the motions of stones, cannon balls, and planets.

Hobbes's views on biochemistry, neuroanatomy, and even physics are, not surprisingly, naive, but it would be a mistake to dismiss him on that account. What he is doing is what many have done since with vastly improved scientific knowledge. Often it is easier to study a trend in its earliest moments, when its essential nature is still readily apparent and before it begins to bristle with technicalities. For this reason Hobbes is particularly valuable, because he writes so clearly and expresses himself so unguardedly.

Modeling himself on Galileo, Hobbes proceeds to reduce everything to motion. In the introduction to the *Leviathan* he says simply, "Life is but a motion of limbs." The same holds true in the life of the mind, which consists entirely of motions communicated through the senses.

All which qualities, called *sensible,* are in the object, that causeth them, but so many several motions of the matter, by which it presseth our organs diversely. Neither in us that are pressed, are they anything else, but diverse motions; for motion produceth nothing but motion. (*Leviathan,* chap. 1)

The unwary reader might imagine that all this amounts to little more than a repetition of Aristotle's principle, that all knowledge begins in perception, but this would misrepresent Hobbes completely. The mind, for Hobbes, is not endowed with an active intellect capable, upon suitable perceptual experience, of going beyond the perceptual data to yield a representation of a causally interacting structure lying beneath appearances.

[Thoughts] are every one a *representation* or *appearance,* of some quality, or other accident of a body without us, which is commonly called an *object.* Which object worketh on the eyes, ears, and other parts of a man's body. . . . The original of them all, is that which we call SENSE, for there is no conception in a man's mind, which hath not at first, totally, or by parts, been begotten on the organs of sense. The rest are derived from that original. (*Leviathan,* chap. 1)

The mind does not go beyond perception at all. Mental life is all "begotten on the organs of sense" as motion, and all thought is simply a continuation of that motion. This means that Hobbes completely set aside Aristotle's distinction between perception and cognition and ran the two completely together. Hobbes, in fact, is the first of our figures to do so. Even more, he ran together cognition, perception, and physiological stimulation of the perceptual organs (or what is sometimes called "low-level" perception). His move means that mental life is under environmental control to a degree that is foreign to Aristotle. It also means that there is no question of the mind getting beneath appearances (accidents) to substantial form. For that matter, it can never get beneath the form of the original physiological stimulation. This whole approach, coupled with the later theory that causality is not immediately given in perception, is going to rule out the possibility that we can ever discover structures of causally interacting components. In Hobbes it is going to lead to nominalism.

In Hobbes's psychology something very curious happens to ideals and to the mind's capacity to grasp them. Remember that it was this capacity that gave rise to Augustine's problem. Commentators on Hobbes frequently refer to the Paduan method of doing science, which was to ignore in one's theory certain complicating factors in the motions of real objects. For example, one could, ignoring friction, make useful measurements of bodies sliding down inclined planes or, ignoring the resistance of the air, of bodies falling from a height. Hobbes employed this way of thinking in his political theory by considering people all living in isolation from each other.

But there was another aspect of Galileo's thought that Hobbes's approach does not touch: its mathematical quality. Galileo believed that mathematics is the key to the universe. In order to employ mathematics, he idealized. For example, to employ Euclidean geometry in kinematics, he represented massive bodies, like a cannon ball or the moon, as a geometrical point: the body's center of gravity. He represented the trajectory of such a body as a Euclidean line. These are but two of the most elementary idealizations that physics uses. I am not sure that such idealizations are absolutely indispensable in physics, but it is clear that they have facilitated theory building enormously and without them physics as we know it today would not exist.

The striking thing about these idealizations is that they belong, in some basic sense, in the *theory* of physical bodies, not in physical bodies themselves. To take a crude example, the center of gravity of a bicycle is almost certainly located not in a physical part of the bicycle but in the space enclosed by the main triangular frame. Something similar holds for most massive bodies, like a bullet; its center of gravity is almost bound to be located in the spaces between the subatomic particles. Even more to the point, there is no physical object that is as small as a Euclidean point. It follows that the idealizations that we are talking about are contributed by the mind, rather than imposed on the mind by the external world.

The decision to do psychology on the model of kinematics meant, among other things, that there would be no ideals in the objects of psychological study, although some ideals might well be posited in the theory of psychology. This last move would be to follow the lead of Galileo, in whose work, as we have just seen, ideals are not in physical bodies but in the theory of physical bodies. The fact that Hobbes was aping Galileo in this matter showed up soon, in Hobbes's objections to Descartes's *Meditations,* in connection with the concept of a Euclidean triangle. Such a triangle is an ideal, which cannot be realized in the physical world. Yet everyone studying Euclidean geometry is expected to have such a concept. Allow that, and you allow idealizations in the mind, that is, in the object of psychological study. In the *Meditations* Descartes had written about a triangle,

Although there may nowhere in the world be such a figure outside my thought, . . . there is nevertheless in this figure a certain determinate nature . . . which is immutable and eternal, which I have not invented, and which in no wise depends on my mind. (*Meditation 5*)

Here Descartes is alluding to the mathematical commonplace, which gave us Augustine's problem. This Hobbes cannot accept, partly because it admits idealizations in the mind and partly because if there is no such triangle in the physical world, there is no physical source for the motion of which the supposed concept must consist.

If the triangle exists nowhere at all, I do not understand how it can have any nature. . . . The triangle in the mind comes from the triangle we have seen, or from one imaginatively constructed out of triangles we have beheld. (Third Set of Objections to the *Meditations,* objection 14)

Descartes did not dignify this with an answer. Earlier he had said in another connection, "I can see nothing here than needs an answer." He did not even say that much about Hobbes's remarks on the triangle. Descartes was clearly right, because he could not have replied without being rude. Hobbes and Descartes had similar exchanges on several other related matters, such as our idea of God as an infinitely powerful being. Hobbes denied that Descartes could have such a notion, since it could not be conveyed to the mind by any experience of a finite universe. But I will not go into detail.

The trouble for Hobbes runs deep here. Its source is the decision to model psychology on kinematics. Hobbes does not himself, so far as I am aware, propose ideals in psychological theory on a par with those in the theory of kinematics. Perhaps if he had, the true nature of his move would have been apparent to him. Much later, psychologists filled the gap and proposed such ideals as an individual's true IQ: the average score obtained by the individual over infinitely many intelligence tests of the same sort, without learning. But the point is not the existence of ideals in psychological theory. It is, rather, that Hobbes has introduced an intolerable torsion. For he has made it impossible in principle to handle or conceptualize the psychological activity of the scientist who appeals to ideals in order to advance science. Scientists are up their necks in idealizations of all sorts, and Hobbes has to deny their existence or explain them away.

Even if we allow that there may be no ideals in the object of study in any natural science except psychology, there has to be provision for them there. Psychology must be studied in the manner appropriate for psychology.

But, one can almost hear the protest, psychology aims to explain the ordinary, everyday operations of the mind. Is it so serious if it fails to handle the rather special mental operations of physicists? The protest seems to me to harbor the misguided assumption that scientific thought is remote from ordinary thought. The truth seems to be the contrary: scientific thought is just ordinary thought applied more doggedly and more resourcefully. But I let that pass.

Let us, in conciliatory mood, lay aside the upper reaches of the natural sciences and confine ourselves to more mundane things. Take the geometry that children study in school. There the idealizations of point, line, and plane surface are essential. They are expected of everyone and, as far as anyone can tell, they cause no problem to children. In fact, the difficulty runs in the opposite direction. There is a branch of psychology, stemming from Piaget's work, that explores the geometrical concepts of children. Children have to learn that a polished table is not a plane surface in the geometer's sense; the table surface is a complex of microscopic bumps and hollows.

Ideals also enter into the conceptualization of probabilities, and there is a psychological literature on people's understanding of probabilities. Sharp ideals are also necessary for the understanding of measurement, and error of measurement—even in such ordinary activities as carpentry and cooking. There are clear ideals of grammaticality in sentences, without which linguistics and psycholinguistics would be impossible.

In other everyday activities ideals of a less sharp character abound. Teachers try to grade exams perfectly fairly, and students expect them to try, even though both realize that the ideal is unattainable. Politicians are supposed to aim at ideals of justice; parents at doing the best for their children. It matters not that some give up on the ideals; we blame them for giving up. We are often severe on ourselves if we sense that we are doing so. We become depressed and guilt ridden if we suspect that our behavior falls far short of the ideal. At times ideals can be deadly. Young women who suffer from anorexia nervosa seem to be plagued by the belief that their bodies depart dreadfully from some ideal form. The motor mechanic must understand how the various parts of a car are supposed to function in order to mend the car.

Advertisers seem to understand all this very well. Advertisements for men and women's clothes, for makeup, for motorcars, toothpaste, cigarettes, and soft drinks appeal to ideals of beauty, grace, freedom, freedom from care, and general well-being. Montreal in winter is bedecked with travel advertisements showing beautiful men and women besporting themselves beneath palm trees under azure skies on the shores of some tropical island. On that island there is no sign of arthritis or of nasty bugs. An obvious evocation of the Garden of Eden! Northrop Frye calls this whole business "stupid realism," because such bliss is offered for a mere $350.

There is no need to multiply examples further. It is clear that to rule ideals out of the subject matter of psychology is to render much of everyday thought and experience incomprehensible. It is simply wrong-headed. I should add that as far as I can see, these remarks do not apply to physiological psychology, but they apply to very many other areas. The root trouble is the decision to model psychology on something that is not psychology. Hobbes modeled it on kinematics. His successors modeled it in turn on mechanics, chemistry, thermodynamics, telephone exchanges, and biology. The current fashion is to model it on computers. Before adopting any such strategy, we should ask ourselves, What happens to the ideals if we adopt that approach?

Hobbes's kinematic approach led him to make perception, cognition, and physiological stimulation of perceptual organs all of a single piece. This inevitably led to the view that what the members of a species have in common is nothing but a set of common perceptual features or, even more radical, that they give rise to similar physiological stimulation. This rather than that they consist of a common structure of causally interacting components, a structure that must be discovered beneath the perceptual appearances. Everywhere else in science the search is for such structures. It is ironic that the attempt to model psychology on physics should end by making psychology radically different from physics.

Like many psychologists who base species exclusively on input to the perceptual organs, Hobbes did not seem to believe that there is any set of perceptible features that is essential for membership in a species. With this, we see full-blown nominalism in its modern form:

Some [names] are common to many things, *man, horse, tree;* every of which, though but one name, is nevertheless the name of diverse particular things; in respect of all of which together, it is called an *universal;* there being nothing in the world universal but names; for the things named are everyone of them individual and singular. (*Leviathan,* chap. 4)

I do not believe that this passage can withstand logical analysis, mainly because a word like "tree" refers not to any particular tree but to the kind TREE, to which each particular tree belongs as a member, but I do not wish to get bogged down in logical problems. Instead, I note that Hobbes's position creates difficulties for handling Plato's problem of truth, difficulties of which Hobbes was aware. He attempts to handle them by saying that even if there are no such things as human nature and animal nature apart from the individuals that are humans and animals, there are the words "man" and "animal," and these, for some reason, he believes to be eternal.

Similarly the proposition *man is an animal* will remain eternally [true] because the terms are eternal; but if the human race perishes, human nature will no longer exist. (Third Set of Objections, obj. 14)

Descartes was not impressed by this explanation, and I don't think we should be either. If all humans were to perish, what, on Hobbes's account, would happen to the words "man" and "animal," and what would "man" then mean? What would there be for it to refer to? But, you say, Socrates is dead, and yet his name is still with us. True, but if the name still names Socrates, then Socrates must somehow have been rescued from utter annihilation. The way this happens, I believe, is that "man" names a kind to which belong all the men that ever were, are now, and ever will be. Such a kind is an abstract object that is not affected by the fate of Socrates or indeed of the whole human race. But this is just the sort of object that Hobbes is seeking to dispense with, because abstract objects send out no sights or sounds, nor do they impinge on the perceptual systems. They have no place in Hobbes's world, nor can they be represented in the mind, as Hobbes construes it. Add to this the view that it is not words as physical objects that are eternal, but words as types, that is, as abstract objects. Hobbes would like none of this.

This concludes our brief study of Hobbes. We have seen how his decision to model psychology on kinematics led him to conflate cognition, perception, and physiological stimulation of perceptual organs in a manner that we have not seen before in these reflections. This, in turn, led him to rule ideals out of the subject matter of psychology, since ideals are not presented to us perceptually—with, as we saw, disastrous results for most of psychology! We ended by noting his nominalism and the difficulties that his approach creates for any attempt to handle Plato's problem of truth and the fundamental contradiction of psychology. If there is a moral for psychology to be drawn from the study of Hobbes, and I believe there is, it is that one should not do psychology in the model of any other science; one should be guided by what one finds in psychology itself.

Addendum Characterizing Contemporary Psychology

Since I claim a special affinity between Hobbes and contemporary psychologists (CPs), a brief note sketching the main trends in contemporary psychology, as I see them, might help. I will confine myself to those trends that are most closely related to the main themes of these reflections. There are many CPs who do not conform to the main trends as I describe them, and things are changing rapidly. Still, I hope that the sketches are accurate enough, at least as regards majority opinion at the present time.

• CPs do not make a principled distinction between perception and cognition. They run the two together, holding that cognition is just further and perhaps deeper processing of the type that goes on in perception.

• For CPs, then, the learning of a concept is the abstraction from the perceptual array of a set of perceptual features that will serve in the recognition of members of a category. I should add that with the collapse of learning theory (based mainly on the study of conditioning of rats in mazes), there no longer is any broadly accepted theory of learning. Psycholinguists are generally well aware of Plato's problem of learning, usually described as Quine's problem. Psycholinguists are also sensitive to what is called the "problem of learnability" in relation to syntax. To handle these difficulties, they posit unlearned structures and constraints, which go some distance in handling Plato's problem of learning. That problem is much less familiar to workers in other areas of psychology.

• Apart from some personality theorists, mostly not seen as mainstream, ideals do not feature in contemporary psychological theories. CPs see themselves as studying the *facts* of performance. They take the facts to be unrelated to the ideals, which they usually assign to someone else. Again, psycholinguists are something of an exception. There is little awareness of Augustine's problem among CPs.

• As far as I know, there is no awareness at all of Plato's problem of truth among CPs.

Bibliographical Note

Hobbes, T. (1651/1962). *Leviathan, or The Matter, Forme, and Power of a Commonwealth Ecclesiasticall and Civil.* Edited by M. Oakeshott. New York: Collier.

13

René Descartes: Medieval Man of the Renaissance

Biographical Note

René Descartes (1596–1650) was born at La Haye, Touraine, now called "La Haye Descartes." His father being a magistrate of the high court, the family was comfortably off. Descartes attended a celebrated college run by Jesuits at La Flèche in Anjou, where he studied a wide range of subjects including mathematics, physics, and philosophy. He learned to write beautiful Latin. On leaving school he led a gay life in Paris for three years and then became more serious. He joined the army of Maurice of Orange (an important figure in the history of Holland). While in winter quarters at Neuberg on the Danube, he seems to have suffered a crisis of skepticism: was he justified in holding onto anything he had been taught or come to believe? He rescued himself by developing a new approach to philosophy. He devoted the rest of his life to mathematics, philosophy of knowledge, and natural science, making fundamental contributions in any area he touched. The end of his life was sad. Queen Christina of Sweden invited him to come to Stockholm and teach her philosophy according to his new method. She insisted on lessons at 5 A.M. on winter mornings in inadequately heated apartments. The easygoing Descartes caught pneumonia the following February, 1650, was bled by a physician (a hazardous business), and died. He wrote several philosophical works. The most important for psychology are his *Meditations on First Philosophy* and his *Discourse on the Method of Rightly Conducting the Reason*.

We will begin by looking at Descartes's discussion of a piece of wax in the second of the *Meditations,* because it makes a fundamental point about the relation between perception and cognition. The example had been used by St. Augustine in a similar context, but Descartes's use is more forceful.

Let us take, for example, this piece of wax: it has been taken quite freshly from the hive, and it has not yet lost the sweetness of the honey which it contains; it still retains somewhat of the odour of the flowers from which it has been culled; its color, its figure, its size are apparent; it is hard, cold, easily handled, and if you strike it with the finger, it will emit a sound. . . . But notice that while I speak and approach the fire what remained of the taste is exhaled, the smell evaporates, the color alters, the figure is destroyed, the size increases, it becomes liquid, it heats, scarcely can one handle it, and when one strikes it, no sound is emitted. Does the same wax remain after this change? We must confess that it remains; none would judge otherwise. What then did I know so distinctly in this piece of wax? It could certainly be nothing of all that the senses brought to my notice, since all those things which fall under taste, smell, sight, touch, and hearing, are found to be changed, and yet the same wax remains. (*Meditations,* II)

The point of this vivid passage is that the notion of a piece of wax cannot be constructed out of purely perceptual data, since we know (or assume) that a piece of wax can remain the same piece of wax despite changes in all perceptual properties. This is in flat contradiction to Hobbes on the issue, and Descartes's claim seems inescapable if one agrees that the piece of wax survives all these perceptual changes.

He goes on to say that what our perceptual systems place us in direct contact with are perceptual properties, not with the substance in which they inhere. He likens substances to men seen from an upper window. One says one sees men in the street below, when all one sees are hats and coats. How do we know that beneath the appearances there is a piece of wax that remains the same when the appearances change? This is the work of the mind. The wax proper is invisible to the perceptual systems; "it is my mind alone that knows (*percipere*) it."

With this distinction in mind we can proceed to Descartes's skeptical crisis. In Descartes's time it was becoming common to make a distinction in perceptual properties (or qualities, as they were called at the time) between what came to be called "primary qualities" and "secondary qualities." The gist of the distinction is this: properties are primary if our perceptual representations of them resemble them; they are secondary if they do not. Galileo, for example, had listed size, shape, number, and motion as primary; as secondary he listed color, sound, odor, and the like. By being overgenerous, we can convey the idea in modern terms. If an object presents the appearance of a rectangle, it probably is rectangular (at least one surface of it probably is). In other words, some objects give rise to an impression of rectangularity because they really are rectangular.

If one allows, for the sake of argument, that the impression the object gives rise to is a mental representation of it, one can then say that the object and the mental representation resemble each other. What gives rise to the impression that an object is red? It was learned well after Descartes's time that the relevant property is a configuration of electrons in its outer shell that causes the surface to absorb light of other wave lengths and reflect red light. The conclusion that philosophers were drawing in the seventeenth century—largely on the basis of speculation—was that red is a subjective property, that red does not exist outside the mind, and consequently that surfaces and people's color impressions of them never resemble each other. The general point was that secondary properties are deceptive in that reality does not resemble the mental impressions people form of them. Primary properties, however, are as they appear to be, and so our impressions of them are veridical.

This way of thinking led to serious difficulty, as we will see when we come to Bishop Berkeley. We should be on the alert, however, for the supposed primary properties were those that Galileo needed for his kinematics. Here is another case of psychology paying the wrong sort of attention to physics. Which is not to deny that psychologists should learn from physicists and chemists the physical properties that the perceptual systems detect, but the task of discovering how the mind represents them is a vastly different one.

The supposed distinction between primary and secondary qualities may well have been at the root of Descartes's skeptical crisis. After all, if we believe that perception misleads us about half the time, why should we trust it at all? We would not entrust ourselves to someone who told us lies about half the time. Descartes's way out of utter despair was ultimately a religious one. It was that we have an innate idea of an infinite God, which Descartes argues must be veridical. It is God who guarantees the veracity of our beliefs when we have employed our minds at their very best. For in such circumstances if we were still in error, the error would have to be attributed to God, who would have fitted us out with deceiving minds. This is how Descartes in his system transposes the divine illumination found in Augustine's. It is interesting that in this connection Descartes recalls the claim of Genesis that we bear the "image and likeness of God" (*Meditations,* IV). But we will not follow Descartes's theological foundations. More interesting to psychologists is how Descartes expressed his skeptical problem.

He noted that even if an evil genius was bent on deceiving him, he, Descartes, would still exist ("Cogito, ergo sum"), so his belief that he existed was sound. What about the objects he perceived about him?

> I had ideas of many thing that are sensible and corporeal, for, although I might suppose that I was dreaming, and that all that I saw or imagined was false, I could not at the same time deny that the ideas were in my thoughts. (*Discourse*, part 4)

The point seems innocent enough. Macbeth in his disturbed state thought he saw a dagger. He could truthfully say, "I thought I saw a dagger." The claim would have been true, even if there was no dagger to be seen. Trouble arises only if he were to say that there was in his head the image (or idea) of a dagger and that he was seeing this image. To say that Descartes was making this mistake probably exaggerates his position, but it neither falsifies nor distorts it. Elsewhere, when challenged, he wrote, "I take the term idea to stand for whatever the mind directly perceives" (Third Set of Objections to the *Meditations,* obj. 5). For Descartes, "idea" is a term that applies broadly enough that there could be ideas of things that are not physical. Nevertheless, Descartes uses "idea" always to mean a mental representation, and he claims that we are aware of such ideas, even if the objects they seem to represent do not exist.

Everything imaginable is wrong with this way of putting things, or at any rate so I will try to persuade you. We are simply not aware of our mental representations at all; only of what they represent. Otherwise, psychology would be a lot easier than it is. All we would have to do would be to turn our attention to these representations and describe their natures. In other words, introspection would work. But alas, it doesn't.

Obviously, there is a use of the word "idea" that suggests the opposite. One says that one has an idea for an essay or that one is weighing up several ideas for a summer vacation. Notice, however, that an idea for an essay is a description of how the essay might be structured. Through it one learns about the essay or what the essay might be like, not about the mental media for representing essays. One idea for a holiday might be to go to Ireland; another to go to France. Each idea attempts to convey the attractions, the advantages, and the inconveniences of one of the alternatives. They tell one nothing about their own structure, anymore than a television image reveals to the viewer the structure of the electromagnetic wave that conveyed it. The more one studies the television screen, the more one learns about the scenes it presents; one learns nothing of the wave form. Likewise, the more one studies an idea for a vacation, the more one learns about the vacation; one learns nothing about the manner in which the mind represents the information. So it is quite in order to say that we have ideas—of vacations, of how an argument should go, or whatever—but it is a mistake to think that we have conscious access to their structures as psychological entities rather than to the objects they represent.

The point is strangely elusive, so I will make one more effort to be clear. Look at any object in your environment, say a book. You cannot see it unless there is an image of it on your retina and unless the retinal image is projected to the visual cortex. Now the image on the retina is upside-down with respect to the book. You have no immediate awareness of this. Indeed, you have no awareness of any activity in your retina, in your optic nerve, or in your visual cortex. What you are immediately aware of is the book. To think otherwise is to "get the intentionality wrong," which for all his subtle genius is exactly what Descartes did. Crudely put, his skeptical question was, "I have representations of objects external to me; how can I be sure that there is anything out there of the sort they seem to present?"

But, you say, we are sometimes deluded. True. Particularly troublesome are examples when one fancies one remembers doing something one did not do or when one is fast asleep and dreaming. Dreams seem to have exercised Descartes most of all. But none of these offers the tiniest smidgen of evidence against the main point. If one mistakenly "remembers" leaving one's glasses in the bathroom, one has representations of the glasses and the bathroom and of placing the glasses on the bathroom shelf; one has no inkling whatsoever of how the mind displays the relevant information. One is simply not aware of ideas in the sense Descartes intended. "Idea" and "representation" are terms of art coined for purposes of psychological-theory building. They do not belong in descriptions of our awareness at least in the sense Descartes intended.

So towering is Descartes that this error of his cast a very long shadow that reaches to our own day. Almost all the psychologists we look at in subsequent chapters are adversely affected by it: Locke, Berkeley, Hume, Kant, Mill, Brentano. The error surfaces in our own time in the extensive literature on the geometric aspects of imagined shapes and movements. There are hundreds of experiments claiming to tell us about our representations of imagined shapes and movements. The danger is that all they tell us about is the shapes and movements themselves, not at all about the manner in which the mind represents them. I do not say that it is impossible to experiment usefully on our representations of imagined movements; just that it is dismayingly easy to get the intentionality wrong.

Like Augustine, Descartes was a substance dualist. His meditations led him to conclude that he himself was a thinking being (*res cogitans*), whereas his body was an extended being (*res extensa*).

And although . . . I possess a body with which I am very intimately conjoined, yet because, on the one side, I have a clear and distinct idea of myself inasmuch as I am only a thinking and unextended thing, and as, on the other, I possess a distinct idea of body, inasmuch as it is only an extended and unthinking thing, it is certain that this I (that is to say, my soul by which I am what I am), is entirely and absolutely distinct from my body, and can exist without it. (*Meditations,* VI)

Perception pertains to the body; understanding and willing pertain to the soul. There is a great gap between the perceptual and the intellectual, which Descartes takes as marking a distinction between body and mind.

Descartes offers an argument for dualism based on the claim that thought in itself has no spatial dimensions, whereas the body is essentially spatial. One is reminded of Aquinas's argument for dualism based on the claim that our concepts represent substantial forms separate from the matter that individuates them, which he takes as indicating that the mind itself is nonmaterial. Descartes's main argument for the immateriality of the mind, however, is more reminiscent of Aquinas's remarks on infinite adaptability. In his main argument Descartes places all the weight on language. His case is not so much that human beings are capable of constructing and parsing infinitely many sentences, which indeed is impressive, as that they can accommodate their speech to circumstances and occasions in an appropriate manner. This, he believed, no machine could do. Indeed, 300 years before Turing he all but proposed the Turing test (whether a computer could fool people into taking it for a person), but unlike Turing, he was convinced that the machine would be shown to be inferior to the person.

But it never happens that [a machine] arranges its speech in various ways, in order to reply appropriately to everything that may be said in its presence, as even the lowest type of man can do. . . . For while reason is a universal instrument which can serve for all contingencies, these [mechanical] organs have need of some special adaptation for every particular action. From this it follows that it is morally impossible that there should be sufficient diversity in any machine to allow it to act in all the events of life in the same way as our reason causes us to act. (*Discourse*, part 5)

In *Cartesian Linguistics* and elsewhere Noam Chomsky makes effective use of this passage to argue that language is a characteristic specific to human beings. His support for Descartes in this matter seems completely justified. But what about Descartes's claim that the human mind is non-material? Chomsky does not say one way or the other, and truly it is difficult to see clearly here. On the one hand, one has to be peculiarly blinded not to observe that among animals humans have a unique power of adapting to circumstances—witness the myriad inventions that humans have made and continue to make. The adaptability of speech is just the most ordinary evidence of this adaptability, for even people of the most modest abilities demonstrate it continually. On the other hand we simply do not know the limits on biological programming clearly enough to assert with justified confidence that human adaptability surpasses the power of any purely biological program. Perhaps, more modestly, I should say that at least I do not know the relevant limits and leave the matter at that.

Descartes is quite clear about substance dualism, as the citation from the sixth of the *Meditations* shows. And yet he seems to have had some reservations.

Nature also teaches me by these sensations of pain, hunger, thirst, etc., that I am not only lodged in my body as a pilot in a vessel, but that I am very closely united to it, and so to speak so intermingled with it that I seem to compose with it one whole. For if that were not the case, when my body is hurt, I, who am merely a thinking thing, should not feel pain. (*Meditations,* VI)

Descartes does not, however, go over to the property dualism of Aquinas. We can construe Descartes's dualism, among other things, as intended to handle Augustine's problem. Descartes is enormously sensitive to the idealizing properties of the human mind. He is fully aware that ideals cannot be realized in the material world. We have already seen that his views on the matter led to a dispute with Hobbes, who simply denied that there are any such things as ideals in that sense.

From the great wealth of Descartes's writing on the mind, we have studied just three points. The first was the sharp distinction he managed to draw, with the example of a piece of wax, between perception and cognition. The second was his manner of stating his skeptical problem. The significance of his statement is that (to my mind) it makes the psychological error of getting the intentionality wrong—of assuming that ideas or mental representations are the immediate objects of our awareness. It is doubtful whether Western thought has yet recovered. The third point was Descartes's substance dualism. I did not dwell on the amazing similarities in thought between the psychology of St. Augustine and that of Descartes. Although our thoughts were focused elsewhere, I hope that something of the similarity showed through. Nor did I dwell on Descartes's theory of innate ideas, which is not unlike Augustine's. We have not, then, studied Descartes's approach to Plato's problem of learning. Descartes is not at his most original in this connection, and other topics seemed more pressing.

There are some terms to tie down.

Idea   In the period from the Renaissance to the present time, "idea" is generally taken as denoting mental representations. Many of the writers we study, including Descartes, take an idea to be the immediate object of awareness. Our awareness of other things is mediated by ideas. This is what I call getting the intentionality wrong.

Primary and secondary qualities   "Qualities" in this context means perceptual properties. Qualities are said to be *primary* if they resemble the ideas to which they give rise; otherwise they are said to be *secondary*.

Bibliographical Note

Descartes, R. (1968). *The Philosophical Works of Descartes*. Vols. 1 and 2. Translated by E. S. Haldane and G. R. T. Ross. Cambridge: Cambridge University Press. Volume 1 contains both the *Discourse* and the *Meditations*, and volume 2 contains the objections to the *Meditations*.

Chomsky, N. (1966). *Cartesian Linguistics: A Chapter in the History of Rationalist Thought*. New York: Harper and Row.

14

John Locke: A No-Nonsense Developmental Psychologist

Biographical Note

John Locke (1632–1704), born near Bristol in the south of England, was the son of an attorney. He went to Oxford in 1652, where he was turned off by what he called the "vermiculate" philosophy of the schoolmen. He learned something of Descartes's work, which interested him more. He took his B.A. in 1656, lectured in Latin and Greek, and was appointed censor of moral philosophy in 1664. He studied medicine but never practiced in the ordinary sense of the word. He joined the household of Lord Shaftesbury as personal physician in 1667 but did little of a medical nature. During the rebellion against James II, Locke fled to Holland, where he worked to have William of Orange invited to become King of England. Back in England, under William and Mary, he became a retainer of Sir Francis and Lady Masham at Oates in Essex. He also served, with signal success, as commissioner on the Board of Trade. He wrote important treatises on government. His main work on psychology, which was 20 years in the writing, was *An Essay concerning Human Understanding,* published in London in 1689. My interpretation of this much discussed book, let me alert the reader, is what I believe to be the standard one, but it certainly is not the only possible one.

John Locke owed more to Thomas Hobbes than he acknowledged, and more to Descartes than he realized. From Hobbes, who was regarded with misgivings as a free thinker by the well connected, he quietly borrowed the fusing of perception and cognition, together with a slightly modified nominalism and its semantics. From Descartes he caught the confusion that we call getting the intentionality wrong.

More than any philosopher before him, Locke writes like a developmental psychologist. He wonders whether infants have some perceptual experiences in the womb. He speculates on what does and does not pass in the infant's mind. He is deeply concerned with the beginnings and progress of learning. Strangely, the whole process seems uncomplicated. There is none of the Platonic bewilderment that learning should be possible at all. One reason for this is his denial of a gap between perception and cognition, but that is not all.

The furniture of the mind is nothing but ideas, which for Locke are all representations of experience. They all derive from two sources: perception of external objects and perception of internal states and activities (such as thinking and wanting). The first he calls "ideas of *sensation*"; the second "ideas of *reflection*." Among ideas some are primitive, or *simple,* as he called them; others are complex. All ideas, no matter how complex, are constructed from simple ones:

In all that great extent wherein the mind wanders, in those remote speculations it may seem to be elevated with, it stirs not one jot beyond those ideas that sense or reflection have offered for its contemplation. (*Essay,* bk. 2, chap. 1, § 24)

For Locke, as for Hobbes, there simply is no gap between perception and cognition; the two are of a single piece.

Of course, there are problems with this. Locke claims that causality is given immediately in perception. The relevant qualities he calls "powers."

The mind being everyday informed, by the senses, of the alteration of simple ideas it observes in things without . . . and concluding from what it has so constantly observed to have been, that the like changes will for the future be made in the same things, by the like agents and the like ways,—considers in one thing the possibility of having any of its simple ideas changed, and in another the possibility of making that change; and so comes to the idea that we call *power.* (*Essay,* bk. 2, chap. 21, § 1)

It is, of course, a confusion to think that possibilities are immediately evident in perception, and this whole doctrine is going to be demolished by David Hume. Locke, however, seems to have suspected no weakness in his view. I will leave the matter there for the present.

Locke gives the impression that learning is not a special problem. The mind seems to proceed automatically to form complex ideas out of simple ones. From perceiving many horses, each affording a mass of simple ideas, the mind proceeds to form a complex idea peculiar to horses; it forms another complex idea for human beings, another for gold, and so on.

This, if it were correct, would handle Plato's problem of learning, at least for concepts, although one has the impression that Locke did not struggle with the problem as many of his predecessors did.

Complex ideas serve several functions in Locke's psychology. (1) They are the immediate objects of thought when one is thinking about kinds; (2) they are the references of words for kinds; (3) they are the means for recognizing members of those kinds; and (4) they serve as concepts for the kinds, although as far as I know Locke does not employ the word "concept" in this connection. Each of these functions merits a brief reflection.

Knowing the leading role ideas were going to play, Locke defines *idea* in the Introduction to the *Essay:*

It being that term which, I think, serves best to stand for whatsoever is the *object* of the understanding when a man thinks. I have used it to express whatever is meant by *phantasm, notion, species,* or *whatever it is the mind can be employed about in thinking.* (*Essay,* Introduction, § 8)

This is not a slip; he repeats many times that ideas are the objects of thought. This, of course, is an example of getting the intentionality wrong—a malady that I believe he contracted from Descartes. He might perhaps have avoided it if he paid more attention to the "vermiculate" psychology of the Schoolmen. In any event, there is no need to repeat here what was said about the subject in the last chapter.

When he comes to discuss the reference of words, in keeping with his distorted view of intentionality, he lays down that "all words . . . signify nothing immediately but the ideas in the mind of the speaker" (*Essay,* bk. 3, chap. 4, § 1). This came to be called the "ideational theory of meaning." Now we surely do have some sort of representation of horses in our minds, but it is monstrous to hold that it is this representation that we are talking about in the first instance when we talk about horses. Locke's theory seems to have been that "horse" denotes a complex idea of horses in the first place and through that it somehow puts us in touch with horses. But to state the theory is to see that it is abortive. Take a clear case of a representation; take a picture of some person, say Nancy. If we study the picture, we may say of it that the shading the artist employed to represent the edge of Nancy's sleeve is poorly done. It does not follow that we are saying anything whatsoever about Nancy or her sleeve.

By parity of argument, if we were really talking about mental representations of horses, it is not clear why we should be saying anything about horses. But even to state this plaint, I have to assume that the reader will interpret "horses" as flesh-and-blood horses, not as mental representations of horses. This is to assume that Locke's theory is wrong.

Without wishing to flog the general point, I would like to consider one more example: the sentence "Santa Claus lives at the North Pole." Locke would have us believe that "Santa Claus" signifies a complex idea of that fictitious elf in the mind, and that "North Pole" signifies a complex idea of the North Pole. The sentence signifies a mental representation associating the representation of Santa Claus with the representation of the North Pole in some manner appropriate to "lives at." Now ask whether Santa Claus is real? Well, the idea of Santa Claus has to be real for the theory to make any sense; so it would seem that he is real after all. What is more, since there is such an idea in each person's mind, it would seem that there are millions of real Santa Clauses. This obviously is a muddle.

Another way to go would be to say that "Santa Claus" signifies an idea in the first instance but the idea itself signifies nothing. Locke would add that the complex idea of Santa Claus is constructed from simple ideas that we have acquired from various perceptual experiences of real objects. This is more promising, since it relates words to objects in the world through mental states. But then ideas really drop out of the theory of meaning because the real reference of the words is whatever in the world the ideas signify. This, however, is a radical departure from Locke's way of viewing things. It is, nevertheless, a necessary departure if we are to avoid making true a sentence that, as interpreted in the real world, is obviously false, i.e., the sentence "Santa Claus lives at the North Pole." For on Locke's reading, this sentence says that there is a certain mental relation between a representation of Santa Claus in the head and a representation of the North Pole in the head. If that is how one takes the sentence, it is difficult to see how it could be false.

Locke seems to have been impressed with Descartes's discussion of the piece of wax, all of whose perceptual properties changed when it was heated but that remained the same piece of wax. At any rate, he discusses substances as supports for variable perceptual properties in the second book of the *Essay*. He is, however, queasy about the whole notion of substance and makes fun of it. The reason is that in his psychology one cannot know a substance since one cannot perceive it, substance being conceived as a substratum, something that lies beneath perceptual properties and provides a home for them.

> The idea then we have, to which we give the *general* name substance, being nothing but the supposed, but unknown, support of those qualities we find existing, which we imagine cannot subsist . . . without something to support them. (*Essay*, bk. 2, chap. 23, § 2)

So Locke does not deny that beneath the appearances there is something to hold them together, but if there is, we know nothing of it apart from the perceptual properties it supports.

This leads to Locke's well-known distinction between nominal and real essence.

> The measure and boundary of each sort or species, whereby it is constituted that particular sort, and distinguished from others, is what we call its *essence*, which is nothing but that abstract idea to which the name is annexed; so that everything contained in that idea is essential to that sort. This, though it be all the *essence* of natural substances that *we* know, or by which we distinguish them into sorts, yet I call it by a peculiar name, the nominal essence, to distinguish it from the real constitution of substances, upon which depends this *nominal essence* . . . , which therefore may be called the *real essence*. (*Essay*, bk. 3, chap. 6, § 2.) [See the definition of *nominal essence* in the Glossary.]

Notice in this passage the identification of substance with real essence. We saw, in discussing Ockham, the founder of nominalism, that the later Middle Ages came to appreciate the difficulty of discovering the natures of physical objects, like animals, and of stuffs, like water and gold. In Locke, who here follows Hobbes, the difficulty has become an impossibility: one simply can never go beyond appearances. So the underlying nature of horses is utterly unknown; all we can know is the perceptual properties that serve for distinguishing particular horses from other sorts of creatures. This is how Hobbes's nominalism emerges in Locke's theory.

One effect of all this is that it identifies the rule for interpreting a word, its meaning, with the perceptual indices for applying the word correctly. This is an enormous error, as a little reflection reveals. A word like "dog" refers to a kind, that is, to an abstract object that contains as members all the dogs that ever were, are now, or ever will be. In other words, the kind DOG is a set. It therefore gives rise to no perceptual impressions whatsoever, although its members do. One sees a dog and recognizes it to be a dog, but one cannot see the kind DOG. It follows that it is a complete muddle to confound the reference of "dog" with the perceptual indices for applying the word correctly to individual creatures. We must distinguish sharply between the reference of an expression and the means that can be employed for applying it correctly. This is precisely what Locke fails to do, and it is not evident to me that he can avoid doing so inside his system.

The fourth function that ideas serve in Locke's psychology is that of concepts. By "concept" I mean a mental representation that purports to be a definition of whatever falls under the concept. My concept of a dog, for example, is my attempt to represent mentally what defines their nature. It includes the beliefs that dogs are animals, that they are quadrupeds, that they are mammals. Unfortunately, my concept is evidently incomplete, since it does not, as stated, distinguish dogs from cats or badgers. It may also contain erroneous beliefs. I used to believe that dogs were a kind that evolution produced without human intervention. Now I am given to believe that this is not so. At any rate, all I need is an example of some erroneous belief that is part of a concept, and let us suppose that this is one.

There is a serious problem in any theory that identifies the rule for interpreting a word, like "dog," with the concept one may form of the members of the relevant kind. On the ordinary account of a word's reference, if some property is implied by the word, then that property *necessarily* belongs to any individual that correctly falls under that word. Take "girl," which implies female. If some person is a girl, necessarily that person is a female. It follows, we say, in virtue of the very meaning of the word "girl." Return to "dog," identify its meaning with the concept someone (say me) has formed of the kind, and allow that there is an erroneous belief in the concept, e.g., that dogs were produced by natural selection alone. On our reading of Locke, it now follows in virtue of the very meaning of the word "dog" that dogs were produced by natural selection. This is obviously wrong. If it were true, there would be no way to correct me, save brute force, because, on this view, the creatures I call "dogs" really are the result of natural selection prior to human intervention. Of course, it would follow that the word "dog" in my mouth would refer to nothing, there being no creatures answering to my erroneous concept. A strange result!

One way to patch things up would be to say that dogs are creatures that share some set of weighted properties. This is the nominalist move—from a sharp set of criterial properties to some weighted subset of properties. On this revision, my erroneous belief must be given a zero weighting. In other words, it drops out of the picture. This would have the advantage of counteracting the unfortunate effects of my belief on my use of the word "dog." It also has the disadvantage of looking like a trick designed merely to save the identification of meaning and concept. Not a reassuring move!

Meaning and concept should not in any case be identified. As children grow older, we go to great pains to improve their concepts of certain kinds: machines, animals, planets, atomic particles, and so on. This means that we are working on their concepts, not on the interpretations of the related words. The whole process presupposes holding the kinds constant and improving the associated concepts. The kinds are held constant by their names: "dog," "animal," "motorcar," and so forth. But this implies that reference is distinct from concept, since the concepts vary while the reference remains constant. Locke, I fear, has sown dreadful confusion.

Locke's ideas of reflection were also the source of much trouble, since the notion of psychological introspection can be traced to them. [See the definition of *introspection* in the Glossary.] And yet it may be unfair to blame the trouble on Locke alone, because we surely are aware of our own conscious states. What else could the word "conscious" mean? We should look at what Locke himself says:

The other fountain from which experience furnisheth the understanding with ideas is,—the perception of the operations of our own mind within us, as it is employed about the ideas it has got;—which operations, when the soul comes to reflect on and consider, do furnish the understanding with another set of ideas, which could not be had from things without. And such are *perception, thinking, doubting, believing, reasoning, knowing, willing* and all the different actings of our own minds. (*Essay*, bk. 2, chap. 1, § 4)

It seems incontrovertible that the broad picture Locke presents is true. It is part of experience, and therefore an empirical matter, that one is sometimes aware that one is perceiving, thinking, doubting, and the rest. It is just as much a part of experience as are the objects one perceives, thinks about, doubts, and so on. This will play a crucial role in the empirical psychology of Franz Brentano. But there is also in Locke's writing the suggestion that one has direct access to the forms of mental representations. This claim, in conjunction with the doctrine of ideas of reflection, is at the root of belief in introspection. It is misleading because we simply do not have an immediate awareness, or any awareness for that matter, of the forms of our own mental representations or the processes whereby they are produced.

There is an interesting book on introspection by Lyons (1986) claiming that introspection in psychology is more a phenomenon of the English-speaking world than of the Continent. Certainly, neither Wilhelm Wundt nor Franz Brentano, the two German founders of modern experimental psychology, was an introspectionist. The most determined introspectionist was E. B. Titchener, an Englishman. In any event, it is obvious that we need to carefully distinguish among ideas of reflection between what may be called intuition and introspection proper. The distinction would have the effect of protecting what is valuable in Locke's theory of reflection from what can all too readily be confused with it. I will put off the task of clarifying this issue until we come to discuss the work of Franz Brentano.

We began by looking at Locke's use of the word "idea," noting that he distinguished ideas of sensation from ideas of reflection. We saw that he conflated perception and cognition, claiming direct perceptual awareness of causality. We went on to study four functions that Locke expects ideas to perform: (1) to be the direct objects of thought (which gets the intentionality wrong), (2) to be the immediate references of our words, (3) to be our means for recognizing those objects to which our ideas apply, (4) to be our concepts for the relevant kinds and properties. We saw that all four functions are seriously problematic. We ended with a brief look at Locke's ideas of reflection, noting that they gave rise, perhaps through confusion, to introspection in psychology. I did not discuss one major line of the *Essay,* the rejection of innate ideas and principles. That aspect will be prominent in the next chapter, which is largely devoted to Leibniz's discussion of Locke in this connection.

In this chapter three terms figured prominently:

Nominal essence A nominal essence for Locke is an abstract idea of a kind. It is abstracted from perceptual experiences and represents just those properties of the experiences that are distinctive of members of the kind. Nominal essences are opposed to *real essences,* which, for Locke, are unknown.

Ideas of reflection These are representations of the internal operations of the mind, such as thinking, desiring, wondering, and the like. Ideas of reflection are contrasted with *ideas of sensation,* that is, mental representations of external objects.

Introspection This is not a term that Locke uses, so far as I know; it is one that I used in discussing his ideas of reflection. By "introspection" I mean the supposed activity of attending to one's own mental states and operations with a view to learning (1) the form of a representation or the internal structure of an operation, (2) the causal origins in the mind of a mental state or operation, (3) the content of a mental state or the object of a mental operation. (Just for the record, I do not believe that we can succeed in achieving aims (1) or (2); I do believe that we can sometimes succeed in achieving aim (3).)

Bibliographical Note

Locke, J. (1690/1894). *An Essay concerning Human Understanding.* Edited by A. C. Fraser. New York: Dover.

Lyons, W. (1986). *The Disappearance of Introspection.* Cambridge: MIT Press.

15

Gottfried Leibniz and Necessary Truths

Biographical Note

Gottfried Wilhelm Leibniz (1646–1716) was born in Leipzig to an academic family—his father a professor, his mother the daughter of a professor. His university education was mainly in philosophy and law, and he obtained a doctorate in law at the age of 20. He turned down a professorship at that age and entered the service of the Elector of Mainz for a time. After this he spent four years in Paris, devoted largely to mathematics. He then entered (in 1676) the service of the Duke of Hanover, in which he remained until his death. He distinguished himself as a philosopher, psychologist, scientist more generally, historian, and diplomat. With Isaac Newton he shares the honor of having discovered calculus, which marks him as one of the world's greatest mathematicians. His main psychological work is a response to Locke's *Essay,* suitably titled *New Essays on Human Understanding.* Although the writing of it was almost complete by the time of Locke's death, in 1704, it was not published until 1765. It is written in French in the form of a (clumsy) dialogue between Philalethes (Locke) and Theophilus (Leibniz).

There is a breed of thinkers who publish more after their deaths than while alive. They include, most notably, Wittgenstein and, to a lesser extent, Brentano and Husserl. Leibniz was of this number and his *New Essays* is an example of an important work that, although ready for the press, was not sent for publication. He seems to have been put off from doing so by Locke's death. The two men differed radically. Locke saw some of Leibniz's comments on his *Essay* and expressed his disappointment to his Dublin friend William Molyneux thus: "Even the largest minds have but narrow swallows." Perhaps Leibniz's reason for not going ahead with publication was his reluctance to publish what must have appeared as a demolition of Locke's work when Locke could no longer defend himself.

Locke is commonly described as an empiricist, and Leibniz as a rationalist. Both expressions are tricky, being used in a variety of senses. The terms, however, do draw attention to a real distinction, and I propose to employ them in slightly modified form. I propose to employ "radical empiricist" to describe psychologists who, conflating perception and cognition, hold that all our knowledge derives directly from perceptual experience; "rationalist" I will use to describe psychologists who deny that cognition reduces to perception and moreover hold that some concepts and principles of reasoning are unlearned. How these expressions apply to Locke and Leibniz will become clear as we go along. I will devote the whole of this reflection to Leibniz's rationalist response to Locke's radical empiricism.

The weak point in radical empirical theories has always been their account of necessary truths, in particular the truths of logic and mathematics, to deny which would plunge one in chaos. The psychologically relevant feature of these truths is that they do not seem to derive from perception of the external world. Instead, they seem to be necessary to make sense of such perceptions. If this is so, it follows that they cannot have been learned in the manner radical empiricists describe. We will see how this line of thought works in Locke and in Leibniz.

Descartes had said that certain concepts have to be unlearned, since we never perceive any objects that fall under those concepts. Among such concepts he included the concept of God: "eternal, infinite, [immutable], omniscient, omnipotent, and Creator of all things which are outside Himself" (*Meditations*, 3). Another such idea is that of a [Euclidean] triangle, which is never perceived in its mathematical perfection, though objects resembling it to some extent are perceived. He had also spoken about certain laws that God had imprinted on our minds (*Discourse*, part 5). To this Locke proposed what is really an experimental counterargument: see if everyone assents to these supposed unlearned truths and grasps these supposed unlearned concepts. (I use the word "unlearned" rather than "innate," because for something to be innate it must be present at the moment of birth, which is a different matter and one that is tangential to our interests.) Locke was quite certain of the results because "all children have not the least apprehension or thought of them" (*Essay*, bk. 1, chap. 1, § 5). He is certainly right about the results. There will be some children who will not appreciate the difference between a Euclidean triangle and the drawing of a triangle in a geometry book. Locke states in the same chapter the principle of contradiction: "It is impossible for the same thing to be and not to be" (§ 4). Ask any five-year-old whether this principle, so stated, is true, and the best one can hope for is a puzzled look. Locke's reason for invoking such evidence is that if a concept or principle really were unlearned, it would be an essential property that could not fail to be present to the mind. He felt he had abundant evidence that there are no such concepts or principles.

Locke goes on to say that people who propound unlearned concepts and principles usually say that they are evoked, and thus appreciated, only upon suitable experience. For example, they might say that the concept of a Euclidean triangle will not occur to people unless they see triangular drawings and objects. They argue similarly for unlearned principles. In response, Locke says that if this is so, then people will be required to employ reason to discover these principles, but "that certainly can never be thought innate which we have need of reason to discover. . . . So that to make reason discover those truths thus imprinted, is to say, that the use of reason discovered to a man what he knew before . . . it is in effect to say, that men know and know them not at the same time" (*Essay*, bk. 1, chap. 1, § 9). This surely is a problem for the supporters of unlearned concepts and principles. For they are obliged to admit that it is in some sense possible to know more than one is aware of or is able to state. This suggests that one can both know and not know certain things.

None of Locke's appeals to evidence and none of his arguments made an impression on Leibniz. To explain how people might need experience to become aware of some principle that they were supposed to know by nature, Leibniz proposed the analogy of a veined block of marble, as opposed to an entirely homogeneous one. His idea was that the veins render certain figures easier than others to sculpt: those that respect the veins rather than those that go against them. Indeed, it is a common expression that certain choices or lines of thought "go against the grain."

I must confess that the metaphor does not help me at all. Granted suitable experience, one might find it "natural" to conclude that the (proper) part of any object is less than the whole—a proposition that is a likely candidate for unlearned status. But upon suitable experience one might find it equally "natural" to conclude that strawberry jam is tasty—a proposition that no one ever thought of as an unlearned truth. If I am to be convinced of Leibniz's general point, I need something more convincing than this analogy.

Fortunately, Leibniz has many deeply interesting arguments. To begin, he reiterates Descartes's observations about geometrical objects, pointing out that geometrical points, lines, and surfaces are never encountered in the perceptual array; only objects that evoke the ideals. This was also St. Augustine's point, giving rise to what I called Augustine's problem—how can we explain our grasp of ideal concepts, given that they are never exemplified in perceptual experience? This argument rests on the gap between the perfection of geometrical objects and the imperfection of perceptual ones. "Will a perfectly homogeneous and even surface ever be seen?" Leibniz asks (*New Essays,* p. 53). The answer is clearly no. It follows that the concepts of geometrical perfection cannot be derived directly from perception. So how are we to explain them? At this point Augustine appealed to divine illumination acting in the mind. Leibniz appeals to unlearned concepts. The two appear to be saying different things until one realizes that Leibniz makes God the source of such concepts. Upon realizing this, one sees that the distance between the two men is not that great. Augustine has God operating in the mind when one becomes aware of a concept; Leibniz has God's action completed at the moment the mind is formed. Whatever the case, however, such concepts cannot be derived directly from perception, so there has to be an important unlearned content in them.

Leibniz is even more interesting on the subject of unlearned principles. Aristotle had long before taught that in any deductive system some principles must be basic, in the sense that other truths may be deduced from them while they themselves are not deduced from anything more basic. We call such basic principles "axioms." Leibniz may have been thinking of unlearned principles as axioms, but I have a suspicion that he was gesturing toward something more like what we nowadays call natural-deductive systems, that is, rules for operating on sentences (or more probably for Leibniz, propositions). I will try to explain the idea and give my reasons for saying that this was what he was reaching for.

First, an example of a natural-deduction rule. Consider a conversation between Joe and Nancy about a roommate of theirs named "Tom."

Joe   Tom came home some time ago and ate his supper.

Nancy   That's odd, because I see his supper is still in the oven.

Joe   True enough. He hasn't eaten it.

Nancy   But you just said he did.

Joe   No; I said he came home *and* ate his supper. I didn't say he ate his supper.

Nancy   Are you crazy, or something?

What is happening here is that Nancy is, reasonably, applying the deduction rule of *and* elimination. It says that if you are given "*p* and *q*" as true, you can always take "*p*" as true and "*q*" as true. Nancy's consternation is due to the fact that Joe does not seem to be applying that rule.

One point of the example is that if you asked Nancy whether she accepted the rule of *and* elimination, she would probably say she never heard of it. And yet she applies it, instinctively as it were. If this account is correct, and I do not see how it could fail to be, then there is a sense in which Nancy both knows and does not know the rule. She knows it in the sense that she applies it automatically; she does not know it in the sense that she has never thought about such a rule and is bewildered when asked about it. The rule, in other words, is an operating principle in Nancy's mind, but not one that she is aware of. Of course, if she is interested in such matters, she is at liberty to observe her own trains of reasoning and see what principles are operative in them. That, presumably, is what Gerhard Genzen, who first formalized natural-deduction systems (in the 1930s), did. At any rate, operating rules afford an idea of how to respond to Locke's complaint that rationalists were implicitly claiming that people both know and do not know their own basic principles.

It also gives an idea of what Leibniz might have meant when he said, "Everyone makes use of the rules of inference, through a *natural logic,* without being aware of them" (*New Essays,* p. 91). Elsewhere he says that such rules, "even though we give no thought to them, . . . are necessary for thought, as muscles and tendons are for walking" (*New Essays,* p. 84). His basic claim is that we must know certain principles, because "we use them all the time," even though we are unaware of them. He likens their operation to an enthymeme, that is, a chain of reasoning with unstated steps that are necessary for the validity of the chain as a whole. The metaphor is less than apt, since an enthymeme is a sentence or proposition, and such things are inert. They do not of themselves advance the reasoning process. What Leibniz needs is a rule of operation, or procedure, that will in certain circumstances produce a particular effect. This way of looking at the principles in question explains at once why "we use them all the time" or better, why they are operative all the time, and also why we are not aware them, since they are not in the form of sentences or propositions.

This way of construing Leibniz's thought has the added advantage that it supplies a role for experience in the discovery of our basic principles. This seems to me to be altogether the best way of making sense of the line Leibniz is taking. Why, then, did he not simply say that natural-deduction rules as operating principles were what he had in mind? The reason is that it was not until 200 years later that the notion of a natural-deduction rule was conceptualized clearly. A second reason is that it is only with the advent of computers, and after people have attempted to model chains of reasoning on them, that the notion of an operating principle or procedure has become sufficiently clear. With hindsight it is possible to say that Thomas Aquinas was gesturing toward such rules but was unable to state clearly what he had in mind. The same is true of Leibniz.

Let us grant, then, that the mind has operating principles of which it is normally unaware. Why should one say that they are unlearned? Leibniz's answer is profound and carries us to a central position in his logic. The short answer is that associated with each of these operating principles is a necessary truth, and there simply is no way to learn necessary truths directly from perceptual experience. This needs unpacking.

It is crucial to obtain an understanding of how Leibniz conceptualized necessity. Interpreting Leibniz on this matter is controversial, so we will simply base our thinking on, to my mind, the most authoritative treatment of Leibniz on this subject: that of Mates (1986). Leibniz had the idea that besides the world (universe) that actually exists, there are other possible worlds that do not exist. God, he argued, could make any world that does not involve contradiction (such as, that it contains dogs and does not contain dogs). This gives us two ways to construe necessary truths. One is as a truth whose opposite involves contradiction. To illustrate with our example (not Leibniz's), suppose that we allow that "*p* and *q*" is true but that "*p*" is not true. We would land in contradiction because "*p* and *q*" is true just in case "*p*" is true and "*q*" is true. To hold that "*p* and *q*" is true and "*p*" is not true is thus contradictory. The other way to construe necessary truth is really quite close to this. It is that a necessary truth is one that holds in all possible worlds: "These are eternal truths. Not only will they hold as long as the world exists, but also they would have held if God had created the world according to a different plan" (as cited in Mates 1986, 107). This, with modifications that need not concern us, is still the dominant way of construing necessity.

It is clear that we cannot experience all possible worlds. We cannot even experience all the situations in the actual world. It follows that the experience we have had cannot directly tell us what holds across all situations in all possible worlds. It is equally clear that perceptual experience on its own cannot tell us what is contradictory. We never see an area that presents itself at the same instant as red and as not red. For that matter, the presentation of an area as red is not a presentation of it as not green. It follows that perception on its own cannot tell us about contradictions. On its own, therefore, perception cannot be the sole source of our knowledge of contradiction, which is contrary to what Locke must try to make us believe, since in his theory there really is nothing but perception and the association of percepts. [See the definition of *association* in the Glossary.] Whether, then, we construe a necessary truth as one whose opposite leads to contradiction or as one that holds in all possible worlds, Locke's approach to necessary truth is barred. Locke simply does not make adequate provision for our knowledge of any such thing.

Leibniz does not claim that a truth is necessary because it is unlearned. It is not as if these operating principles are blind constraints on thought. Rather, it is that we see that the concerned truths are true. We have sufficient insight to see that going against them would lead to contradiction.

It is this insight, he claims, that distinguishes us from the beasts; it is this insight that shows us not to be mere mechanisms or mere biological clocks (*New Essays,* pp. 51, 67).

Thinking along these lines, Leibniz came to believe that a large part of the mind's conceptual and logical furniture has to be unlearned. Besides logic, he held that the whole foundations of arithmetic and of geometry are unlearned. I believe, on theoretical grounds, that he has to be right about this, although the role of the experience of space, itself to a considerable extent determined by physical nature, is probably larger than Leibniz imagined. Interestingly, developmental psychology is moving in his direction. There are numerous studies that show infants to have an astonishing grasp of numbers. The intuition of space seems also to be largely given by nature. Noam Chomsky is surely right to hold that nature massively prepares infants to deal with language in all its aspects. On and on it goes from one area to the next. More and more psychology is adopting Leibniz's solution to the problems Plato and Augustine posed us: that the main answer lies with unlearned mental structure.

We began by looking at Locke's reasons for rejecting unlearned concepts and principles. We then went on to study Leibniz's rebuttals, beginning with his claim that the mind's idealizing powers cannot be attributed to perceptual experience, since ideals are never encountered in the perceptual array. We construed Leibniz's idea of unlearned principles, principles that one uses without being aware of their nature, as operating principles. We ended by looking at his characterization of necessary truths as those whose opposites would give rise to contradiction and as those that hold in all possible worlds. We saw that either construal rules out Locke's explanation of how we know them to be true. We cannot have experienced all possible worlds and perception on its own cannot be the source of our knowledge of contradiction. We also noted that Leibniz saw our access to necessary truths as that which distinguishes humans from other animals.

It is only fair to advise the reader that I have not touched at all on some major lines of thought, some of them quite strange, in Leibniz's philosophy. Failure to mention them does not indicate irrelevance to psychology. It seemed wiser to concentrate on one line that is of supreme importance.

Here I will define two more terms:

Radical empiricist   I use the term "radical empiricist" to describe a person who runs together perception and cognition, and claims that concepts consist of distinctive features abstracted from the perceptual array.

Rationalist   I use "rationalist" to describe a person who, making a principled distinction between perception and cognition, claims that concepts represent structure that is not given immediately in the perceptual array. Rationalists also believe in unlearned concepts and unlearned operating principles as a basis for all human thought.

Bibliographical Note

Leibniz, G. W. (1765/1981). *New Essays on Human Understanding*. Translated and edited by P. Remnant and J. Bennett. Cambridge: Cambridge University Press.

Mates, B. (1986). *The Philosophy of Leibniz: Metaphysics and Language*. Oxford: Oxford University Press. A masterly work.

16

Bishop Berkeley and the Consequences of Nominalism

Biographical Note

George Berkeley's father and grandfather were English, but they took up residence in Ireland, and George himself was an Irishman. George Berkeley (1685–1753) was born near Kilkenny town and at the age of 10 attended Kilkenny College, which counted Jonathan Swift among its alumni. At 15 he went to Trinity College, Dublin, where he studied, among other things, Greek, Latin, Hebrew, and French. At age 19 he took his B.A., and three years later he won a fellowship. At about the same time he took Holy Orders in the Church of Ireland. In 1713 he went to London and made several trips to the Continent, not returning to Trinity College for eight years. In 1724 he became Dean of Derry. Shortly after, he set out on an abortive mission to found a college in Bermuda. This led to his living for over two years near Newport, Rhode Island. He is thus the first of our figures to visit the New World. Back in London, he was appointed Bishop of Cloyne (Cork) in Ireland, where he spent most of his remaining years. He had seven children, three of whom died in infancy. He was heartbroken when his favorite son, William, died at the age of 14 (in 1751). In 1752 he accompanied his son George to Oxford, where he (the father) died the following year. Most relevant for us are his *New Theory of Vision* (1709) and *Principles of Human Knowledge* (1710). The argument of the latter is somewhat extended in the delightful *Three Dialogues between Hylas and Philonous* (1713). These are his main writings, all completed by the age of 28.

Of all the figures we have considered, Bishop Berkeley is the first who could give a job talk on visual perception in a good department of psychology today and have a fair chance of landing the job. Aristotle would, perhaps, overawe an audience of contemporary psychologists by the depth of his theorizing in the absence of psychological experiment. Hobbes's physiology would put him in trouble. Descartes would appear too remote from experimental psychology, while his physiology would be too out of date. Locke might make a favorable impression, but the developmentalists would cause him more trouble than he could cope with. Berkeley, if he was careful not to advance his metaphysical ideas, could give a talk on visual perception that would impress the vision people. Of course, he could not field questions on current experimental work, but that might be attributed to his coming from Ireland. The force of his observations and conclusions on vision might well be enough to outweigh the blanks in the literature and win him the post. I too would be impressed by his brilliance, but I would have reservations because of his running together perception and cognition, to which we now turn.

Right at the beginning of the *Principles of Human Knowledge* he reveals his *bête noire*—abstract ideas. Abstract ideas, and their baneful effects, arise because people think they can form ideas (in the now familiar sense of mental sketch) of objects that abstract from the individuating perceptual properties of the objects that give rise to them. He gives as example the supposed "abstract idea of extension; which is neither line, surface, nor solid, nor has any figure or magnitude" (*Principles,* Intro, § 8). In other words, the visual presentation of some particular object may include a particular line segment, a particular surface, or a particular solid form. These present, respectively, a certain length, a certain area, and a certain volume. Belief in an abstract idea (or sketch) of extension is belief in a mental sketch of an object in which the line segments have no particular length, the surfaces no particular area, the solid form no particular volume. One might be tempted to think that such an abstract idea could be a line, since a line could exist in all three. Yet the claim was that the abstract idea is not a line. The only other alternative is that the abstract idea is a collection of points that do not form a line, but it is difficult to see why one should treat such a collection as any sort of representation of a line, a surface, or a solid.

Another supposed example of an abstract idea that Berkeley studies is body, which is supposed to represent bodies in general but itself to have no particular shape or magnitude.

By body is meant body without any particular shape or figure, there being no one shape or figure to all animals; without covering, either of hair, or feathers, or scales, etc., nor yet naked. . . . I cannot by any effort of thought conceive the abstract idea above described. (*Principles,* Intro, §§ 9, 10)

Berkeley does not reject general ideas, that is, ideas that "signify" several objects; what he rejects are abstract general ideas. Locke in his *Essay* claimed that he himself had an abstract general idea of a triangle, which was "neither oblique nor rectangle, neither equilateral, equicrural, nor scalenon; but all and none of these at once" (bk. 4, chap. 7, § 9). Locke concedes that this is difficult. Berkeley, who will have none of this, protests that it is not so much difficult as impossible, and of course he is right, provided one means by "idea" what both Locke and Berkeley meant, that is, a mental image that is supposed to resemble what it represents. To convince yourself that Berkeley is right, imagine a horse, but try to imagine it facing all directions at once. It cannot be done.

Unknown to himself, it seems, Berkeley is here echoing the line of reasoning in *De ente et essentia,* the first piece Thomas Aquinas ever wrote. We do not, Thomas says, form more general representations by dropping out particular items of information but by representing them in a more general way. A general representation of an animal that happens to be a horse represents the whole animal, and so does a more particular one that represents it as a horse. There is, however, a major difference between Aquinas and Berkeley. Aquinas is speaking of concepts, which for him are cognitive entities situated at a level distinct from the perceptual, whereas Berkeley's ideas are at the perceptual level. Part of the trouble to which Berkeley draws attention arises from the identification of the conceptual with the perceptual. Berkeley is perfectly correct to insist that you cannot form a single image that resembles animals of all types. Strangely, the belief that you could survived Berkeley's attack. We will meet it again in John Stuart Mill, and through him it made its way into contemporary cognitive psychology.

How, then, is it possible for Thomas Aquinas to speak about abstract concepts? He can because for him concepts, being at the cognitive level, are intelligible outlines (*species intelligibiles*), not images. In explaining what Aquinas meant by this I suggested that the easiest way to understand him is by taking an intelligible outline to be a blueprint. Nothing in the notion of blueprint precludes one blueprint being more specific than another. Take a clothes drier. Any blueprint must specify that the drier has a heating element. But one blueprint may just indicate that there is a heating element with its input and output wires, while another may indicate in addition that it draws 1,000 watts. In this way one blueprint may be more abstract than another. From another point of view, all blueprints are abstract, and in this sense Aquinas can speak about abstract concepts. But this approach is not open to Berkeley, who took from Locke the view that knowledge consists of nothing but percepts, either of sensation or of reflection. Berkeley wholly rejects the idea that perception gives us knowledge of causality, and hence he finds no place for a concept that goes beyond the perceptually given and represents the causally interacting components of an object. It is precisely because Aquinas's intelligible outlines do not consist of perceptual features that the differences among them do not consist of dropping or including such features. The belief, however, that we can reach beneath appearances to natures is as foreign to Berkeley as it is to Locke—and for similar reasons. Berkeley goes one step further than Locke: he denies that there is anything in material objects beyond appearances.

Here is where Locke's chickens come home to roost. Locke got the intentionality wrong, and Berkeley followed suit. Berkeley thus held that what we know immediately are ideas. In Locke, ideas are images of external, material bodies (at least ideas of sensation are); Berkeley denies that the ideas are the images of anything "without the mind." He coins the slogan, To be is to be perceived (*Esse est percipi*). Locke had retained the notion of an utterly unknown and unknowable substance that sustained perceived qualities. Berkeley, with a good deal of justice, wondered what place an unknowable substance could have in knowledge and, finding none, excluded it as an idle wheel. No idea of substance, no substance! What he sees is that if ideas are the immediate objects of awareness, there is no need of an external world of material objects. The external world drops out, so to speak.

Berkeley has the honesty to face up to the implications: "But after all, say you, it sounds harsh to say we eat and drink ideas, and are clothed with ideas" (*Principles,* § 38). True, he responds, but this is entirely due to the bad habit of assuming material substances as the reference of our "familiar use of language." Berkeley offers no cure except to practice seeing things as he does, until the oddness disappears.

Berkeley scholars place great stress on Berkeley's arguments for rejecting the distinction between primary and secondary qualities. Primary qualities, recall, were those objective properties that give rise to ideas that resemble them, so that the adjective that describes the quality also describes the idea. To be square is a supposed example, the theory being that the (visual) idea or image of a square is itself square. Secondary qualities, on the other hand, are those whose ideas do not resemble them, so that the adjective describing the idea does not describe the quality. Red is a supposed example. This whole distinction is a result of getting the intentionality wrong, because Berkeley supposes that we have immediate awareness of the attributes of our representations of things, immediate awareness of ideas. With his penetrating intelligence Berkeley somehow saw that the distinction had to go. If ideas are the immediate objects of our awareness, he reasoned, there is no need of external material bodies. It follows that the definitions of primary and secondary qualities make no sense, there being no material bodies and hence no objective properties. It follows further that there can be no distinction between ideas that represent by resembling something and those that do not. Berkeley gives many additional psychological reasons, based on his theory of perception, for rejecting the distinction, but they are really unnecessary. We will therefore not attempt to follow him, even though his arguments are of psychological interest. Suffice it to say that, with Locke as his starting point, Berkeley was perfectly right in rejecting the distinction.

Berkeley's psychology, like his ontology, is enormously simplified, but at drastic cost. He has no need of an active intellect to generate concepts in connection with given percepts. There is no problem in explaining intentionality, since everything is in the mind, and the impression that we are in touch with material substances outside the mind is an illusion. There is no problem of how we pass beyond the imperfections of perceptual objects to the perfection of ideal ones. There are, for example, no ideal lines, only the lines one perceives or imagines. To be, after all, is to be perceived. He is unperturbed if, because of this, the "very foundations of Geometry are destroyed" (*Principles*, § 131); he assures us that he can salvage all that is useful in the subject. Here too I must beg leave to differ. Calculus works for physicists only because they go beyond the physical to idealized lines, surfaces, and areas. In fairness, however, I should record that in 1734 Berkeley wrote an important paper, *The Analyst*, criticizing the conceptual foundations of calculus. And indeed there was a problem, which took some 200 years to iron out. Some would say it is not completely ironed out yet.

Berkeley is deftly able to make another saving in his psychology. Aristotle had asked how we manage to tell which objects are both white and sweet, how we coordinate information from different perceptual modalities. Berkeley claims that we simply do not do so, and his arguments create a challenge for the theory of perception that so far has not, to my mind, been satisfactorily handled by perceptual psychologists. To follow him, we turn to the *New Theory of Vision*.

He argues, "It is a mistake to think the same thing affects both sight and touch" (*New Theory*, § 136). Of course there cannot be some such thing if there is nothing that affects sight and nothing that affects touch. There can be no such material thing, that is, because God is the agent that supplies us with the perceptual impressions we have. This is a form of divine-illumination theory, but instead of God supplying conceptualizations in connection with perceptual experience (Augustine), Berkeley has God supply the perceptual experience itself. Berkeley concedes, of course, that most people believe that they sometimes see and touch the same object, that they apply the same words to the extensions and shapes of an object regardless of whether they see it or touch it. We say of a wooden square that we see that it has straight edges, four of them; we also say that we can feel all four edges and that they feel straight.

To which I answer, we can no more argue a visible and tangible square to be of the same species, from their being called by the same name, than we can that a tangible square, and the monosyllable consisting of six letters whereby it is marked, are of the same species, because they are both called by the same name. (*New Theory*, § 140)

The argument is correct. The fact that we call the sequence s-q-u-a-r-e and the shape □ by the same name, "square," is no evidence that the objects so named are of the same type. Clearly not, one being a word and the other a geometric shape.

But, you object, those two objects don't even appear to be alike: one has six letters and no sides; the other has four sides and no letters. A visible square and a tangible square, however, seem to be alike, and on occasion to be one and the same object. A visible square and a tangible one at least have the same number of sides. In response Berkeley offers a telling analogy.

I observe that visible figures represent tangible figures much after the same manner that written words do sounds. Now in this respect words are not arbitrary; it not being indifferent what written word stands for any sound. But, it is requisite that each word contain in it as many distinct characters as there are variations in the sound it stands for. (*New Theory, §* 143)

This too is a reasonable argument, even if the number of letters in an English written word is not in perfect agreement with the number of distinct sounds in the spoken word. There is sufficient agreement for us to grasp Berkeley's point, which is that the agreement in the number of sides of a visible square and a tangible one is not conclusive evidence that the two are even of the same species, let alone the very same object. No more are a written word and a spoken word the same species, the one being a visible shape, the other a sound wave. Berkeley's observation is perfectly justified, and psychology will have to dig deep to deal with it.

It is possible to make Berkeley's line of thought clearer by turning briefly to the movies, where we seem to see the heroine and hear her talking. In the cinema, however, there is no one individual that is directly seen and heard. What is seen is a sequence of projections on a screen; what is heard is a series of sounds emanating from loud speakers at either side of the screen. And yet we are seduced by the impression that we are looking at and hearing a single individual, namely the heroine. Of course, when the movie was being shot, a single individual was being photographed and recorded, but this unity of sight and sound is no longer the case when the film is being screened. We can make Berkeley's point by analogy. He claims that there is no individual that we both see and touch, although we have a powerful impression that there is. It seems fair to say that in the framework he inherited from Hobbes and Locke, his conclusion is completely justified. The moral is not that Berkeley is crazy but that there is something dreadfully wrong with the framework.

This line of thought led Berkeley to propose an answer to a question proposed by his Dublin friend William Molyneux—the "ingenious Mr. Molyneux," Berkeley calls him. The description of a single object is justified by an empirical test of Locke's radical empiricism that Molyneux proposed in the form of a psychological experiment—a radical empirical test of radical empiricism! The question goes like this. Suppose that a man of normal intelligence is born blind because of defective corneas and in growing to manhood learns by touch to discriminate spheres from cubes. He also learns the words "sphere" and "cube" and applies them correctly to the objects he touches. If such a man, now an adult, should have an operation to replace his defective corneas by good ones so that he can now see shapes clearly, would he, without further training or further experience, be able to apply the words "sphere" and "cube" correctly to objects that he is allowed to look at but not touch? Many great writers attempted an answer. My own department (at McGill University) gained considerable luster from Donald Hebb's attempt to answer it in *The Organization of Behavior* (1949). Berkeley's answer was clearly decided for him by his theory. The man could not apply the words correctly to the visual objects, because he had not formed the necessary associations between the words and the visual experiences and there simply is nothing that is the common object of vision and touch. Therefore, there is no way for the man to tell a sphere from a cube by vision alone. I am not sure that the matter is settled, but my friend Michael Morgan put together a whole book of responses to Molyneux's question (1977) and ended it with an essay saying, in essence, that Berkeley's response is wrong. Getting the answer wrong, however, takes nothing from the interest of the method followed.

It is instructive to read the *New Theory,* noting the various uses Berkeley makes of language. We have just seen how he used language to rebut the argument for a common object of vision and touch based on the equal number of sides in a visible square and a tangible one. His most interesting use of language is his proposal that what vision yields is a set of representations that are in the form of well-formed formulas in a language of vision. I believe that this proposal is broadly correct, and that the theory of visual perception cannot advance significantly until this is recognized. I propose, then, to devote the little space that remains to a brief sketch of how Berkeley's proposal might be developed. I do not believe that visual objects (apart from written sentences) are formulas in a language; rather I believe that the representations the visual system forms of them are.

Berkeley's reasons for the proposal of vision as language arise from inside his theory as a whole. The proposal is a good deal more interesting than the reasons. Nevertheless, we should at least obtain a glimpse of his reasons. The main one is that visual representations cannot represent by resembling, as Locke and Hobbes taught, because for Berkeley there are no objects to resemble. It follows that visual representations do not achieve their purpose, of guiding us in our actions, by resembling anything. Berkeley noticed that the same is true of words in natural languages. The word "sphere" is no more spherical than the word "cube," yet "sphere" serves very well to characterize spherical objects just as the word "cube" serves to characterize cubical ones. This all leads to the following:

> Upon the whole, I think we may fairly conclude that the proper objects of Vision [with the intentionality wrong] constitute the Universal Language of Nature; whereby we are instructed how to regulate our actions, in order to attain those things that are necessary to the preservation and well-being of our bodies, as also to avoid whatever may be hurtful and destructive to them. . . . And the manner wherein they signify and mark out unto us the objects which are at a distance is the same with that of languages and signs of human appointment; which do not suggest the things signified by any likeness or identity of nature, but only by an habitual connection that experience has made us to observe between them. (*New Theory*, § 147)

Of course, Berkeley means not objects that really are at a distance from the viewer, only objects that appear so.

Berkeley's reason for calling vision the "universal language of nature" is that he believed that it is the same for all peoples, no matter what language they speak. The claim is that Japanese speakers, English speakers, Chinese speakers all share precisely the same visual experiences when looking at the same visual objects. And so the language of vision "is not liable to that misinterpretation and ambiguity that languages of human contrivance are unavoidably subject to" (*New Theory*, § 152).

The depth of Berkeley's proposal can only be hinted at here. Take the visual perception of a green square. The first thing the visual system does is to distinguish a figure from the adjoining background and type it as a square (present it as squarelike)—all at the perceptual level. That is, the visual system presents the figure as a square. This corresponds to the function of count nouns at the linguistic level, because the extension of such nouns is a set of individuals with the relation of identity holding among them. The visual system presents the attribute of being green as inhering in the square and as individuated by it (there may be several green squares in the scene). This corresponds to the function of the adjective "green" in language. Green squares are a subset of squares, which are individuated by square and not by green. In addition, the presentation of the attribute as inhering in the figure corresponds to "green" being predicated of "a square" in language, which corresponds to the predication of "to be green" of the square, which corresponds to the English sentence "The square is green."

We cannot go further here, but I trust that the idea comes through. It has the advantage of not suggesting either pictures or models in the brain, where there are no eyes to see them or fingers to feel them. It is in keeping with Berkeley's general point that visual representations do not represent by resembling—a point that research on visual color and shape strongly suggests. This point has the added advantage that it represents the output of vision as formulas, and one can begin to think about how we might translate them into other appropriate sentences, English ones for example. If one demands that a real language be one in which the user can compose as well as interpret, one can regard visual imagination as providing for the process of composition in the language.

We owe a lot to this strange man, Bishop Berkeley. Better than anyone else he demolished the erroneous doctrine of abstraction in connection with perception. We are in his debt for defining in his philosophy the position known as idealism, that is, the position that there are no material substances "without the mind." Not that the position is attractive, but we need a clear example of an idealist. He revealed that idealism lies hidden in the radical empiricism of Hobbes and Locke. We also learned the challenge he posed to perceptual psychologists about the integration of information across perceptual modalities and the problem of making provision for an object that is accessed by several different perceptual modalities. Perhaps most important for the future of psychology is his proposal to regard visual representations as formulas in a language of vision. One last debt may be mentioned: he wrote concisely and beautifully. Where he is wrong, he is clearly wrong. No small merit!

Bibliographical Note

Berkeley, G. (1709–13/1965). *Berkeley's Philosophical Writings*. Edited by D. M. Armstrong. New York: Collier-Macmillan. See especially *A New Theory of Vision* (1709), *Principles of Human Knowledge* (1710), and *Three Dialogues between Hylas and Philonous* (1710).

17

David Hume: Some Consequences of British Empiricism

Biographical Note

David Hume (1711–1776) was born in Edinburgh, attended its university for a time, and spent a great part of his life there, in the time of that city's greatest intellectual flowering. Urged by his father, he began the study of law at Edinburgh University, but detesting law, he left the university at the age of 15. He tried his hand at business in Bristol for a few months, unsuccessfully, and left for France, where he embarked on a course of private studies (1734–1737). This period resulted in the work for which he is most famous: *A Treatise of Human Nature*, published in three volumes in 1738–1740, when he was still in his twenties. Anxious for literary fame, he was disappointed by the book's reception, complaining later that it "fell dead-born from the press." Failing to obtain a chair of philosophy at Edinburgh University, he spent several years abroad as the secretary of General St. Clair. In 1752 he became librarian in Edinburgh's Advocates Library and took to writing history. From 1763 to 1766 he served in the British Embassy in Paris, and from 1767 to 1768 as Undersecretary of State in the Northern Department. He returned to Edinburgh in 1769, where some seven years later he died of cancer. The principal sources for his psychology are the *Treatise* and a revision of the first part of that book published in 1748 and known today by the title he gave the second edition (1751), *An Enquiry concerning Human Understanding*.

In no philosopher I am familiar with does psychology dominate so totally over ontology as in David Hume. We do not find in Hume the fertility of new ideas that we find in Berkeley, but we find an even greater determination than Berkeley's to get to the bottom of Hobbes's and Locke's psychology. The results, if alarming, are of prime importance, because they reveal the natural consequences of adopting such a psychology. We will look at just two of his results: the annihilation of the notion of cause as it is generally conceived and the loss of belief in a self that remains the same from one day to the next. These are by no means all that we lose in adopting Hobbes's and Locke's psychology, but they are enough to illustrate the consequences as a whole. The consequences are all the more surprising and instructive for the fact that both Hobbes and Locke considered themselves to be the plainest thinking people and the least duped by the perilous subtleties of the Cartesians and the medievals, to whom the Cartesians looked back for so much. The consequences that we have already seen in Berkeley and those that we will now study are such that no plain-thinking commonsense person would accept. There surely is a lesson of some sort in all this.

In seeking to annihilate the common conception of cause and the associated ones of energy and force, Hume realized that he was going against "the inveterate prejudices of mankind" (*Treatise,* bk. 1, sect. 3, p. 166). He was, in fact, flying in the face of common sense, to which he preferred the psychological theory that he learned from Locke, whose "fundamental principle, [was] that all ideas are copied from impressions" (*Treatise,* bk. 1, sect. 3, p. 163). By "impressions" he merely means the direct deliveries of Locke's sensation (external) and reflection (internal). Hume's whole case against the common conception of cause is that perception never reveals directly any causal activity or causal energy or causal nexus. This is something that I have touched upon several times but reserved a fuller discussion for when we came to Hume. No one showed more definitively than he that there is no direct perception of cause and effect, as these terms are commonly understood. I agree completely with Hume's analysis of the perceptual evidence, though not with the skeptical conclusion he draws. Since the treatment of the subject in the *Enquiry* is fuller, for our study of causality I turn mainly to that book.

Hume often illustrates his case with the movement of billiard balls, which, he allows, seem to impel each other to motion upon contact. But, he observes, all we perceive is motion: not energy, force, or inertia. We can make his point even more vivid if we think of a man cycling a bicycle. We almost fancy we perceive the pressure he exerts on the pedals. But we don't really. All we see is the motion of his feet and the simultaneous motion of the pedals. Yes, you will say, but what if I am the cyclist? I can then feel the effort I put into my legs to make the pedals go around. Hume is unimpressed.

> The resistance which we meet with in bodies, obliging us frequently to exert our force, and call up all our power, this gives us the idea of force and power. It is this *nisus* [pressure], or strong endeavor, of which we are conscious, that is the original impression from which this idea is copied. . . . This sentiment of an endeavor to overcome resistance has no known connection with any event: What follows it, we know by experience; but could not know *a priori*. It must, however, be confessed, that the animal *nisus*, which we experience, though it can afford no accurate precise idea of power, enters very much into that vulgar, inaccurate idea, which is formed from it. (*Enquiry*, sect. 8, part 1, § 53, fn.) [See the definition of *a priori* in the Glossary.]

As I understand the argument, the remark about a priori knowledge is for the following purpose. Hume believes that if we had direct experience of causally efficacious energy, we would thereby, even without observing any effect, know that it would produce change. But, he argues, we never have such a direct experience. We experience, rather, an effort in our bodies and, associated with it, the motion of objects we are in contact with. It is this experience of an association between effort and motion, and nothing else, that gives rise to the impression, illusory according to Hume, that energy has passed from our bodies to the moving objects. That this impression is illusory is further evidenced by the fact that there is no resemblance between our feeling of effort and the motion of the objects we are in contact with.

This, he holds, is particularly obvious in the association between acts of the will, which are mental, and movements of our bodies, say twiddling one's thumbs, which are physical. Anatomy teaches that innumerable events intervene between the two—activities of nerves, muscles, and tendons. "Can there be a more certain proof, that the power by which this whole operation is performed, so far from being directly and fully known by an inward sentiment or consciousness, is, to the last degree mysterious and unintelligible?" (*Enquiry*, sect. 7, part 1, § 52).

While at the purely perceptual level Hume's analysis is fully accurate, his way of dealing with the issues harbors some serious misconceptions. Perhaps the most serious misconception arises in connection with his view about a priori knowledge of cause, energy, force, power, and the like. It is the idea that if we know any of these, we can know them in isolation from the others. This he makes explicit in the next citation:

According to these explications and definitions, the idea of power is relative as much as cause; and both have a reference to an effect. When we consider the *unknown* circumstance of an object, by which the degree or quantity of its effect is fixed and determined, we call that its power: And accordingly, it is allowed by all philosophers, that the effect is the measure of the power. But if they had any idea of power, as it is in itself, why could not they Measure it in itself? (*Enquiry*, sect. 8, part 2, § 60, fn.)

This is really quite unreasonable. Force (or power) is a primitive in dynamics, and its reference and concept are determined, to the extent they are, by a whole system of interrelated concepts. For example, physicists tell us that force = mass × acceleration. As Hertz realized, it is the set of equations in which the various primitive expressions occur that determines the references of the expressions. It is out of order to ask that each be defined on its own or observed and measured in isolation from all others. This does not mean that Hume was unjustified in his perceptual observations; it just means that he was not entitled to demand that each term be considered in isolation, much less that it be so measured. For this reason he is not entitled to employ this line of argument to further his case against causality. And yet the demand for isolation forms a central part of his attempt to demolish the common conception of causality and to yield the conclusion that he expresses so colorfully: "Upon the whole, there appears not, throughout all nature, any one instance of [causal] connection which is conceivable by us. All events seem entirely loose and separate" (*Enquiry*, sect. 7, part 2, § 58).

This all leads Hume to the following definition of *cause:*

An object precedent and contiguous to another, and so united with it in the imagination, that the idea of one determines the mind to form the idea of the other. (*Treatise*, bk. 1, part 3, p. 172)

According to this definition, all that A's causing B amounts to is that A precedes B, is contiguous to it, and our experience has given rise to an association such that the thought of A evokes that of B and the thought of B evokes that of A. Causality, as the vulgar conceive of it, is illusory, a trick of the imagination.

How serious is Hume's conclusion for science? The answer can only be totally devastating. Hume's psychology prohibits positing theoretical entities that elude perception: atoms, subatomic particles, photons, gravitons—a great part of modern science! Moreover, scientists when they are not attempting to be philosophers instinctively believe that they are getting at structure—the causally interacting components of the objects they study—whether they be physicists dealing with the subatomic world, chemists dealing with the atomic one, or biologists dealing with the world of living matter. Hume tells them that their beliefs are illusory, that at best they learn only regularity of patterning, the rest being imagination. Whenever older psychologists think of causality, they are apt to recall the work of the Belgian psychologist Albert Michotte. Michotte constructed animated cartoons to study the phenomenology of causality. The question he asked is, What gives rise to the *impression* that A caused B? Typical cartoons of his presented A moving to touch B and B moving off. The variables Michotte studied were the lapse in time between A's touching B and B's moving, the direction of B's motion in relation to that of A, B's velocity relative to A's, and the like. Subjects knew that in no case did A actually cause B to move. They were asked to say merely when it appeared to do so. Interestingly, people had no trouble distinguishing the appearance of causality from "real" causality. Michotte's studies seem to me among the most elegant and interesting carried out in this century. Nevertheless, they do not refute Hume. Hume could reasonably say that they merely extend, with improved methods, his (Hume's) analysis of the psychology of causation, adding that all there ever is to causality is a certain type of mental association.

I believe that in the Hobbesian and Lockean framework, Hume's case is utterly inescapable. There is no direct perception of the exchange of energy in causation. It follows that one is presented with just two alternatives: either causality as we commonly conceive it is illusory, a trick of the imagination, or we allow that the human mind is able to reach beneath appearances and discover realities that are not directly given in appearances. Most people will choose the second alternative, but in doing so, they implicitly reject the Hobbesian and Lockean line in psychology. I would merely add that I find it ironic that Hobbes's decision to do psychology on the model of the leading science of the day, kinematics, should in the not so long run (100 years) render the concept of science, as Galileo and Hobbes himself understood it, illusory.

Hume was impressed with Berkeley's arguments (of which we saw something in the last chapter) against the existence of material objects that give rise to perception though they themselves are independent of perception. One reason for following Berkeley was that the common view would require a causal connection between the supposed material objects and perceptions, and Hume had dispensed with causality of that sort. Little wonder, then, that he accepted Berkeley's general position and rejected "the double existence of perceptions and objects" (*Treatise*, bk. 1, part 4, sect. 2, p. 211). That is, he agreed with Berkeley that there are no objects independent of perception.

Now it is possible to read Hume so as to deflect some of the skeptical impact of his work. If so inclined, one can cite a famous remark of Hume's: " 'Tis in vain to ask, *Whether there be body or not?* That is a point, which we must take for granted in all our reasonings" (*Treatise*, bk. 1, part 4, sect. 2, p. 187). And yet the whole tendency of the *Treatise* is in the opposite direction. I find it easier to follow Hume if, with most people, I read him as saying that there are no external objects of perception and there is no identity of percepts from one occasion to the next, that is, if I read him as attempting to give an acceptable account of what underlies the ordinary expressions that there are such objects and that they have identity over time. In any event, I am less concerned to give an original and scholarly reading of Hume than to read him as he has usually been read. For it is that ordinary reading that has influenced psychology.

The root of Hume's thinking about identity is easy to understand. There are no external objects of perception, only the percepts themselves. These come and go in our minds, and at times, when we are unconscious or in dreamless sleep, they seem to disappear completely. Take the percept of a desk that I have now and had yesterday but did not have during the intervening night. What is identical from yesterday to today? Not an external desk, according to Berkeley and Hume, since there is no such thing. The only candidate is the percept. But what makes a percept formed yesterday and one formed today identical? Nothing, just as the image of a desk drawn on the blackboard yesterday and then erased is not identical with a new image of a desk drawn there today. All we can have is similarity of images. That is all that Hume allows for percepts. Within the terms of his theory this position is inescapable.

But, you are bound to protest, it was I who perceived the desk yesterday and I who perceived it again today, so there is something else that is identical from one occasion to the next, namely me. Not so fast, Hume responds: "We must altogether reject the opinion, that there is such a thing in nature as a continued existence, even when it no longer appears to the senses" (*Treatise*, bk. 1, part 4, sect. 2, p. 214). It follows that there is nothing corresponding to me while I am unconscious or in dreamless sleep. We do not have to infer this, for Hume is nothing if not explicit on the point:

When my perceptions are removed for any time, as in sound sleep; so long am I insensible of *myself,* and may truly be said not to exist. (*Treatise,* bk. 1, part 4, sect. 4, p. 252)

He says a few pages later, "The identity, which we attribute to the mind of man, is only a fictitious one" (p. 259).

This means that the David Hume who went to bed in the evening was not the same person as the David Hume who got out of it the following morning. I am not sure that this position can be coherently stated, since we have to wonder about what it is that notices the similarity between the Hume that went to sleep and the Hume that woke up, but there is little question that the position is Hume's. He points to similarity as the main reason for supposing identity. Because the David Hume who went to bed resembled closely the David Hume that woke the following morning, the imagination fills the gap: "The imagination is seduced into such an opinion only by means of the resemblance of certain perceptions" (*Treatise,* bk. 1, part 4, sect. 2, p. 209). Elsewhere he states that the idea of a continued existence is "entirely owing to the imagination" (p. 193).

Thus the same agent is responsible for both the illusion of a connection, other than association, between cause and effect and the illusion of identity, including personal identity, across gaps in perceptual contact. Once again, the conclusion follows inescapably from the psychology that Hume learned from Hobbes and Locke. There obviously cannot be any percep-

tual evidence for the existence of something that is beyond the reach of
our perceptual systems. If you find the conclusion repugnant, as I am sure
you do, you have to reconsider the psychological premises on which it
is based. Plainly put, the sort of personal identity we all assume is not
given immediately in perception. If we believe in such identity, we must
be prepared to admit that the mind is able to reach beyond appearances
to entities that continue to exist even when they are not being perceived,
entities that have identity across numerous perceptual gaps.

I believe that if followed in depth, no notion is so important for psychology as that of identity. Aristotle tried to make provision for it by
means of substance, which is not directly perceptible but remains constant beneath many changes in appearance. Hume rejected the notion of
substance as an "unintelligible chimera" (*Treatise,* p. 22), and indeed
Aristotle's idea is not satisfactory. And yet Hume makes no provision at
all for identity—with catastrophic results. My own conviction is that to
handle identity correctly, we need the notion of kinds. Kinds and their
members mutually determine each other. But I leave further discussion
of this topic for later, in the chapter I call "Extroduction." Suffice it here
to say that kinds, being abstract objects, are not given in immediate perception, although perception has its part to play in our discovery of kinds.
Hume would not accept the theory of the Extroduction. He would reject
kinds precisely because they are not perceived. This failure of minds to
meet cannot be helped, I fear.

We have traced to its end Hume's exploration of what is sometimes called
"British empiricism" in two matters. That radical empiricism, begotten
by the determination to escape the "idle subtleties" of the ancients and
to build on the surest foundation of common sense, ended in intellectual
shipwreck. It led Hume to dismiss causal connections and even the notion
of personal identity reaching across periods of sleep—two conclusions
that are, to say the least, disconcerting to commonsense people. One obvious moral for psychology can be put in the form of a query: is it wise to
conceive the study of ontology and that of psychology as being separate
from one another, as is the practice today among philosophers and psychologists? Another query can be put thus: how much of David Hume
(and British radical empiricism) survives in contemporary psychology?

Here I define two more terms that are important for our study:

A priori   A concept or a belief is said to be known a priori if it is brought to experience by the mind, rather than derived from experience.

A posteriori   A concept or belief is said to be known a posteriori if it is derived from experience, rather than brought to experience. A posteriori and a priori are contrasting and complementary notions.

Bibliographical Note

Hume, David (1738–40/1967). *A Treatise of Human Nature*. Edited by L. A. Selby-Bigge. Oxford: Clarendon Press.

Hume, David (1748/1962). *Enquiries concerning Human Understanding*. Edited by L. A. Selby-Bigge. Oxford: Clarendon Press.

Michotte, A. (1946/1963). *The Perception of Causality*. Translated by T. R. Miles. New York: Basic Books.

18

Thomas Jefferson and the Declaration of Independence

Biographical Note

Thomas Jefferson (1743–1826), a Virginian, was orphaned at the age of 14 and raised thereafter by his wealthy and influential maternal relations, the Randolph family. He studied law at the College of William and Mary. After graduating, he stayed on in the college to benefit from the conversation and companionship of Dr. William Small, his main mentor. Through Small, a Scotsman, he became acquainted with the writings of Francis Hutcheson (1694–1746) and Thomas Reid (1710–1796). Hutcheson, an Irishman, was a Presbyterian minister who was chosen to be professor of moral philosophy at the University of Glasgow. Reid, a Scotsman and likewise a Presbyterian clergyman, also became professor of moral philosophy at Glasgow. Jefferson drafted Virginia's *Declaration of the Causes and Necessity for Taking up Arms* in 1775 [see Jefferson, 1943] and the American Declaration of Independence in 1776 [see Wills, 1978]. He succeeded Benjamin Franklin as U.S. ambassador to France and, on returning to America, became Secretary of State in Washington's cabinet. In due course he became the third president of the United States. In retirement he helped found the University of Virginia. The buildings he designed for it are deemed among the finest examples of architecture in North America. In addition, he was for the time a man of considerable scientific and technological knowledge on an astonishing number of fronts.

These reflections on the Declaration of Independence will have to serve as our introduction to the Enlightenment. The Declaration, though penned by Jefferson, who was not a Christian, has a strangely Christian ring to it. This is due to the influence on it of two Presbyterian clergymen, Francis Hutcheson and Thomas Reid, who though in some respects typical Enlightenment men, were atypical in being devout Christians. More typical of the Enlightenment were the Frenchmen Voltaire, La Mettrie, d'Holbach, Diderot, Helvetius—free thinkers and materialists all of one sort or another. It is inevitable, then, that viewing the Enlightenment through the eyes of Jefferson, we come away with an impression that is not true of the movement as a whole. Such an impression, however, is nonetheless valuable, for after all, the Declaration may well be the Enlightenment's most enduring and influential monument.

We are, naturally, interested in the psychology implicit in the Declaration, rather than the document's legal import. For the psychology, I will rely heavily on a remarkable book by a political scientist well versed in the history of ideas, Gary Wills's *Inventing America* (1978), which works out the Enlightenment background in detail. There are other ways in which this chapter departs from the pattern of most of the other chapters. It deals more with moral reasoning and moral judgment than with speculative knowledge. It also concentrates on certain seminal expressions in an important text rather than on an explicit psychology. In this respect the chapter resembles more those on Genesis and the New Testament than, say, those on Descartes and Hume. We begin by looking at part of the preamble that Jefferson wrote to the main sections of the Declaration. The part that most concerns us was adopted almost without change by the Congress.

When in the course of human events it becomes *necessary* for one people to dissolve the political bands which have connected them with another . . . , a decent respect to the opinions of mankind requires that they should declare the *causes* which impel them to the separation.

We hold these *truths to be self evident:* that *all men are created equal;* that they are *endowed by their creator with inherent and inalienable rights;* that among these are life, liberty and the *pursuit of happiness:* that to secure these rights, governments are instituted among men . . .

The expressions on which I propose to comment I have italicized. The only change that Congress made in this part is that they replaced "inherent and inalienable rights" with "certain unalienable rights." The passage before us, then, is familiar from the final version.

Jefferson said not that the time had come to separate from England or that it would benefit the colonies to do so, but that there were causes that rendered it necessary. This suggests a clear grasp of the issues involved and the idea that any level-headed person would see that in view of these causes there was no alternative. Wills gives an interesting interpretation of this statement against the background of Newton's mechanics and Enlightenment hopes, engendered by Newton's success, to develop a range of mathematically precise sciences of human nature in politics, education, ethics, and psychology. Newton's mechanics, remember, specified causes of motion, whereas in Galileo's kinematics no causes were specified.

We often think that Sir Francis Galton, in the second half of the nineteenth century, began the movement of mental measurement, and indeed he was more precise than his predecessors. But Jefferson, like many of his contemporaries, believed one could measure such things as the general happiness of society, and he also believed that one could compute with such measurements. Jefferson and his contemporaries were among the original time-and-motion people. Jefferson himself was forever measuring the amount of work one person could do in a unit of time. He also believed in measuring mental ability and in selecting the ablest students for advancement in education. Hutcheson even believed that a useful algebra of ethics could be developed. In many ways the emergence of "scientific" psychology 100 years later is prepared in the theories and practices of the Enlightenment. The Enlightenment in turn looked back not only to Newton, who gave it a boost, but also to Hobbes, who first proposed that the sciences of human nature should be modeled on physics. In the Enlightenment, Hobbes's idea took off. And Jefferson wanted the Declaration to echo and build upon the scientific ideas of the times.

"We hold these truths to be self-evident," wrote Jefferson, and Congress accepted his words. There was a technical sense of "self-evidence" in Locke, who declared, roughly, that truths are self-evident if they are tautologies, that is, if the predicate is implicit in the meaning of the subject term. As an example, if a person is a girl, she is female. This is not what Jefferson means by "self-evident"; his idea derives rather from that of Reid. Reid's *Inquiry into the Human Mind on the Principles of Common Sense* (1764), of which Jefferson possessed a copy, takes its departure from common sense, as the title suggests. For Reid, common sense is rooted in perception, which places us in contact with external objects rather than with mental entities. So much is evident to any person, old or young, he believed. Common sense also gives us the basic principles of morality. But common sense is not to be identified with the average or commonplace. It is, rather, the sense that emerges in a community. For, Reid held, individual and community constrain each other—a thoroughly Christian notion, as we saw in the reflections on the New Testament, and not surprising in a Christian clergyman. Reid did not value formal education, especially in connection with either perception or common sense. He held that the wisdom of the community was equally available to all. It is, we might be inclined to say, a normal output of the faculty of social cognition, granted normal experience in a community. It is only in the realms of reason and science that people draw apart and formal education makes a significant difference. Examples of truths that are self-evident from the standpoint of common sense are, Do not offend people needlessly, and Make some provision for the future. These are not self-evident in Locke's system; they are in Reid's. And so, Jefferson and Congress believed, are the truths described as self-evident in the Declaration. Viewed from the standpoint of Plato's problem of learning, this means that Jefferson and Congress believed that, at least in the area of social cognition, children are endowed by nature with mental structures that make the relevant sorts of learning inevitable, granted normal social experiences.

The first such truth is "that all men are created equal." No claim could more clearly indicate the influence of the Bible. It was certainly the wisdom of Jefferson's community that human beings are created and that there is but a single Creator (assumed in the next phrase). Today Jefferson could not state these points so confidently, and in some societies they would not be accepted at all. The Declaration is a more thoroughly Christian document than Jefferson perhaps realized. This is particularly interesting in view of the much vaunted separation of church and state in the United States. The claim that all men are created equal has cast a long shadow over American psychologists, who, more than their English counterparts, have been uneasy with the notion of genetically conditioned individual differences in intellectual and personality traits.

It is all the more important, then, to inquire in what sense Jefferson and Congress held that all human beings are equal? We are not equal in sex, height, hair color, or mathematical ability. The answer that Reid gives is that we are all equal in moral sensibilities—again provided that we have grown up in a healthy community. There is something of this confidence built into the notion of a jury in the Anglo-Saxon legal tradition. Twelve folk collected from the community at large are thought to be as sound a source of moral judgment and of judgment about certain matters of fact (guilty versus not guilty) as the most learned lawyers or professors. The jury are not expected to be experts on points of law; they are expected to be as expert as anyone can be in judging human action. This is tantamount to saying that there is no such thing as expertise in the area. This is Reid's point; he held that the philosopher and the fool were here on equal footing. And Jefferson's "State a moral case to a ploughman and a professor. The former will decide it as well and often better than the latter, because he has not been led astray by artificial rules" (Wills, 1978, 185). This is a claim of fundamental importance for the psychology of the development of moral reasoning. I might add that the belief implicit in the Declaration is widely denied in the psychological literature stemming from the work of Jean Piaget and Laurence Kohlberg. That literature argues for substantial differences in powers of moral reasoning and moral judgment among adults in a single community. What is more, that literature seeks to characterize expertise in the area of moral reasoning and moral judgment. Here I can do no more than draw attention to the discrepancy with the Declaration, adding that implicit in the Declaration is the belief that the development of powers of moral reasoning is something akin to the development of linguistic skills: nature places constraints on what can be learned; but just as nearly everyone masters the idiolect of their speech community, so nearly everyone develops competence in the exercise of moral judgment—at least in relation to actions in which they themselves are not personally involved.

It has become fashionable in certain circles to speak disparagingly of *folk psychology,* by which is meant our commonsense understanding of each other. The idea behind folk psychology is that we all judge character and interpret actions, those of others as well as our own, in the light of an everyday understanding of human nature, including suppositions about the beliefs and desires that guide actions. Certainly this understanding, though serviceable, does not amount to a scientific theory. Hence the disparaging remarks. Reid's commonsense philosophy rejected the belief that it is possible to tighten this commonsense understanding to the status of an exact science in which there could be experts. In this he was opposed to the main forces of the Enlightenment. Jefferson, however, had absorbed both Reid's common sense and the more general Enlightenment view. And so, unless I am mistaken, there is in the Declaration a tension between a frame of mind that highly values folk psychology and a frame of mind that values an exact science of human nature. The tension is also reflected in the ambivalence of a certain skepticism in the public's attitude to psychologists, particularly clinical psychologists, along with a willingness to turn to them when things go seriously wrong.

People are not equal in reasoning and scientific ability, but they are equal in moral sensitivity, Reid would say. They are equal not as regards the head but as regards the heart. Jefferson too mistrusted the head: "In short, my friend [my head], as far as my recollection serves me, I do not know that I ever did a good thing at your suggestion, or a dirty one without it" (Wills, 1978, 190).

Where equality in moral sense seemed not to hold, Jefferson believed that the explanation lay in circumstances. Many whites among his contemporaries believed blacks to be unreliable and dishonest. Jefferson held that observed dishonesty and unreliability among blacks was due to their treatment at the hands of whites:

Whether further observation will or will not verify the conjecture that nature has been less bountiful to them [blacks] in the endowments of the head, I believe that in those of the heart she will be found to have done them justice. That disposition to theft with which they have been branded must be ascribed to their situation, and not to any depravity of the moral sense. . . . We find among them numerous instances of the most rigid integrity, and as many as among their better instructed masters, of benevolence, gratitude, and unshaken fidelity. (Wills, 1978, 223–224)

This is surely an interesting psychological claim. Jefferson has been criticized for keeping some 200 slaves. Although he was a benevolent master, his slaves still endured much misery. This is not a trivial charge, as it indicates a certain inconsistency of theory and action. Nevertheless, it is the theory that most concerns us.

Besides the psychological theory needed to explain what was implicit in the claim that all human beings are equal, there is the very claim itself. The Declaration obviously echoes Genesis. In fact, it can be read as making psychologically concrete the respect in which all humans are equal. Genesis teaches that all humans descended from Adam and Eve are created in the image and likeness of the Creator. Reid, and with him Jefferson, can be read as seeing in moral sensibility the main image of the Creator.

The moral characteristics that Jefferson finds to admire in blacks—rigid integrity, benevolence, gratitude, unshaken fidelity—have an Enlightenment ring to them. In Hutcheson's system, benevolence is the core and the others follow. Benevolence is the desire to do good to others even without the prospect of personal gain. Today we have replaced "benevolence" with "altruism." Persons imbued with benevolence would, by their very natures, not betray those whom they wished to help, nor would they show themselves ungrateful. The rest of altruism follows from benevolence. But what is this but a secularized form of Christian love? What distinguishes it from Christian love is the absence of an explicit principle that one should love one's fellow human beings for the love of God. That principle, however, may have been implicit in Jefferson's conception of public service.

Interestingly, Jefferson identifies an act of doing good to others as an act of promoting one's own well-being.

It is instinct, and innate that the moral sense is as much a part of our constitution as that of feeling, seeing, or hearing; as a wise creator must have seen to be necessary in an animal destined to live in society: that every human mind feels pleasure in doing good to another. . . . The essence of virtue is in doing good to others. (Wills, 1978, 204)

From this point of view, there is, then, no conflict between pursuing one's own good and pursuing that of others. All things work together unto good.

This is, of course, a claim of enormous significance for the theory of mental health. It may not be an easy matter to choose what is good for other people, even with their cooperation. Presumably also a certain detachment is required of those who succeed in doing good, because to demand gratitude would spoil things. The Gospels have stern advice for those who aim to do good to others (e.g., "Do unto others as you would have them do unto you"), and there is no reason to believe that Jefferson would have found fault with any of it.

Among the self-evident truths is that every person is endowed by the Creator with "inherent and inalienable rights." In other words, one's basic rights do not derive from the law. Rather, governments and laws are set up to secure these rights. These basic rights are ideals at which governments and laws must aim. Governments and laws are just only to the extent that they manage to respect and secure these rights.

Basic rights function as innate needs arising from the very constitution of the individual. Experiencing those needs ourselves and growing up in a community of persons who also experience them, we come to appreciate what is demanded of each member of society. This shared humanity guides our efforts at benevolence.

Among the basic rights are "life, liberty and the pursuit of happiness." Not the right to property, mind you, as Locke claimed. Jefferson looked askance at inherited property and privilege, and even at the patenting of ideas. All this he saw as completely secondary to life, liberty, and the pursuit of happiness.

These inalienable rights place corresponding obligations on their possessors. People are not at liberty to give up their lives or liberties, or to abandon the pursuit of their own happiness. Basic rights also impose correlative duties on governments. Hutcheson saw them as "essential limitations in all governments" (Wills, 1978, 229).

Among the three inalienable rights the pursuit of happiness alone needs comment. Hutcheson propounded the slogan "the greatest happiness of the greatest number" (Wills, 1978, 150). Jefferson wrote, "The general happiness is the supreme end of all political union" (Wills, 1978, 252). He was fully aware that it is not easy to measure the happiness of a people, and he offers to a friend about to travel in Europe advice that still warms the heart for its realism and humanity:

Take every possible occasion of entering into the hovels of the labourers, and especially at the moments of their repast, see what they eat, how they are clothed, whether they are obliged to labour too hard; whether the government or their landlord takes from them an unjust portion of their labour; on what footing stands the property they call their own. (Wills, 1978, 158–159)

To Lafayette he recommended the same practices even in his native France:

You must ferret the people out in their hovels, as I have done, look into their kettle, eat their bread, loll on their beds under pretense of resting yourself, but in fact to find out if they are soft. (Wills, 1978, 159)

We have seen an aspect of Scottish Enlightenment psychology as reflected through Jefferson in the opening sections of the Declaration of Independence. We saw a belief in social science that does not come to full flower for another century. We saw the commonsense psychology of Reid reflected in the claim that there are self-evident truths—evident to all persons brought up in society, regardless of educational advantages or intellectual brilliance. The claim that all human beings are created equal incorporates just this view of psychology: that all are equal in heart, even if not equal in head. Human beings are also equal, the Declaration holds, in inalienable rights that include the right to life, to liberty, and to the pursuit of happiness. For Jefferson, to pursue one's own happiness is not selfishness, since he identifies one's own happiness with doing good to others. The psychology implicit in all this owes far more to traditional Christianity than to the influence of Hobbes that is so evident in much of Enlightenment thinking.

Bibliographical Note

Reid, Thomas (1764/1817). *An Inquiry into the Human Mind on the Principles of Common Sense.* Glasgow: W. Folcener.
Wills, Gary (1978). *Inventing America.* New York: Doubleday.

19

Immanuel Kant and the Foundational Stance in Psychology

Biographical Note

Immanuel Kant (1724–1804) was born in Königsberg (now Kaliningrad) in East Prussia (now divided among various states), lived there almost his whole life, and died there, aged 80. His father, a saddler, was a man of modest means. Nevertheless, Kant managed to study at the Collegium Fredericianum (a high school) and the University of Königsberg. For lack of funds he accepted positions as tutor in better-off families for a period of about 10 years. He kept up his studies and obtained a master's degree from his university in 1755. This enabled him to give up tutoring and become *Privatdozent* at the university, continuing in straightened circumstances. He never married. He taught physics, mathematics, and physical geography, in addition to philosophy. In 1770 (aged 46) he was appointed to the chair of logic and metaphysics, still at the University of Königsberg, and his financial worries ceased. He wrote many books that still, to a considerable extent, dominate philosophical thought and in one way or another exercise an influence on psychology. His final years were plagued by a form of mental deterioration that some have thought to be suspiciously like Alzheimer's disease. We will work mainly from two of his books: his most celebrated book, *Critique of Pure Reason* (1781) and his *Logic,* prepared for publication in 1800 by G. B. Jäsche from notes Kant wrote around 1782 for his course on logic.

Kant is one of those systematic and original thinkers that, by the force of their theory, change the intellectual atlas. After reading him, psychology somehow looks different. One finds one has new points of view, often without noticing, some useful and some suspect, but all interesting. His achievement is especially noteworthy, since he never left East Prussia. No sabbatical leaves, no visiting professorships, no conferences! He was, however, what none of our other figures from the Renaissance to his time was: a life-long university teacher.

In Kant we will study just two issues: how we come to know necessary truths about nature and the relation between logic and psychology. Both are foundational for psychology. Both bring us squarely into contact with Plato's two problems of learning and of truth and into contact with Augustine's problem relating to the idealizing properties of mind.

We came across the notion of necessity in our look at Leibniz, for whom the main form may be called logical necessity, or freedom from contradiction. Such freedom can be conceptualized as a possible world, a world that God could have created because it did not involve contradiction. Kant is concerned about a different sort of necessary truths, namely the laws that happen to obtain in our universe. For example, it is a law that the speed of light is a constant, some 186,000 miles per second (at least so physicists believe). So far as we know, another universe might have been created, with compensating changes elsewhere, in which light travels at some other speed—say 180,000 miles per second. At least the concept does not seem to be contradictory. Nevertheless, physicists believe that at all times and places in our universe, light has traveled at about 186,000 miles per second, and always will. We can put the idea of necessity that Kant is interested in like this: necessity in relation to laws of nature means holding "at all times" (*Critique*, A 145) in the universe as it actually is. Newton's laws of motion were thought to be of this sort. For example, the law of inertia made a claim about all physical bodies in the universe at all times: every body continues in a state of rest or of uniform motion in a straight line unless acted upon by a force impressed upon it. Such laws serve as axioms in physics from which conclusions can be validly drawn. The whole structure of Newton's physics, which so impressed Kant and his contemporaries, depended on there being such laws and upon our being able to know them. Nothing essential in the general picture has changed since Kant's day, although the laws of motion themselves have been revised by Einstein.

The problem for psychology is immediate. We cannot experience the motions of all physical bodies at all times. How, then, can we know laws? Kant was deeply versed in the then available writings of Leibniz, and he was particularly taken with Leibniz's application of his theory to psychology in the *New Essays* (responding to Locke), which was published for the first time as late as 1765, when Kant was over thirty years of age. The

New Essays made a great stir. Kant was even more preoccupied with the writings of David Hume. In a letter addressed to Herder, he actually ranks Hume as the most important philosopher. These two writers, Leibniz and Hume, posed for him a dilemma: either allow with Leibniz that we know laws that hold in the external world of nature and give up the Hobbesian, Lockean, Humean line in psychology, or accept that psychology and give up knowledge of laws of nature. What does he do? He holds onto knowledge of laws of nature and constructs a radically new psychology, which he believes to be compatible with such knowledge.

The new psychology, he claims, is tantamount to a Copernican revolution (*Critique*, Pref., 2nd ed., p. xcii). Roughly, what Kant proposes is this. We do not extract the laws of nature from insight into objective nature; we impose the laws on the objective world. The major source of the laws is the human mind.

If intuition [of external objects] must conform to the constitution of the objects, I do not see how we could know anything of the latter *a priori*; but if the object (as object of the senses) must conform to the constitution of our faculty of intuition, I have no difficulty in conceiving such a possibility. . . . We can know *a priori* of things only what we ourselves put into them. (*Critique*, Pref., 2nd ed., pp. xvii and xviii)

We saw in the chapter on Hume what *a priori* means. The main point that Kant wants to make is that those regularities that we attribute to nature as laws are not regularities that we derive from nature itself but ones that we contribute because of the constitution of our minds. And since we bring our minds to all experience of physical bodies, we have an explanation of how we (seem to) discover regularities in nature. Kant is confident that with due attention we can discover the constitution of the mind.

He is equally confident that we cannot discover the constitution of material bodies as they really are in themselves. He simply says, "We can have no knowledge of any object as thing in itself, but only insofar as it is an object of sensible intuition, that is, an appearance" (*Critique*, Pref., 2nd ed., p. xxvi). How often have we not heard, especially from people in artificial intelligence, that all we can know of the external world is the way our minds represent it? There is in this observation, particularly when used to discount the objective properties of nature, more than an echo of Kant.

Not that Kant is a complete idealist, as were Berkeley and Hume. He believes that there really is a material world out there and that it triggers our perceptual experiences. To think otherwise would be to accept "the absurd conclusion that there can be an appearance without anything that appears" (*Critique,* Pref., 2nd ed., pp. xxvi–xxvii). It is just that about that external world we know absolutely nothing beyond its existence; all we know are the constructions and interpretations we impose on it.

From all this it follows that unknown to themselves, physicists, chemists, and other scientists are all doing psychology. The whole of science is really a description of the human mind. Kant's own enterprise was to describe the psychology that makes science possible. He would not, I fear, have been happy with my formulation. He had a poor view of psychology, as we will see in the next section, and thought of his enterprise as metaphysics. Psychology he saw as describing the mere facts of physical experience, whereas he saw himself as describing the universal conditions of such experience. We will see that he is not entitled to this distinction and that my description of his enterprise is really quite accurate.

One very important respect in which Kant's psychology departs from Hobbes's, Locke's, Berkeley's, and Hume's psychology is that he posits, whereas they deny, a radical division between perception and cognition. Perception in Kant's system is a fundamental psychic experience with its own perceptual laws, but it is not the whole of our knowledge of the environment, nor can cognition be taken as mere rearrangements and recombinations of perceptual data. Cognition goes well beyond perception. This is where the a priori play their part. Perception triggers the conceptual operations of the mind, which include the contributions of properties that go well beyond perception. A great part of the *Critique* is a study of these contributions. They include the concept of causality, which Hume had shown is not immediately given in perception. Kant agreed, but he denied that causality is merely a matter of priority, contiguity, and constant conjunction. It is a new phenomenon contributed by the human mind. Kant would have been delighted with Michotte's studies, claiming that Michotte made precise the perceptual preconditions for the mind to impose the a priori concept of causality. Indeed, in the Gestalt tradition to which Michotte belonged, stemming from Franz Brentano through Christian von Ehrenfels, the Kantian connection is entirely appropriate.

With the a priori Kant hopes to solve one of the great problems that has run through our reflections, the problem of learning. He decided that there is no learning the properties of external objects, only learning the mind's own properties. And the manner in which the mind contributes these is determined by the constitution of the mind. He goes as far, he believes, as any person can go toward solving the problem of truth, because the only notion of truth that is effective for him is that of the agreement of thought with "the universal and necessary rules of understanding" (*Critique,* B 84). For Kant, truth is not an agreement between propositions and the way the world is, independent of how we construe it. Truth is rather an agreement between a proposition and the fundamental principles of thought. There is more to the problem of truth than this, since Kant does not explain how any thought remains forever in agreement or disagreement with the universal rules. But he might claim to have brought some light on the matter.

Kant's handling of Augustine's problem, the idealizing properties of mind, has already surfaced in his claim to discover the universal and necessary rules of thinking. It is best handled, however, in connection with our second theme: the relation between logic and psychology. To begin, we should look at how he conceptualizes logic:

Logic is the science of reason not only as to mere form but also as to matter; a science *a priori* of the necessary laws of thinking, not, however, in respect of particular objects but all objects *generatim;* it is a science therefore of the right use of the understanding and of reason as such, not subjectively, i.e., not according to empirical (psychological) principles of how the understanding thinks, but objectively, i.e. according to *a priori* principles of how it ought to think. (*Logic,* p. 18)

Leave aside, for the moment, the remark about psychology. No logician today would mention thought in the definition of logic, nor describe logic as the "necessary laws of thinking." By the way, the necessary laws of thinking are contrasted with contingent aspects. Contingent aspects relate to such matters as whether I think about money, say, or psychology; necessary laws are everywhere operative in all thought, at all times.

This immediately raises a problem. How is it possible to reason erroneously? If the laws of logic are to thought as the laws of dynamics are to the motion of physical bodies, there is no place for failure, miracles apart. Kant faces the issue squarely:

How error in the formal meaning of the word, however, is possible, that is, how a form of thinking contrary to the understanding is possible, that is difficult to comprehend; as indeed how any force should deviate from its own essential laws cannot be comprehended at all. (*Logic,* p. 59)

The best Kant can do to explain error is to appeal to distraction, perceptual error, inadvertence, and the like—performance factors, as they are sometimes called. Clearly, something is wrong.

If the aim of logic is to reflect on and discover the laws of thought, why is logic not part of psychology? The next quotation, giving Kant's answer, brings us to the core of our reflection:

Some logicians presuppose *psychological* principles in logic. But to bring such principles into logic is as absurd as taking morality from life. If we took the principles from psychology, i.e. from observations about our understanding, we would merely see *how* it *is* under manifold hindrances and conditions; this would therefore lead to the cognition of merely *contingent* laws. In logic, however, the question is not one of *contingent* but of *necessary* rules, not how we think but how we ought to think. The rules of logic, therefore, must be taken not from the contingent but from the necessary use of the understanding, which one finds, without any psychology, in oneself. (*Logic,* p. 16)

Just to be on the safe side, we will have a quick look at "taking morality from life." The point is that you cannot determine from the way people actually behave how they ought to behave. If the Kinsey Report establishes that most married men cheat on their wives, it does not follow that they ought (or ought not) to do so. At first sight, then, it might seem reasonable to make a distinction between the facts about human behavior and the ideals.

Kant seeks to make the corresponding division between the facts of mental life (understanding and reasoning) and the ideals. He also proposes an associated division of labor, which we can express in the following relation: Psychology is to deal with facts in the same way as philosophy deals with ideals. I do not know who originated this division of labor. It is central in Kant's thought, and after him it is commonplace. It is still the standard conception of how philosophy and psychology relate to each other, how they divide the labor between them. To philosophy go all the ideals, of logic, of ethics, of aesthetics; to psychology (and perhaps the other social sciences) go the related data, the related facts.

This is utterly and disastrously muddled. Just think for a minute. Either it is a fact of mental life that the mind has access to ideals of interpreting (understanding) and reasoning, or it is not. If it is, by the terms of the supposed division of labor, the ideals must be part of psychology's concern—which contradicts the supposed division. If it is not, it doesn't matter which discipline is concerned about the ideals. We would then know nothing whatever about them, and anyone should be ashamed of pretending to discuss them. The same applies in connection with the other ideals, but I will not hammer the point home. Kant's division of labor is destructive of both philosophy and psychology.

His division is what justifies the lofty disdain of some philosophers for psychologists, as people who spend their time grubbing around among the frequently sordid facts. It equally justifies the dismissal of philosophy by some psychologists as airy nonsense. But that is not the way things should be. The division is a travesty of serious scholarship.

One major voice that has been raised against the division is that of Noam Chomsky. He insists that in the area of language both linguists and psycholinguists share the task of describing linguistic competence, that is, the ideals of grammaticality for the particular language one is studying and the universal constraints on the rules that can occur in a natural language. By and large linguists and psycholinguists have heeded his advice. But elsewhere in what is called "cognitive science" the position is far different. Many psychologists argue, for example, for a complete division between (ideal) decision theory and psychological decision theory. Ideal decision theory they assign to mathematicians; the decisions ordinary people take they assign to psychologists. This has the unfortunate effect of suggesting that mathematicians are not ordinary people and that the basics of their way of thinking are not available to ordinary people. Once again, we must ask whether it is a fact of mental life that the human mind has access] to the basis of mathematical decision theory. If it is a fact, then it is incumbent on psychology to account for such access as well as for whatever decisions people take in everyday practice. If it is not a fact, the whole of mathematical decision theory is an illusion. It is my impression that the division between ethics (philosophy) and mental health (psychology) is if anything more complete and, of course, more dangerous. The enterprise of ethics, as I understand it, is concerned with the principles of how we ought to behave so as to advance the welfare of all. This must involve a notion of what the welfare of all is. One cannot but wonder if that does not include mental welfare. In fact, clinical psychologists seem to think far more about mental illness than about mental health. Many psychology departments give courses on abnormal psychology; it is far rarer to find a course on mental health. Yet mental illness is comprehensible only against a backdrop of mental health. This matter too I will have to put aside, until we come to the chapter on Freud, where it will receive a fuller airing.

In this chapter I confined myself to just two issues in Kant's writings that are relevant for psychology. The first was his account of how we can know necessary truths about nature. Studying this problem led Kant to his "Copernican revolution": the source of such necessary truths is the human mind. While he does distinguish cognition from perception, his approach depends essentially on getting the intentionality wrong. The result is, if we were to believe him, that physics is really psychology in disguise. Incidentally, Kant's work on the conceptual a priori that the mind contributes when perception occurs is enormously interesting, which is not to say that he got it right. The second theme shows that Kant attempted to drive a wedge between the theory of idealizing properties of mind and psychology. Kant assigns the ideals to philosophy and the "facts" to psychology. We saw, or at least I attempted to show, that the proposed division of labor is incoherent, although it is still popular among contemporary psychologists.

Bibliographical Note

Kant, Immanuel (1781/1929). *Critique of Pure Reason.* Translated by N. Kemp Smith. London: Macmillan.

Kant, Immanuel (1800/1974). *Logic.* Edited by G. B. Jäsche and translated by R. Hartman and W. Schwarz. New York: Bobbs-Merrill.

20

John Stuart Mill: A Contemporary Psychologist

Biographical Note

John Stuart Mill (1806–1873) was the son of a famous philosopher, James Mill, who with Jeremy Bentham founded the movement known as Utilitarianism. John Mill, the eldest of James Mill's children, was born in London, where he spent the greater part of his life. James was a stern father, who set John to study Greek at age 3, Latin and arithmetic at 8, logic at 12, and political economy at 13. John in turn had to teach the younger children. At 17 John Mill received a position in India House working for the East India Company (which governed India). He worked for the company until its extinction in 1858. Still in his teens, he founded the Utilitarian Society, joined the London Debating Society, and worked for the *Westminster Review,* a serious Benthamite periodical. Then and for the rest of his life he worked for radical reform. At 20 came a spiritual collapse: a sense of the emptiness of life. He was cured by taking to poetry and by falling in love with a remarkable woman, Harriet Taylor. Unfortunately, she was the wife of John Taylor and remained so until her husband's death in 1849. Although John Mill and Harriet Taylor were inseparable from the first, she was faithful to her first husband throughout the years of their marriage. Upon John Taylor's death, John Mill and Harriet Taylor married, in 1851. Harriet died in 1858 after seven happy years of marriage, bequeathing to him her daughter, Helen Taylor, as the companion of his declining years. John Mill's claims on the historian of ideas relate mainly to the domain of politics and political theory. He was the first to speak in parliament for giving women the vote. He made an unpopular speech in support of the Republican side in the American Civil War. He spoke on the side of abused Irish tenants and advocated fair play for all in Canada. We will pay most attention to his *System of Logic* (1843), which, as we will see, has important psychological content. His psychological views are further developed in his *An Examination of Sir William Hamilton's Philosophy* (1865).

John Stuart Mill was an admirable man—upright, honest, courageous, and humane. His *Autobiography,* edited by his stepdaughter but scheduled for publication only after her death, must endear him to all its readers. He was not, however, a great logician, and his influence on psychology far outstrips his originality as a psychologist. Yet so faithfully does contemporary cognitive psychology mirror him that it is essential to study his thought. Doing so affords us an opportunity to study the contemporary scene at one remove, as it were, and thus with added objectivity.

We cannot even touch on all the aspects of Mill's work that one might reasonably hope to see in a chapter such as this. Perhaps the most important omission is Mill's views on the origins of our knowledge of logical and mathematical principles. He believed that both derive in a fairly direct manner from perceptual experience. For this he received a well-known drubbing from Gottlob Frege and Edmund Husserl, whom most people judge to have shown that Mill was seriously in the wrong. The interested reader will find the relevant texts in Frege's *Foundations of Arithmetic* (1884) and in the prolegomena to Husserl's *Logical Investigations* (1900). We will confine ourselves to two topics: Mill's account of abstraction and his handling of the difference in meaning between the way we interpret common nouns and adjectives. His views on both scores are vigorously alive in contemporary cognition.

Mill's general doctrine of abstraction is one we have encountered several times, most recently in discussing Locke and Berkeley. In essence, it is that children are confronted by a stock of individuals, at first in no kinds whatsoever. They then notice "circumstances" (perceptual properties) in which the individuals resemble, or fail to resemble, each other. On this basis they form various categories of individuals.

Mill says that two individuals (or objects) are as many as the mind can conveniently compare at one time. We mark the perceptual features in which the two agree, placing them in the same kind if the agreement is "remarkable."

Having advanced thus far, when we now take in hand a third object, we naturally ask ourselves the question not merely whether this third object agrees with the first, but whether it agrees with it in the same circumstances in which the second did? (*System,* bk. 4, chap. 2, § 3)

This is supposed to yield us the kind DOG and the associated concept of dog. We are supposed to reach the kind ANIMAL by an extension of the process:

Sometimes, again, we find that the same conception will serve by merely leaving out some of its circumstances; and by this higher effort of abstraction we obtain a still more general conception. (*System,* same para.)

He goes on to say,

A person of clear ideas is a person who always knows in virtue of what properties his classes are constituted, what attributes are connoted by his general names. (*System,* bk. 4, chap. 2, § 5)

I do not believe one will find a clearer statement of the standard theory of abstraction.

It is not necessary to rehearse here Thomas Aquinas's demolition of the whole approach in *De ente et essentia* or what was said in this connection in the chapters on Locke and Berkeley. In one way, it is a measure of Mill that he takes this abstraction line so unguardedly, in view of the work of Thomas Aquinas, which he may not but should have known, and the work of Berkeley, which he certainly knew. I will direct our attention to a couple of features of the general theory that Mill brings out clearly. Both have to do with his belief that our experience is originally of a stock of unclassified individuals that we classify on the basis of similar perceptual features.

Mill's text is replete with such expressions as "individual things" and "objects." What precisely can these be? If you are asked to count the objects in a room, you may begin with some chairs, a desk, and a lamp. Then you notice that each chair has four legs, each of which can be called "a thing." There are also the screws holding the parts together. On a little reflection you observe that the wooden parts of the chair are composed of cells, each of which is a thing, and the cells of atoms, etc. Should you count a chair as one thing distinct from its parts? You come to realize that you don't know how to begin, let alone end, your count. You don't know what to count as "one thing" because the uncontrolled notion of "thing" is without precise meaning. It is not just vague; it seems to crumble beneath your gaze.

Nor is it the case that there is the kind THING out there lurking just beyond the reach of this uncontrolled notion. There cannot be an individual that is not properly individuated from other individuals or one for which there is no truth of the matter as to what is and what is not identical with it. Let us adopt the slogan, No individual without individuation and identity! [That is, we do not know what to count as an individual unless we have a concept that tells us what its defining qualities are.]

It is no defense to respond that if we asked children, or even unreflecting adults, to count the objects or things in a room, they would count a whole chair as one and ignore the legs. That merely demonstrates that they are not working with an uncontrolled concept of a thing. Most probably they are assuming a kind corresponding to perceptual figures, or gestalts, an entirely different matter from the supposed uncontrolled notion of a thing!

It follows that the general picture of infants' confronting a stock of unclassified individuals and learning to categorize them is simply incoherent. If the approach is to work at all, children have to start out with the kind PHYSICAL OBJECT, corresponding to perceptual figures or gestalts. Now, if you have the general kind PHYSICAL OBJECT, can you construct from it without more ado the kind DOG, containing as members physical objects that satisfy certain perceptual conditions? Can you then construct the kind ANIMAL, containing as members physical objects that satisfy a smaller set of perceptual conditions? This is precisely the question that Thomas Aquinas and Berkeley answer with a thundering "No." I will not repeat their arguments here. There simply is no determining the kinds DOG and ANIMAL simply from the application of perceptual predicates to the kind PHYSICAL OBJECT. It takes a lot more machinery to establish those two kinds and to set up the proper relation between them. More of this in the Extroduction.

Mill's theory of abstraction runs perception and cognition together. It is also an attempt to handle Plato's problem of learning. On both counts it fails.

Mill adds another remark, almost by the way, that has become a commonplace of the psychological literature on concept formation and the learning of word meanings. It relates to the purposes for which we seek to establish kinds in the first place.

The conceptions, then, which we employ for the colligation [tying in bundles] and methodization of facts, do not develop themselves from within, but are impressed upon the mind from without; they are never obtained otherwise than by way of comparison and abstraction. (*System*, bk. 4, chap. 2, § 2)

My reason for citing this passage is to draw attention not to the running together of perception and cognition but to the claim in the opening clause. The purpose of kinds, he states in effect, is to serve as principles of order and economy in our mental lives. Today how often do we not read that our perceptual experiences are so abundant, so varied, so chaotic that we have need of organizing principles? Categories or kinds are thought to be just that, exactly as Mill says here. Now this, as we have begun to see, is quite inadequate. We simply have no access to any individuals at all without kinds to handle individuation and identity. Of course, kinds, when recognized, serve as organizing principles. But this is nugatory compared with their major purpose: to individuate the members of the kind. It is as though we were to say that the purpose served by having a federal government in Canada is to occupy the government buildings in Ottawa. Of course the government occupies the government buildings, but it seems wrong-headed (or perhaps cruelly cynical) to offer that as the reason for having a government.

The second aspect of Mill's psychology that concerns us is closely related to the first. It is his views of the meaning of such general words as "dog" and "black" and how the two differ from one another. First the meaning.

To begin, Mill makes a good start by getting the intentionality right. Words, he says, refer not to ideas in our heads but to objects in the world. This is a strong point in his favor. But which objects in the world? Here his theory begins to fall apart in instructive ways, because he takes words like "dog" or "stone" to be a sort of generalized name. In the following passage he seeks to distinguish between proper names, like "Freddie," and generalized names, like "dog."

Other objects, of which we have not occasion to speak so frequently, we do not designate by a name of their own; but when the necessity arises for naming them, we do so by putting together several words, each of which, by itself, might be and is used for an indefinite number of other objects; as when I say, this stone: "this" and "stone" being, each of them, names that may be used of many other objects. (*System,* bk. 1, chap. 2, § 3)

The idea can be made clearer with an example. Whereas "Plymouth Rock" is a proper name that designates one particular stone and no other, Mill thinks that "this" and "stone" are names that can designate many things. The general effect can be presented, a little brutally but nonetheless correctly, if we replace "this" by something that really is a name, say "Tom," and replace "rock" with another name, say "Dick." Then the sentence "This stone is Plymouth Rock" would become "Tom Dick is Plymouth Rock." This, however, is not a sentence at all. Something has gone drastically wrong.

The trouble is manifold. "This" and "stone" form a single noun phrase in "this stone." There is a syntactic relation between the two words, which Mill misses completely. The syntactic relation is reflected in the semantics. "This" is an indexical that picks out a particular individual in a kind—there being no other individuals in that kind that at that moment are the object of attention—and "stone" specifies the kind of that individual. "Stone," then, does not designate any stone at all; rather, it designates the kind to which all stones belong. If you insist on treating it as a name, and you may well want to, you have to see that it names a kind, the kind STONE.

Failure to recognize this is all but ubiquitous in the current literature on cognition. It is not only a fundamental error in logic; it obscures a fundamental aspect of word learning and word use. Words like "stone" do not name any stones at all; they name abstract objects to which certain concrete objects belong. Let us look a little more closely at this.

Why say kinds are abstract? The point can more easily be made with a word like [the count noun] "dog," because we are more aware of dogs coming in and out of existence than of stones, but nothing essential hangs on the switch to "dog." We employ the word "dog" to speak indifferently about dogs dead, dogs living, and dogs yet to be born. We need it to be able to say things like, "Mary Queen of Scots had a dog hidden under her skirts when she was beheaded," and we mean the same by "dog" as when we say, "The family next door has a dog," or "I hope that the dog next door will father some dogs next year." The word "dog" does not change meaning as new dogs are born and old ones die. It follows that the reference of [the count noun] "dog" is fixed once and for all. The reference is not affected by the fate of particular dogs; it stands outside the system of causally interrelated events in the universe. That is precisely what we mean by an abstract object.

Turn now to children learning such words as "stone" and "dog." Although their learning is guided by perception and although the objects that serve to fix the reference are concrete objects, the reference itself is not. It is an invisible, intangible object that is in dialectical relation with concrete stones in one case and with flesh-and-blood dogs in the other. To posit such abstract kinds is as fundamental and as natural for the human mind as breathing is for the human chest. Notice that there is no constructing the kind STONE by perceptual or even conceptual means. The kind has to be as objective as Plymouth Rock itself, unless we are to leave stones with no objective provision for individuation and identity.

Mill is already in serious logical difficulty, but he creates even more when he turns to adjectives. Ignoring grammar again, Mill places adjectives, like "white," on an equal footing with common nouns, like "animal." The only difference between the two is in the number of perceptual features entering into the related concepts.

> There are some classes, the things contained in which differ from other things only in certain particulars which may be numbered, while others differ in more than can be numbered, more even than we need ever expect to know. . . . White things, for example, are not distinguished by any common properties except whiteness. . . . But a hundred generations have not exhausted the common properties of animals or of plants. (*System,* bk. 1, chap. 7, § 4)

The disregard for grammar is ominous and, not surprisingly, trouble shows up immediately in the semantics. If asked to count the animals in a farm, you may object that the task is too onerous if, in addition to the cows and horses, you are expected to count the worms and the flies. But at any rate, it is determinate what counts as one animal. The reason is that "animal" provides for individuation and identity. Matters are quite different if you are asked to count whatever is white on the farm. Should you count a white horse as one white, or should you count separately the whites of its eyes, each white hair, the separate pigments in each hair, etc.? This task is not just onerous; it is impossible. There is nothing to guide you in what to count as one white, precisely because white on its own makes no provision for individuation and identity.

Once again, the neglect of grammar results in a fundamental distortion of children's task in learning to interpret adjectives. They have to realize that "white" on its own is assigned no reference; that it acquires a reference only in conjunction with a suitable noun. "White" in conjunction with "animal" ("white animal") picks out a subset of animals; in conjunction with "paint" it picks out a subset of paints. Because of this, well-known logical problems arise. Although every man is an animal, a white man is not a white animal—white animals being exemplified by white horses, white mice, white rabbits, all of a very different hue from white men.

Once again, Mill is not alone in running together the semantics of common nouns and adjectives. One finds the same move in contemporary writing on cognition. Errors of so fundamental a nature, however, are crippling.

We have not strayed from Mill's treatment of concept formation as abstraction and his account of words as names for perceptually accessible individuals. In both contexts he ignored grammar, with catastrophic results. In both contexts he missed the essential role of those abstract objects, kinds, that make provision for individuation and identity. The result was failure to appreciate fundamental properties of the human mind. We noted that modern psychology has inherited his standpoint on both issues.

Bibliographical Note

Mill, J. S. (1843). *System of Logic*. London: Longman's.

Mill, J. S. (1924/1944). *Autobiography of John Stuart Mill*. New York: Columbia University Press.

Frege, G. (1884/1950). *Foundations of Arithmetic: A Logico-mathematical Enquiry into the Concept of Number*. Translated by J. L. Austin. Oxford: Basil Blackwell.

Husserl, E. (1900). *Logical Investigations*. Vols. 1 and 2. Translated by J. N. Findlay. London: Routledge and Kegan Paul. The Prolegomena to the *Logical Investigations* is contained in the first volume.

21

Charles Darwin: The Newton of Biology

Biographical Note

Charles Robert Darwin (1809–1882) was born, in Shrewsbury, to financial security, not least because of a maternal connection with the Wedgwood (pottery) family. He never had to earn his living. He was the grandson of a famous physician, biologist, and poet, Erasmus Darwin, and second cousin of the statistician and mental measurer Sir Francis Galton. Charles tried medicine in Edinburgh University and theology in Cambridge, but he took to neither. He was passionate about zoology, and he accepted the post of naturalist, without pay, on H.M.S. *Beagle* during its voyage around the world, which included long periods in South America and the Galapagos (1831–1836). The rest of his intellectual life was devoted to making sense of the data he gathered during this trip, supplemented, to be sure, by extensive reading and continuing observations of animals and human infants. On returning to England after the voyage, he lived for some years in London and then retired to a country house in Kent, where he lived the quiet life of a scholar and family man. He wrote extensively on many subjects, but his main fame rests on two books: *The Origin of Species* (1859) and the extension of its theory to human beings in *The Descent of Man* (1871). The first of these led to a famous debate in Oxford between T. H. Huxley, on the evolution side, and Samuel Wilberforce, opposing. Both were considerable figures: Huxley, a rising young biologist, and Wilberforce, a bishop and third son of William Wilberforce, who was possibly England's most celebrated reformer at an earlier time and the main force behind the abolition of the slave trade. Charles Darwin's studies led him to a materialistic view of human beings and to discreetly abandon the religion of his young days.

Charles Darwin's influence on psychology may be compared to that of Galileo and Newton at an earlier period. Nothing was the same after his books had been digested by the intellectual world. He is at the origin of an even greater intellectual revolution than that of Copernicus, since

Darwin's writings touched human beings' conception of human nature more immediately and more intimately than did the work of Copernicus and the physicists.

I will not dwell on the purely biological aspects of Darwin's work: his development of the theory of natural selection and the related theories of random mutations and fitness for survival, and his lack of any sound theory as to how fitness is communicated to offspring. The first move to supply that want was taken by Georg Mendel. The adequacy of Darwin's theorizing is still the subject of intense debate among biologists. Nevertheless, it is my impression that most biologists accept Darwin's broad picture of the origin of species and the descent of man. I will turn now to the impact he had on psychology.

His whole approach, details aside, is that all of life, including human life, consists of various combinations of material elements. Moreover, all the combinations are the result of natural selection, which is a continual press toward whatever combinations prove fitter to survive and reproduce themselves. Grant this, and one must grant that human beings emerge on the face of the earth by the exercise of purely material forces on purely material stuff. It follows that there is no place for a nonmaterial constituent of any sort in human nature. This position is incompatible with either substance or property dualism. It powerfully supports the materialistic psychology of Hobbes, Locke, and Hume, and undermines the dualism of the ancient and medieval worlds, which are continued in the psychology of Descartes and Leibniz.

Darwin was not content with his general theory but sought to show that human mental powers were extensions of those that are to be found in other species of animals: "My object . . . is to show that there is no fundamental difference between man and the higher mammals in their mental faculties" (*Descent*, p. 446). He proceeded to compare civilized humans with "savages," and the latter with various sorts of mammals. He admitted to a certain difficulty in the undertaking: "The difficulty arises from the impossibility of judging what passes in the mind of an animal" (*Descent*, chap. 3, p. 460). Undaunted by the difficulty, however, he concludes the following in relation "to the higher animals, especially the Primates":

All have the same senses, intuitions, and sensations,—similar passions, affections, and emotions, even the more complex ones, such as jealousy, suspicion, emulation, gratitude, and magnanimity; they practice deceit and are revengeful; they are sometimes susceptible to ridicule, and even have a sense of humor; they feel wonder and curiosity; they possess the same faculties of imitation, attention, deliberation, choice, memory, imagination, the association of ideas, and reason, though in very different degrees. (*Descent,* p. 456)

The evidence for all this is a series of anecdotes about various animals and (supposed) savages. One such will have to stand for all. Darwin cites a certain Houzean who crossed the arid planes of Texas with his two dogs. The dogs, when thirsty, would go looking for water in hollows, even when no vegetation suggested the presence of water and when they could not have had a scent of water, because there was no water in those hollows. "The dogs behaved as if they knew that a dip in the ground offered them the best chance of finding water" (*Descent,* p. 454). This is offered as evidence that dogs can reason, perhaps as follows: Water tends to collect in hollow places. Here is a hollow place. Therefore, I should look down here for water.

This is not Darwin's statement of the reasoning in question but mine. Darwin suggests that what was operative in the dogs' minds was an association between the experience of hollows and that of water. Given the association, "a cultivated man would perhaps make some general proposition on the subject; but from all that we know of savages it is extremely doubtful whether they would do so, and a dog certainly would not" (*Descent,* p. 455).

Now reasoning is an operation on sentences. There are two varieties. The first is proof-theoretic, where the operations are specified purely in terms of the well-formedness rules for some language and the rules that authorize certain transformations of the language's formulas on the basis of their purely linguistic properties. The second is model-theoretic, where the sentences, being interpreted, have truth conditions, and the permissible transformation of sentences that are supposed true yields new sentences that cannot then fail to be true. In other words, sound model-theoretic transformations preserve truth. Since the dogs are described as using their knowledge of the world, Darwin must be interpreted as attributing to them model-theoretic reasoning. And yet he denies that they entertain general propositions. The overall position seems incoherent.

Darwin seems to be thinking about associations of ideas, which he mistakes for reasoning. This is a howler, as we can see when we look at ideas that really are associated, in the sense that the evocation of one tends to evoke the other. For many people, *white* is associated with *black* in the sense that when they are presented with the word "white," the first word that occurs to them is "black." Yet no one would reason from the fact that some book's cover is white that it is therefore black.

The remark about "savages" is unfortunate, because no people, no matter how removed from the technical advances of the Western world, is devoid of natural language and all people make general statements in the language they speak. There simply is no language in which the means are lacking to express the equivalent of a general statement such as "Water is good to drink."

Darwin also argues that animals have "abstract concepts . . . at least in a rude and incipient degree" (*Descent,* p. 464). As evidence he reports, "But when a dog sees another dog at a distance, it is often clear that he perceives it is a dog in the abstract; for when he gets nearer his whole manner suddenly changes, if the other dog be a friend" (*Descent,* p. 460).

There is in this a good deal of confusion. Let us pass over Darwin's running together of perception and cognition in the style of Mill and focus of his notion of *abstract.* Again, it is the familiar notion of an image that represents just those perceptual features that are common to the members of some species. This is Mill's approach too, and there is no need to repeat what we now know to be wrong with it. Could it be, just the same, that dogs have a "rude and incipient concept" of a dog? Well, what is the concept of dog that anyone has? It is one's attempt to characterize, in the appropriate theoretical language, the nature or structure of dogs. One way to put this is that a concept aims to specify a set of necessary and sufficient conditions, expressed in appropriate theoretical language, for membership in the kind. The species DOG contains as members all the dogs that ever were, are now, and will ever be. Can we with any confidence claim to know that dogs have a shot at such a concept? Can we with any confidence claim to know that they do not? Of course not. We are totally in the dark, and Darwin was right when he said that it is "impossible to judge what passes through the mind of an animal"—even so familiar an animal as a dog.

Equally, when some present-day psychologist claims that the chimpanzee Sarah learned a symbol synonymous with the English word "banana," we must ask, "Did Sarah use it to denote the kind that contains as members all the bananas that ever were, are, and will be?" It would be irresponsible to answer either way.

There is the usual comment about savages: "the hardworked wife of a degraded Australian savage, who uses very few abstract words" (*Descent*, p. 460). Darwin fails to recognize that even "dog" and "banana" are abstract words; they denote abstract entities, as we saw in the discussion of Mill. It is not profitable to pursue Darwin further on the mental faculties of humans and other animals. We simply have no grounds for accepting or rejecting his claims, and neither, it would seem, did he. All he has to go on is anecdotes and anthropomorphizing.

Another sense in which Darwin influenced psychology is that his theory favored nominalism. One supposition of Aristotelian psychology is that each kind has its own nature, which is instantiated in each member of the kind. The nature of a dog is an essence for dogs; it is thought of as the structure that any animal cannot fail to have if it is to manifest all the activity of a dog. It is also a principle of stability and separation: Aristotelian species are fixed once and for all; and each species is separate from all others. The nature proper to the species is handed on from generation to generation and preserves the separateness between that species and all others. The relevance of this for psychology was that the mind's task was to discover these natures.

Darwin's approach is radically different. The species that exist at any one time are distinct from one another, but these species emerged by small steps from distant ancestors that were different in species. So species are not as fixed as the Aristotelians, and even the taxonomists like Linnaeus, imagined. Moreover, Darwin emphasized variability within a species, where Aristotle and Linnaeus emphasized uniformity. It is only if there is variability within a species that natural selection can favor some members over others and thus lead to the survival of the fittest. Darwin was no metaphysician, yet his whole approach favored nominalism rather than essentialism. In psychology, this meant that the mind's task was not to discover an essential nature, since the existence of any such thing was denied, but to discover something else that holds a species together and differentiates it from other species. Success in this enterprise, and even in deciding on reasonable guide lines about what is being looked for, has proved as elusive for modern biologists as for their medieval predecessors (see the essays in the excellent collection by Elliott Sober [1984, sect. 7]). In psychology two responses to the problem have dominated: one is the family-resemblance approach of Wittgenstein, which looks to a weighted collection of attributes some number of which are shared by all the members of a species; the other is the prototype approach, which looks to some members as most typical of the species, others being included in the species on grounds of similarity to the prototype. In either approach there is no question of an essence common to all members of a species. In the Wittgensteinian approach there may be no set of features that all the members of a species share; in the prototype approach the members may resemble the prototype to varying degrees.

You may want to know how this nominalism sits with the claim that, by handling individuation and identity, kinds (species) play an indispensable role both in ontology and psychology. Surprisingly, it does not disturb that claim. The crucial element in that claim is kinds; concepts that capture (or fail to capture) an essence for the members of the kind are secondary. The reason for this is psychologically important and needs to be brought out.

Assume the basic postulate, which I have attempted to motivate in the chapter on Mill, that kinds are necessary to handle individuation and identity. Then take any kind, say DOG, and ask for its concept. One might find that dogs are animals that satisfy certain conditions. No problem yet, because ANIMAL handles individuation and identity for the individuals one is describing. Next ask for the concept for the kind ANIMAL. One might find that animals are living creatures that satisfy certain conditions. Again, there is no problem: the kind LIVING CREATURE handles the identity and individuation of what one is talking about. Sooner or later, however, one must run out of suitable kinds and employ some such word as "thing" or "object," which, being in that context uncontrolled and conceptually uncontrollable, appeals in effect to individuals outside any kind that one can specify, and this at the most general level. This means that there is no provision for the individuation and identity of what one is attempting to talk about. This is fatal. The remedy is to take kinds and their members as logically prior to concepts. Concepts, then, are not constitutive of kinds; they relate to already constituted kinds.

If kinds exist in the extramental world and our basic access to them is not through concepts, how do we know that kinds exist? The answer to this question can be whatever the biologists tell us: perceptual similarity, possibility of interbreeding, separation from other species, and so on. We should not, however, confuse the means for learning of the existence of a species either with the species so identified or with the concept of the species. These are all distinct, and it is vital for psychologists to recognize the distinctions.

There are several other mutually interrelated respects in which Darwin influenced psychology. Here we cannot do much more than list them. Darwinism, emphasizing variability within a species, clearly gave an impetus to the study of individual differences in psychological traits. The main initiator of this movement was Darwin's own second cousin, Sir Francis Galton. He contributed greatly to the mental-measurement movement and the statistical analysis of mental measurements.

Darwin's claim that humans shared ancestors with other species, such as primates, encouraged the development of physiological psychology. There the primary objects of study are rat brains, cat brains, monkey brains, and so on. The belief here is that there is important overlap in neural structure and neural activity between human brains and the brains of other animals and discoveries about the brains of other animals contribute to our understanding of human brains.

More subtly, Darwin's work on the historical origins of species legitimized historical explanation. Biologists, for example, are fond of "explaining" the mammalian eye by demonstrating a number of its antecedents: light sensitive cells, light sensitive cells associated with a lens, etc. The historical approach has done much, among other things, to "validate" the developmental approach in psychology: witness numerous studies of concept formation, language learning, child-parent attachment, and a host of other topics. These studies have often enriched psychology, and they owe a lot to the inspiration of Darwin. They do not, however, owe everything to him. Locke was deeply interested in psychological development. Indeed, the whole movement called British empiricism is based on certain beliefs about the origin of ideas. Nevertheless, Darwin's influence was important.

More generally, Darwin's influence led to the biologizing of psychology, just as Newton's led to the mechanizing of psychology. This is especially evident in the work of the line of experimental psychologists (especially Ebbinghaus and Titchener) that followed and set aside the founding fathers, Wundt and Brentano. The new line, contrary to the views of both Wundt and Brentano, denied any fundamental distinction between biology and psychology. Later still, Watson founded the behaviorist movement on a physiological (biological) discovery: Pavlov's conditioned response. Watson, quite consciously, wanted to model psychology on biology. Darwin's general influence can also be seen in such institutional phenomena as that at McGill University the department of psychology is housed in the Stewart Biology Building, as though to proclaim that psychology is a biological science, on a par with botany, zoology, and genetics!

Darwin's general influence also shows up in queasiness about intuition among psychologists. As Darwin said in effect, one has no intuition about what passes in the mind of nonhuman animals. Biologists, therefore, are unable to appeal to the intuitions of animals, and many psychologists, in sympathy as it were, eschew appealing to human intuition. We must leave the subject of intuition and its role in psychology, however, until we come to Franz Brentano.

Darwin's influence on psychology is at least as massive as that of Newton. It had the effect of dislodging dualism. We saw something of Darwin's psychological arguments for the continuity of psychology from animals to humans. The arguments were not impressive. One has the impression that with British empiricism, psychology became significantly less sensitive to the basic operations of the human mind in comparison with the psychology of the ancient world and that of the Middle Ages.

Darwinism, with its emphasis on variability in a species, favored nominalism. In psychology, this led to the approaches known as family resemblance and prototype theory.

In conclusion, I presented a list of several general respects in which Darwin influenced psychology. These included an impetus toward physiological psychology as we know it today; mental measurement and the study of individual differences; developmental psychology; the biologizing of psychology, treating psychology as a biological science; the neglect of intuition in psychology. There has been benefit in all this as well as harm. We have not yet fully digested the message of this extraordinary man.

One new term in this reflection will be especially important in later reflections:

Association   The associations that particularly interest psychologists are mental associations. These are thought of as relations among mental objects where the evocation of one tends to evoke the other with which it is associated. For example, the occurrence of a mental representation of the word *boy* may evoke a mental representation of the word *girl,* or the mental representation of a person's name may lead one to imagine the person. It is important to appreciate that only mental objects are related by mental associations. There cannot be a mental association between a person and the person's name, for instance, neither being a mental object.

Bibliographical Note

Darwin, C. (1859/1993). *The Origin of Species by Means of Natural Selection, or The Preservation of Favoured Races in the Struggle for Life.* New York: Random House.

Darwin, C. (1871/1989). *The Descent of Man and Selection in Relation to Sex.* New York: New York University Press.

Sober, E. (1984). *The Nature of Selection: Evolutionary Theory in Philosophical Focus.* Cambridge: MIT Press. A useful collection of theoretical papers on biology.

22

Wilhelm Wundt: The Founder of Experimental Psychology

Biographical Note

Wilhelm Wundt (1832–1920) was the son of a Lutheran pastor in Mannheim, Germany. He was tutored from an early age by a Lutheran vicar, to whom he became attached and who was the main companion of his childhood. Wundt studied medicine at the universities of Tübingen, Heidelberg, and Berlin with a view to becoming a physiologist. He worked for some time in Berlin in the Physiological Institute of Johannes Müller, the leading physiologist of the day. In 1856, back in Heidelberg, he took his doctorate and became *Dozent* in physiology there. In 1858 Hermann von Helmoltz took over the Physiological Institute in Heidelberg, and they spent 13 years together. Thus Wundt had a prolonged association with the two foremost physiologists of his day. In 1874 Wundt was called to a chair of philosophy at the University of Zurich. In 1875 he was made professor of philosophy at Leipzig University, where he remained until his death, some 45 years later. In 1879 he opened the first laboratory for experimental psychology. He trained a host of young psychologists, many of whom went on to occupy chairs of psychology in Europe or America. In 1900 he was made rector of Leipzig University. Despite failing eyesight, he continued lecturing until 1917 and continued writing until his death. His scholarly output was phenomenal. It covers the fields of physiology, physiological psychology, logic, ethics, perception, and philosophy in general. Apart from some articles, his major psychological work was his 10 volume *Völkerpsychologie* (1904–1923), each volume about 600 pages. A more concise source for his views about the nature of *Völkerpsychologie* is the third volume of his *Logik* (1893–1895).

Neither time nor psychology has been kind to Wilhelm Wundt. Although psychologists revere him as the founder of experimental psychology, few have read a page of his work. Besides, all that psychologists knew of him for a long time they learned in the pages of Boring's *History of Experimental Psychology* (1929), for about 50 years the dominant textbook in the field. Boring was a student of E. B. Titchener at Cornell, and Titchener had been Wundt's student in Leipzig. It is clear that Titchener, despite protestations to the contrary, disliked Wundt and rejected the major part of Wundt's psychology. Although Boring's book is a serious work of scholarship, it sees Wundt through Titchener's unfriendly eyes. The result is a major distortion of a major figure. It is only in recent years that psychologists have begun to set the record straight (see particularly Jahoda, 1993). In the English-speaking world the process has been hindered to some degree by the lack of English translations of most of Wundt's writings, and those that have been translated are mostly not in print.

The very quantity and diversity of Wundt's work has also militated against balanced sketches of his ideas in more recent textbooks. William James, who could be acerbic, described him in unflattering words: "Cut him up like a worm, and each fragment crawls; there is no *noeud vital* in his mental medulla oblongata, so that you can't kill him all at once" (cited in Murray, 1988, 205). The remark, though unkind, reflects the view of Wundt that has obtained since the end of the last century. It is instructive to trace some of the reasons for this incomprehension.

Wundt taught a form of dualism that is sometimes called psychophysical parallelism. In essence, this is the theory that cognitive life and physiological life progress independently of each other. There is no causal interaction between the levels. At each level there is causality appropriate to that level: psychic causality to explain the flow of ideas and events at the cognitive level, physiological causality to explain the flow at the physiological level. This implies a radical separation between cognition and physiological stimulation of perceptual organs, to say the least.

As one would expect, this view betokens a rejection of belief in the unification of the sciences. In his article on the division of the sciences Wundt (1889) remarks that it is not the object of study that guides the division. He gives as example a trade agreement between two countries, which can be the object of a juridical study or an economic one. He finds that sciences fall into two types: natural sciences (*Naturwissenschaften*) and mental sciences (*Geisteswissenschaften*). The German word *Geisteswissenchaften* was coined to translate John Stuart Mill's use of "moral

sciences" (in the sixth book of his *System of Logic*), but the German word
is best translated back into English as "mental sciences." The ground of
the division is as follows:

Accordingly, to the natural sciences belong all those disciplines in whose exploration facts are studied without regard to the participation of a thinking and pur-
poseful agent, while to the mental sciences belong all those subjects in which
facts are studied whose existence depends essentially on such a subject. (Wundt,
1889, 33)

Prototypical of natural sciences are physics and chemistry; prototypical
of mental science are cognitive psychology, economics, and anthropology. To natural science belongs physiological psychology; to mental science belongs psychophysics. At least in his early writings, Wundt claimed
that the mental sciences and the natural sciences are complementary.

With such a distinction, closely associated with dualism, Wundt ruled
out the doctrine of the unity of science that was advocated by Ernst Mach
and the logical positivists, who later adopted Mach's standpoint. Logical
positivists actually embarked on the enterprise of producing the International Encyclopedia of Unified Science. It was inevitable that the generation of psychologists that embraced logical positivism—prominent
among them Hermann Ebbinghaus, Oswald Külpe, and E. B. Titchener—
should discount Wundt's distinction, together with its associated dualism. They found Wundt old-fashioned and, in relation to cognition,
irrelevant.

There was also a clash between Wundt and some of his students on the
subject of introspection as a research method in psychology. He was particularly uneasy with the introspective methods that were becoming popular, often supposedly in imitation of his own work, in the laboratories
of his younger contemporaries. In his early *Beiträge zur Theorie des Sinneswahrnehmung* (Contributions to the theory of sense perception)
(1862), he wrote,

Introspection, however, is totally insufficient, when one's intention is to go back
to the beginnings and to the causes of [conscious] phenomena. . . . For the phenomena of consciousness are composite products of the unconscious psyche.
Their nature is such that—once they have already entered consciousness,—they
will seldom allow conclusions concerning their formation. (Translation by T.
Shipley, 1961, 57; I substituted "introspection" for Shipley's "self-observation"
(*Selbstbeobachtung*).)

He maintained this skeptical attitude throughout his life. In an article devoted entirely to introspection Wundt (1888) lays down that no object can be inspected unless at the time of inspection it is available for inspection—a certainly inoffensive principle! But attempts at introspection arrest the inner operations of mind, and all that remains for inspection is the recollected phenomenon, not the phenomenon itself. Such a recollection he called a "wellspring of deception." He did not, of course, rule out all use of memory in the study of mental phenomena. After all, in tachistoscopic studies of perception, subjects have always been shown stimuli and asked to report what they *saw*. This means that subjects have to apply to memory to describe their perceptual experience. Wundt is all for careful experiment of this sort. But here subjects are reporting not on mental entities but rather on objective ones. Since other people can perceive the same objects, the objects are in the public domain. Trouble arises mainly when the phenomena to be reported on are not in the public domain, although even then carefully planned experiments may lead to useful results.

In another lengthy article Wundt returns to the attack and excludes from the ambit of legitimate introspection "the interpretation of the significance" of conscious phenomena (1907, 321). In this article he is exercised about the whole method of questioning subjects about their mental states—as people with questionnaires so often do—and seeks to lay down conditions under which the approach is likely to be fruitful. He suggests the following:

• The subject must, as far as possible, be in a position to know precisely when the phenomenon to be observed commences (individuation of phenomenon).
• The subject must, as far as possible, be able to observe the phenomenon and follow its progress in a state of raised attentiveness.
• It must be possible to repeat the phenomenon in similar circumstances (reliability).
• The conditions under which the phenomenon appears must vary with variations in the conditions employed to evoke it (validity).

These are extremely exacting conditions, showing that Wundt was anything but a technique-happy researcher. He viewed much of the experimental work that was being reported as pseudoscientific (1907, 334). I will leave further discussion of introspection for the next chapter, where I will examine Brentano's distinction between inner perception and introspection.

I will devote the space that remains in this chapter to Wundt's major work, *Völkerpsychologie*. He attributes the word itself to a philosopher-linguist pair, Lazarus and Steinthal, working in the middle of the nineteenth century. Since I do not know any equivalent English word, I propose to use the German one, hoping that the meaning will become clear as we go along. As a hint, it may help to think of *Völkerpsychologie* as ethnic psychology.

Psychology is, by its nature, the theory of the soul or mind. Obviously, there are individual minds: each person has one. Is there any such thing as the psychology of a whole people distinct from the psychology of the individuals who make up the people? Wundt's answer is an unhesitating "Yes," and it would seem that he is right, because there are psychological phenomena that are incomprehensible if an individual is viewed in isolation. A human being is an essentially social creature—a claim that we encountered in the chapter on the New Testament—for Christianity presents humans as created in the image of a God, that is, as a trinity of persons. Wundt does not allude to this but rather says,

The subject matter [of *Völkerpsychologie*] is all those products of the mind that result from communal human activity manifesting the interactions of many individuals, rather than the properties of individual consciousness. This feature will serve in what follows as the main distinguishing characteristic of *Völkerpsychologie*. (Wundt, 1904/1923, vol. 1, p. 3)

To begin to understand Wundt, consider natural languages, a favorite example of his to which he devotes the first two volumes of his *Völkerpsychologie*. It might appear that each person in a society comes to know the society's language, and there's an end of it. Maintaining this would be a mistake. To learn their native language, children must align themselves with the society that speaks it, seeking to obey the grammatical rules of that people and to mean by its expressions what the people mean. This attitude has important consequences. To adapt an example from Tyler Burge, suppose that a doctor tells your friend Tom that he has arthritis of the knees, and suppose that some time later Tom develops a pain in the thighs and, not being versed in medicine, comes to believe that the arthritis has spread to his thighs. He even tells his friends this. Does Tom have arthritis in the thighs? Clearly not, because arthritis is a disorder of the joints, not of the muscles. Perhaps what he now suffers from, without realizing it, is rheumatism. From this it follows that the meaning of "arthritis" for Tom is not fixed by his own beliefs or by any particular mental states of his. Not even God could determine the content of Tom's beliefs involving arthritis if all he had access to were the semantic rules in Tom's head.

It does not take from the efficacy of the example that "arthritis" is a technical term. Such terms are not different from others in ways that are relevant to Wundt's concerns. All children get some words wrong or slightly so early in their language learning. Our right to correct them presupposes their desire to conform to the community. Children's willingness to revise their rules of interpretation is incomprehensible apart from the same presupposition.

Moreover, a language like German is not the product of any individual. It emerges from the communicative interactions of a certain community. Its development is constrained and guided by certain psychological laws that operate only in communicative interactions among members of that community. Wundt (1904/1923, vol. 1, p. 3) rightly dismisses Esperanto as a possible counterexample. It was elaborated by a single individual, but Wundt dismisses it as a counterexample, not on the grounds that it is artificial, but because it borrows extensively at all levels (phonology, morphology, syntax, lexicon, and semantics) from existing languages that have come into existence by the unconscious operation of many people's linguistic faculties. It is uncanny how closely Wundt's thinking here foreshadows that of Noam Chomsky, who has also set for linguists the task of discovering the unconsciously operating rules that constrain the development of natural languages and guide individual children in learning them. Chomsky calls these rules "Universal Grammar."

Chomsky emphasizes the lawlike status of these rules and so does Wundt. Throughout, Wundt sets himself the task of specifying the laws that are operative across all peoples, not just in one people. The general laws must, of course, hold for development in a single people. This fact yields an important division in emphasis within *Völkerpsychologie:* between the general rules that govern development and their operation in particular cases (Wundt, 1921, 4). This is parallel to Chomsky's search for the universal rules of grammar on the one hand and the application of these general rules in particular languages like English or Japanese on the other.

Wundt claims that there can be no conflict between the laws of *Völkerpsychologie* that control communal activity and psychological laws that relate exclusively to individuals (Wundt, 1921, 13). Far from impeding each other, the two sets of laws collaborate. In fact, the psychology of individuals is essentially related to *Völkerpsychologie*.

The child of a cultural community is surrounded by inescapable [community] influences over what spontaneously passes in that individual's mind. . . . For this reason *Völkerpsychologie* is developmental psychology in the principal sense of the word. (Wundt, 1913/1916, 4)

So far the only example of *Völkerpsychologie* we have considered is language. This is Wundt's lead example too, but the scope of *Völkerpsychologie* is very broad:

This program is in fact as broad as can be. Not only language, myth, religion, and mores, but in addition art and science, the growth of culture in general and its particular branches, even the historical coming to be and disappearance of particular peoples as well as of the human race as a whole are among the objects of this future science. (Wundt, 1921, 3–4)

Within its scope fall folklore, folk tales, comparative religion, anthropology, and the history of legal systems. Wundt would have seen the chapter on the Declaration of Independence as an essay in *Völkerpsychologie* because, even though the document came from the pen of one man, it was accepted by the whole Congress, and besides it sought to distill a *mentalité* that had developed in Enlightenment America.

Freud and Jung made ample use of myth and comparative religion to explore properties of the psyche. (It would be interesting to know the extent of these men's debt to Wundt. A glance through the indices of the various volumes of Jung's collected work—and he is the more relevant of the two—reveals numerous references to Wundt's experimental work but none to his *Völkerpsychologie*.) To my mind, the neglect of such material in psychology as a whole is a pity. The discipline of social psychology has opted almost exclusively for an experimental approach in neat little laboratory settings. Wundt argued that major areas of psychology are inaccessible to such experimental work on its own. Wundt would urge them to study such data as folk tales.

Psychologists to whom I have spoken about this say that if one were to study folk tales, one would have to appeal to insight for their psychological significance and that psychologists in such a case would have no objective evidence for any conclusions they might draw. They feel that they would be obliged to proceed more like literary critics than scientists. But this seems both narrow-minded and unnecessarily pessimistic. A story like Cinderella has been told for thousands of years throughout the Indo-European world, and stories similar to it have been found in other parts of the world. Such a story survives only if generation after generation of children love to hear it, and generation after generation of parents like to tell it, again and again. The empirical base for psychological conclusions is in the hundreds of millions. True, the data, the story itself, have to be interpreted, but then so do the data of any psychological observations or experiments. Among the psychological conclusions from Cinderella must be the yearning for fairy-tale justice and the desire for a divine protector (a godmother) who is in touch with one's innermost feelings and can respond to them, who sees a plan and purpose for one's life and rewards openness to such a plan. But where are the experimental or observational controls? one can almost hear psychologists protest. The obvious controls are the stories that disappeared, for there is a natural selection of fairy tales. But there are other controls in other fairy tales. If one fairy tale suggests some general property of mind, one can see whether other fairy tales bear out the suggestion. Surely the study of fairy tales would be at least as profitable as many of the laboratory tests of minitheories that one comes across in the literature? Wundt thought so.

There is a secondary strand in Wundt's *Völkerpsychologie* that should be mentioned, although I find it a little ominous, especially in view of what happened later in Nazi Germany. It is his theory of the individuality of a people, of what makes them different from another people. This is one of the concerns of nationalists. For my part, I instinctively feel that if individual differences show up, one is missing the core of the subject. To give him his due, Wundt seems to have shared this feeling. Nevertheless, individual differences are real, and so are differences among cultural communities; and Wundt is quite right to draw attention to them. I noticed nothing racist in his reporting of them.

Wundt has provided us with three ideas which, because of their importance for psychologists, are in need of being repeated—all the more so for the fact that they are not widely appreciated, especially as having been advocated by Wundt. One, there is a deep and principled division between cognitive psychology and physiological psychology. Two, introspective methods are of only the most limited value. Three, there are major aspects of psychology that are evident only through social interactions, and these cannot profitably be studied in laboratory experiments, especially in experiments on individuals viewed in isolation. I myself believe that if one is aware of the social nature of some phenomenon, one can usefully employ experiments to explore the phenomenon in an individual—as for example in word learning. At the same time I believe that the psychological community has almost totally missed Wundt's greatest contribution to psychological research and theory—his *Völkerpsychologie*. Observing this, one cannot but wonder about the sincerity and the depth of the claim that Wilhelm Wundt is the father of modern psychology.

Bibliographical Note

For Wundt himself it is difficult to find translations of the relevant work. For this reason I list references to some of his works in the original German:

Wundt, W. (1888). Selbstbeobachtung und innere Wahrnehmung (Introspection and inner perception). *Philosophische Studien* 4: 292–309.

Wundt, W. (1889). Über die Einteilung der Wissenschaften (On the division of the sciences). *Philosophische Studien* 5: 1–55.

Wundt, W. (1907). Über Ausfrageexperimente und über die Methoden zur Psychologie des Denkens (On interrogations in experiments and on methods for [studying] the psychology of thought). *Psychologische Studien* 3: 301–360.

Wundt, W. (1921). *Probleme der Völkerpsychologie*. Stuttgart: Alfred Körner.

The following histories of psychology or ideas are important for the themes of this chapter:

Boring, E. G. (1929). *A History of Experimental Psychology*. New York: Appleton-Century-Crofts.

Murray, D. J. (1988). *A History of Western Psychology*. Englewood Cliffs, N.J.: Prentice-Hall.

Jahoda, G. (1993). *Crossroads between Culture and Mind: Continuities and Change in Theories of Human Nature*. Cambridge: Harvard University Press.

23

Franz Brentano: Intuition and the Mental

Biographical Note

Franz Clemens Brentano (1838–1917) was born in Aschaffenberg, Germany, into a distinguished literary family. He was gifted in music, painting, sports and in his physical person. Most of all, he was gifted intellectually. He studied philosophy in Munich, Würzburg, and Berlin, where he worked under the great Aristotelian scholar, Trendelenburg. His doctoral thesis on Aristotle's metaphysics was published in 1862. The degree was from the University of Tübingen. At that point he joined the Dominican Order (Thomas Aquinas's order) and was ordained priest in 1864. Two years later he habilitated and became *Privatdozent* at the University of Würzburg. His thesis, *Aristotle's Psychology, with Special Reference to his Doctrine of Nous Poietikos*, is still one of the most important commentaries on Aristotle's *De anima*. In 1869 he prepared for the German bishops at the first Vatican Council a historical document on papal infallibility, advising against the definition of the doctrine. In 1872 he left the priesthood, the Catholic religion, and his post in Würzburg—not because of papal infallibility but because he believed the doctrine of the Trinity to be incoherent. At this stage he wrote his most important book, *Psychology from an Empirical Standpoint* (1874). In 1874 he was appointed professor of philosophy in Vienna. In 1880 he married. Under Austrian law it was not clear that a priest could marry and hold a government post. To be on the safe side, Brentano resigned his chair with the assurance that it would be given back to him, took out Saxon citizenship, and married in Leipzig. He was never reinstated as professor, and he had to return to the University of Vienna as *Privatdozent*. His wife died in 1893, and in 1895 he left Vienna and moved to Italy. In 1897 he married a second time. His eyesight failed in his declining years, and his wife helped by taking dictation. His unpublished writings were extensive. Brentano was an extraordinary teacher. His students included Carl Stumpf, Anton Marty, Edmund Husserl (founder of phenomenology, whom he drew away from mathematics), Sigmund Freud (for two years), Kasimir Twardowski (inspirer of the famous Polish school of logic),

Alexius Meinong (founder of the first psychological laboratory in Austria), Christian von Ehrenfels (originator of gestalt psychology), Franz Hillebrand (perceptual psychologist), T. G. Masaryk (founder and first president of Czechoslovakia), and Graf Hertling (later Chancellor of Germany). Besides his *Psychology* (1874), his most important work for us is his *Deskriptive Psychologie,* published as late as 1982 but containing the notes for his lectures in Vienna for the years 1887–1891.

Time has not been unkind to Brentano, but psychology has. Unlike Wundt, Brentano inspired a devoted circle who continued after his death to re-edit his writings with numerous additions from his unpublished papers and to put together new books from the unpublished work. In some ways his publication rate increased after his death. Moreover, a philosophy professor at Brown University, Roderick Chisholm, has orchestrated a series of English translations. So the greater part of his work is still available in reasonably priced German editions and now also in English translations. He is, however, better known to philosophers than to psychologists, who for all I can see scarcely read him at all. To redress the balance a little, we will look at just two aspects of his work: (1) his conception of what psychology is and how it can be studied and (2) his doctrine of intentionality, grounding a principled distinction between cognitive and physiological psychology.

He begins his *Deskriptive Psychologie* with a distinction between descriptive psychology and physiological psychology. We will study this distinction in the second section of this chapter; here we concentrate on descriptive psychology, which he describes in the opening words as "the science of the mental life of humans; that is, that part of experience that can be grasped in inner perception. It seeks to specify exhaustively the elements of human consciousness and, as far as possible, their interconnections" (*Deskriptive Psychologie,* p. 1). Our first task will be to understand what he meant by "inner perception" and to see what types of phenomena it is thought to embrace.

First, inner perception must not be taken for introspection under a new name. Brentano is even firmer than Wundt in rejecting introspection. In the interests of clarity, let me try again to specify the types of phenomena that the introspectionists hoped to determine scientifically by introspective methods.

1. The form of mental phenomena themselves, as distinct from what they might represent

2. Mental or other activities causally involved in the formation of such phenomena

In relation to (1), we already saw Wundt's observation that when we seek to attend to some mental phenomenon, we inevitably end up attending not to the desired phenomenon itself but to our recollection of it. To this Brentano adds,

> If someone is in a state in which he wants to observe his own anger raging within him, the anger must already be somewhat diminished, and so his original object of observation would have disappeared. The same impossibility is present in all cases. It is a universally valid psychological law that we can never focus our *attention* upon the object of inner perception. It is only while our attention is turned toward a different object that we are able to perceive, incidentally, the mental processes that are directed towards that object. (*Psychology*, p. 30)

This passage needs careful analysis. It makes the important claim that mental phenomena themselves, rather than what the phenomena are about, can never be the direct objects of attention. Here is how I understand Brentano's point. If you see a cow, for example, the cow is the object of your vision, and you may attend to her as much as you wish. You are also aware, *incidentally*, that you are seeing her, not imagining or touching her. You are further aware, *incidentally*, that it is you, not your friend, who is having this experience of seeing. The cow is the object of outer perception; the facts that you are seeing, not touching, and that it is you who is having the experience are given incidentally in inner perception. Perhaps here Brentano is echoing a remark of Aristotle's in the *Metaphysics* (book 12, chap. 9) "Knowledge and perception and opinion and understanding always have something else as their object, and themselves only *by the way*" (1074b, 35–36).

Hopes of being able to examine the form of a mental representation and its causal origins in the mind arise from what I call getting the intentionality wrong. This is the type of confusion that suggests that when we imagine Ronald Reagan, we are looking at a mental picture of him. Instead, of course, we are picturing him in a certain way. We can describe how we picture him to be, what properties we imagine him to have. On the basis of immediate experience alone we can say nothing whatever about the form of the mental representation involved in imagining him.

As to item (2) in the introspectionist's ambitions (mental causes of mental phenomena), we saw Wundt's denial that we are ever conscious of the causal antecedents of a mental phenomenon. Brentano in *Deskriptive Psychologie* professes great affection for physiological psychology precisely because it can often illuminate such causal antecedents. But physiological processes are in the realm of natural science, and its objects of study are not given in inner perception.

So Brentano is drawing a distinction between introspection, which he rejects, and inner perception, upon which he bases the greater part of psychology proper because he identifies psychology proper with descriptive psychology and not physiological psychology. It would be useful at this stage to bring Brentano's notion of inner perception into clearer focus. Perhaps he would have been wiser to have used "intuition" instead. Etymologically the word "intuition" derives from the Latin visual-perception word "intueri" (to look upon), but it has been extended to cover propositions that present themselves as true without any consciousness of a proof. Some intuitions in mathematics, physics, and other sciences need to be proved before they are accepted; others are so fundamental that proofs are made to depend on them. The latter we may call "basic intuitions."

That basic intuitions are what Brentano intended by "inner perception" is readily seen in the following (exaggerated) remark: "The truth of inner perception cannot be proved in any way. But it has something more than proof; it is immediately evident" (*Psychology*, p. 140). The absence of proof indicates intuition; being immediately evident, which he explicitly takes as a sign of infallibility, betokens basic intuition. He is, of course, mistaken about infallibility. The evidence of intuition has to be weighed in the light of the relevant theory as a whole, and that may well have experimentally derived elements in it. But I let this pass.

Further evidence that Brentano equates inner perception with intuition is to be found in the following passage, where the two expressions alternate, as though they can be made to substitute for one another. The general subject of discussion is whether thought is concerned with particulars or universals.

What Locke calls reflection and what we call *inner perception* does not afford us examples of individual *intuitions*. For *inner perception* no one can state any characteristic that individuates *intuition*. (*Psychology*, p. 199; emphasis added)

Later Brentano clearly extends inner perception (intuition) beyond Locke's reflection and uses it to cover aspects of all sorts of perceptual experiences.

Can I be more explicit about the objects of inner perception? Again in the interest of clarity, but with little hope of completeness, I suggest the following:

a. The modalities involved in a perceptual experience (seeing versus hearing)

b. The subject of a psychological experience (the self)

c. Emotional states accompanying a psychological experience

d. The adequacy or inadequacy of a linguistic structure, the interpretation of a linguistic string, the perceptual processing of an object, a mental operation (e.g., drawing an inference)

e. Propositional attitudes of believing, doubting, wondering about, fearing, wanting something

Item (a) is, of course, Aristotle's sense that is common to the external senses. We have already said something about item (b). In this connection Brentano alludes to Descartes, as one might expect. In discussing introspection, Brentano referred to anger (item (c)), noting that we are aware of it incidentally when we are attending to something else. Naturally, he would include other emotional states among the objects of inner perception.

Item (d) needs some unfolding. Our inner perceptions of the adequacy or inadequacy of a linguistic structure are what are called "linguistic intuitions." English speakers have the intuition that, for example, "The dog spoke to the man" is a grammatical (though fanciful) sentence and "The spoke dog to man the" is ungrammatical. Most English speakers would be unable to specify precisely what is right with the first and wrong with the second. Yet it is a condition on any grammar of English that it accept the first as grammatical and the second as ungrammatical. Brentano makes provision for this sort of intuition in the remark, "The elements of our mental lives, that is, the various simplest constituents, are to be found in combination in our *conscious intuition*" (*Deskriptive Psychologie*, p. 2). Among the elements are words, and their structural combinations are the subject of evaluation in inner perception. Brentano touches on the intuition relating to being well formed in the claim that not only are we aware of elements of consciousness but we are also aware of the manner of their combination (*Deskriptive Psychologie*, p. 10, where the word used for the interrelations among elements is *Verbindungsweise*).

We also have intuitions about whether we have understood a string of words. These intuitions are of basic interest for cognitive psychology. For example, we know by intuition that we can refer, by means of a proper name, to someone who is not present at the time or to someone who is long dead. We also know by intuition that we can say, "The president of the United States was born in Arkansas," although we are quite aware that he was not president at the time of his birth.

We have intuitions as to whether or not we have succeeded in properly processing some perceptual object. There is a famous black-and-white picture of a Dalmatian among leaves that is difficult to "see." Intuition tells us when we have not seen it and when we have. Or take the example of a face and a smile, which in combination yield a smiling face. We have an intuition that the smile inheres in the face, not the face in the smile. We know by intuition that the face can exist without the smile, but not the smile without the face. Lewis Carroll was deliberately playing with this intuition in the passage about the smile of the Cheshire cat.

We are also aware, through intuition, of our attitudes to the various propositions that we entertain in our minds, whether we are just wondering about them, whether we doubt their truth, whether we accept them as true. And we have basic intuitions about what inferences are valid. If we did not, logic would be impossible, as would indeed any systematic thought at all.

Brentano claimed that he was the first to draw the distinction explicitly between introspection and inner perception (*Psychology*, p. 30). The distinction is fundamental, since introspection is illusory whereas inner perception is the main guide to the psychology of perception and cognition, and much else besides. Experiments are useful, to be sure, in making precise various aspects of inner perception, but the role of experiment is subsidiary to that of inner perception.

Chomsky has always spoken about linguistic intuitions as empirical, and Brentano uses the word "empirical" in a similar way. Intuitions are empirical in the sense that they are part of experience. That is why Brentano could call his book *Psychology from an Empirical Standpoint*. Only what we defined earlier as radical empiricism (sometimes referred to, impishly, as industrial-strength empiricism) would exclude such intuitions from being part of the data for an empirical psychology. Indeed, to exclude them is to decide to do psychology blindfolded with both hands tied behind one's back.

Stressing the foundational role of intuition, Brentano naturally confines descriptive psychology to the mental life of human beings. Not having any access to the intuitions of other animals, there is no possibility of developing a psychology of them parallel to what can be developed for human beings. Brentano, then, is firmly opposed to biologizing psychology at anything except the physiological level, not that he is against biology, just that the biological stance rules out the very heart of descriptive psychology. He stands at the opposite pole from E. B. Titchener, who wrote in an influential article about "sensations and affections," which he took to be the basis of all of mental life: "That [the] underlying processes are psychical in character is, so to speak, an accident; for all practical purposes they stand upon the same level as digestion and locomotion, secretion and excretion" (Titchener, 1898).

Brentano, like Wundt, insisted on a fundamental distinction between natural sciences and mental sciences. Brentano, however, reserved the status of mental science for cognition alone, because there alone, he thought, investigators have the sure-footed guidance of intuition of the type we have been considering. That gives one ground for the distinction, but not the principal one. In this connection he proposes a celebrated criterion for distinguishing the mental from the physical (or physiological). His favorite formulation is that the mental is characterized by "reference to something as an object" (*Psychology*, p. 97). This expression needs unfolding.

Since Brentano was so steeped in Aristotle, we can look to Aristotle for guidance about Brentano's thought. In *De anima* (bk. 3, chap. 3), recall, Aristotle characterized cognition as the area where the predicates "true" and "false" are applicable. Now "true" and "false" are semantic notions; they apply only when sentences are interpreted. This means that the terms in them must be assigned references. For example, "Freddie is an animal" as a string of words is neither true nor false. Of such a string as a purely linguistic entity one can reasonably ask whether it is grammatical, but not whether it is true. Interpret "Freddie" as denoting a certain domestic animal, "animal" as denoting a certain kind of living creature, "is a" as specifying the relation of membership between the creature picked out by "Freddie" and the kind picked out by "animal." Then it makes sense to ask whether the sentence so interpreted is true. The crucial step was assigning references to the terms. But this step is merely assigning them objects as references.

By characterizing the mental as those states and events in which there is "reference to something as an object," Brentano is reaching back to Aristotle. Brentano is really saying that mental states and events, and nothing else, express truth conditions. They describe the world as being in a particular way, which may or may not be the way the world is. Nothing else, he claims, describes the world in such a way; nothing else has that relation of aboutness to the world's states of affairs. Brentano means this in a very strong sense. If he is right, the divide between the mental and the physical is so complete that there is no reducing the mental to the physical; that is, there is no defining the primitives of the theory that describes the mental in terms of the primitives of the theory that describes the physical or, for that matter, the physiological.

What would entitle Brentano to claim so radical a division between the mental and the physiological? The answer cannot be that he was a dualist and so believed that human beings have nonmaterial as well as material constituents. This is certainly compatible with denying the possibility of reducing the mental (the cognitive), on the supposition that the mental lies on the nonmaterial side. Brentano believed that the mental does lie there, and he was a dualist. But he saw things the other way round. He was a dualist because he believed that the mental could not be reduced to the physiological. So we return to the question: what entitles Brentano to claim a radical division between the mental and the physical?

I must confess that the question places me in a quandary because I believe that Brentano is right (a) that there is a fundamental division between the theory of the mental and that of the physical (or physiological) and (b) that the theory of the mental does not reduce to that of the physical (or physiological), but I do not know Brentano's reasons for these positions and Brentano, at least in later years, would reject the reasons I can give for agreeing with him. Brentano realized that something was wrong with what he had said on the matter, because he returned to the topic again and again in letters and dictations right up to his death. It was as though he realized that his distinction between the mental and the physical was his most important contribution but also that he had not nailed it down. The best I can do is to give my own reasons for the distinction and say why Brentano would have rejected them.

In the chapters on Locke, Hume, and Mill we saw arguments that there is no reference to an individual without the support of a kind to provide for its individuation and identity. We agreed with the slogan, No individual without individuation and identity. Now kinds, as we saw, are abstract entities. They play no part in the system of causally interrelated events in the universe. And yet the logical form of the simplest interpreted sentence must make appeal to such entities. For example, "Freddie is an animal" cannot be interpreted unless provision is made, through a suitable kind, for the individuation and identity of Freddie. Thus the logical form of that sentence must specify at least this much, that Freddie in the kind DOG is an animal.

We are forced to deny that reference to Freddie as an object can be reduced to physiology precisely because physiologists cannot, in the context of their discipline, explain how certain neurological states or events make the proper sort of contact with an abstract entity. Notice that the physical objects that causally trigger my visual perception of Freddie are cells in a certain portion of the surface of his body. But these cells are not Freddie. Freddie remains Freddie even if he has a haircut and all those cells are removed. Remember Descartes's wax. To my mind, the fundamental reason for rejecting the reduction of the mental to the physiological is the essential role of kinds in the mental. This is not to advocate dualism, because I do not see how positing a nonmaterial constituent in human beings helps to explain the right sort of contact with abstract entities. In any event, I believe that there is no escaping Brentano's conclusion that cognitive psychology is fundamentally distinct from physiological psychology. In the spirit of Brentano one can say that cognitive psychology requires a new primitive, reference, and that the main, if not exclusive, guide to it is intuition.

Why should Brentano object to this? In later years, after about 1904, he came to deny the existence of certain classes of "objects" that he had previously allowed. Among them were collections. He knew about Cantor's theorem in set theory, which, as Brentano says, would allow you, from the existence of three stones, to claim the existence of infinitely many objects—for example, three pairs of stones, three pairs of pairs of stones, and so on ad infinitum. He reacted by denying the existence of collections as distinct from the individuals that make up the supposed collection (see, for example, Brentano 1977, 366–367). From this point of view his position is similar to that later advocated by Goodman and Quine (1947, sec. 4). But the kinds of which we have been speaking are collections, and so Brentano would have denied their existence. In my view, he would have been wrong to do so. Nevertheless, his denial means that my account of how the mental differs from the physiological is not his.

For all that, I believe that both positions that we find in Brentano are correct and that their importance for psychology is foundational. He claimed that there is a radical distinction between the theory of the mental and that of the physiological. Very many philosophers of mind today accept this position. Some it leads to deny the reality of the mental, which to my mind is unfortunate. It is my experience that many psychologists, especially physiological psychologists, would deny the distinction, usually without having examined what is thought to be special about the mental. This rejection of Brentano has obtained for over 100 years. As evidence of that, just one observation. When Brentano's *Psychology* appeared, Hermann Ebbinghaus (who was to establish the first psychological laboratory in Berlin) began his studies of memory. Instead of studying memory for childhood events, for poetry, or the like, he studied the learning and recall of nonsense syllables. No reference to something as an object! This allowed him to make neat experiments, but from Brentano's viewpoint, he purchased neatness at the expense of worth and interest—at least for the theory of cognition.

The other theme that we took from Brentano was the indispensable role of intuition (inner perception) in approaching the mental. It seems that when psychologists became aware that introspection is not a useful way to study the mental, as Brentano and Wundt had warned, they failed to distinguish between intuition and introspection, and threw out the baby with the bath water.

It is my belief that the theory of perception and cognition, which are at the core of psychology, cannot flourish until psychologists recognize the justice of Brentano's claims in these two matters.

Bibliographical Note

Brentano, F. (1874/1973). *Psychology from an Empirical Standpoint.* Translated by A. C. Rancurello, D. B. Terrell, and L. L. McAlister. London: Routledge and Kegan Paul.

Brentano, F. (1977). *Die Abkehr vom Nichtrealen.* Edited by F. Mayer-Hillebrand. Hamburg: Felix Meiner.

Brentano, F. (1982). *Deskriptive Psychologie* (Descriptive Psychology). Edited by R. M. Chisholm and W. Baumgartner. Hamburg: Felix Meiner.

Titchener, E. B. (1898). The postulates of a structural psychology. *Psychological Review* 8: 449–465.

Goodman, N., and Quine, W. V. (1947). Steps toward a constructive nominalism. *Journal of Symbolic Logic* 12: 105–122. Reprinted in N. Goodman (1972), *Problems and Projects,* pp. 173 198.

24

Sigmund Freud and the Concept of Mental Health

Biographical Note

Sigmund Freud (1856–1939) was born in Moravia (now in the Czech Republic, then in the Austro-Hungarian Empire) to parents who came from Galicia (now part of Poland). When Sigmund was young, the family moved to Vienna, where he attended high school and university. At the university of Vienna he took an interest in philosophy (two years of Brentano's lectures), anatomy, and physiology (in which he published several papers). With some reluctance he eventually opted for medicine. After qualifying, he studied Charcot's approach to mental illness in Paris and then set up as a psychiatrist in Vienna. In the late 1890s he founded psychoanalysis, over which he presided until his death. His later life was made difficult by cancer of the jaw, and his closing years by Hitler's annexation of Austria. In 1938 he fled with his immediate family to England, where he died in September 1939, just after the outbreak of the Second World War.

First a very brief sketch of Freud's theory of personality, after which we will study just one topic: Freud's neglect of the theory of mental health (as opposed to mental illness). The insight we gain by studying the neglect of mental health is not peculiar to Freudian psychoanalysis: it applies equally to all branches of psychotherapy, including clinical psychology. The insight, however, comes through in sharpest relief in the context of Freud's own methods and writings. In this study we will be considering psychoanalysis in relation to St. Augustine's problem, that is, how Freud handles ideals of personality and human behavior. But first the theory of personality.

The original matrix from which the infant's personality grows is the Id. The Latin pronoun *id* means the same as the English pronoun *it*. The word, by its very poverty, is meant to indicate a neglected aspect of personality that is remote from the probings of consciousness, its origins and functioning being subconscious. In the Id dwell all inherited drives. Of these there are two basic ones: the pleasure drive (which is positive and includes the sexual urge) and the death drive (which is negative and includes a subconscious death wish as well as other urges that are subversive of the individual's well-being).

Out of the Id develops the Ego (the Latin word for self). The Ego, which embraces a great many processes that are conscious, is begotten from the Id by means of "perceptions which are received from without and conscious processing from within," both being "conscious from the start" (*The Ego and the Id*, p. 20).

The third constituent of the Freudian personality, called the Superego (above the Ego), also develops out of the subconscious Id. It corresponds to what ordinary people call conscience. It comes about through a process of identification between children and their parents. There are separate processes for boys and girls; we will restrict ourselves to boys. Freud's idea is that little boys desire their mothers as sexual partners but find the way blocked by their fathers, who can be quite punitive. The result is a conflict called the Oedipus complex (King Oedipus being a mythological figure who slew his father and married his mother—both actions performed unwittingly, and therefore without the consciousness of what he was doing, in the myth). The resolution of the Oedipus complex depends on a boy's repressing his sexual desire for his mother and accepting his powerful father's attitudes. This, according to Freud, is the origin of all morality in the boy. Morality is a psychological dodge to avoid punishment by a powerful father and to gain some rewards by currying the father's favor, all this by doing what the father approves of. The idea of God, for Freud, is nothing more than a displacement from a visible and finite father to an invisible and infinitely powerful father in the sky. Guilt is a form of anxiety at having violated the dictates of the Superego; it owes its origin to fear of paternal punishment.

What are we to make of all this? Opinion is sharply divided. Inside the psychoanalytic movement certain segments of the theory are held by some with religious fervor. Many outsiders, especially among professional psychologists, are wholly unconvinced. Some of this is due to the fact that Freud's methods have left these psychologists dissatisfied. Freud has had some highly publicized bad press at the hands of philosophers of science, notably Karl Popper (1983), and Adolf Grünbaum (1993), although these distinguished philosophers do not agree on what is the matter with Freud's scientific methods.

Instead of following the main lines of dissatisfaction with Freud, which have to do with the adequacy of the evidence for the conclusions he proposed, I wish to take a different tack. To introduce it, I note that Freud excommunicated one of his early disciples, Alfred Adler, on the grounds that Adler was paying attention to phases of psychic development in normal, nonpathological personalities. In other words, Adler was studying normal personality development.

Now Freud was a physician with a strong suit in physiology. He knew that in medicine, disease is studied in the context of the normal. Medics in training are grounded in the anatomy and physiology of the normal body. Pathological states are understood as departures from the normal; the job of therapists is understood as replacing pathological states with normal ones. Remove consideration of the normal, and both the training of medical students and the practice of medicine are incomprehensible.

Let me make this concrete. The surgeon who hopes to correct a defective knee must know the normal knee, must know what the knee is supposed to be like. Not that knowledge of the normal knee gives immediate skill in curing defective ones; just that such knowledge is essential to knee surgeons. Doctors who specialize in respiratory disorders must be able to tell, with reasonable confidence, the X ray of a diseased lung from that of a normal one. The ability to do so cannot be gained by studying nothing but X rays of diseased lungs.

Freud turned his back on this aspect of medicine and claimed to concentrate exclusively on the pathological. It is as though he believed that in the normal, well-adjusted person, the deeper secrets of the mind are veiled and that the pain and distress of neurosis are needed to tear the veil and reveal the hidden depths. And he insisted that his disciples follow suit. In fairness, he saw himself as reversing a trend: where others had dismissed neurotic states and actions as mere nonsense, he took them seriously and tried to understand them. Perhaps he feared that attention to the normal tended to result in dismissal of the neurotic, and that this tendency had to be resisted. With a writer like Freud, it is difficult to be sure. At any rate, the result was the dismissal of the study of the normal, and with it, I fear, the possibility of understanding the abnormal. The basic reason is that opposites have to be grasped in a single act of insight; they are too interdependent to be grasped in isolation from each other.

Freud was, of course, aware that he was open to criticism for dismissing the normal from the scope of his studies. In his popular *Psychopathology of Everyday Life* he adverts to the criticism and claims that his studies of the slips and mistakes made by perfectly normal people in everyday circumstances went a long way to redress the balance. This, however, is completely misguided. The book concentrates exclusively on mistakes. One might as well claim that from the exclusive study of normal people stumbling, one could develop an adequate theory of how normal people manage to walk.

Perhaps I ought to add that this aspect of Freud's approach to personality disorders is by no means unique. My own experience has been mainly in university departments of psychology with clinical psychology programs. Typically, such departments pay little attention to Freud. Yet few departments (if any) give courses on mental health or make a serious and systematic attempt to help students to conceptualize what mental health is. Instead, they study various forms of personality and behavior disorders, and they study possible lines of therapy. To be sure, courses are given elsewhere in these departments on normal perception, learning, cognition, and even personality. But none of these courses either on its own or in combination with others amounts to a conceptualization of mental health.

Nothing in the foregoing should be taken as denying that the normal is illuminated by the study of the abnormal. Often a knowledge of what can go wrong and how serves to underline what happens when things go right. The normal and the abnormal are in a dialectical relation. They mutually help to determine each other. This in turn implies that exclusive attention to the abnormal subverts the process of understanding the abnormal. As a doctor with a background in normal physiology, Freud should have been able to see this. So why did he not see it? A difficult question to answer with confidence, and yet the attempt to answer it will,

I believe, lead us to a special property of mental health that will repay the effort.

When people study the normal knee or the normal lung, they seek to delimit what its states and operations are when it fulfills its functions. The corresponding study of human persons and their behavior would seek to delimit what persons ought to be and how they ought to behave if they are to fulfill their functions. But what might these functions be? Clearly they are not, in the first instance, the functions that society pays them to perform. Rather, they are those functions that most closely touch their status as persons. This is going to take some teasing apart.

If a man works in a garage, his skill as a motor mechanic will not concern the mental therapist—except insofar as it subtends, or fails to subtend, the man's ability to act in other respects. What other respects? The list would include, as circumstances demand, ability to act as a husband, as a father, as a son, as an employee, as a friend. It would include the ability to deal with life's successes and disappointments in a balanced manner; to rejoice over good fortune and have compassion with bad; to handle lethargy, anxiety, and ambition. How, then, should one act as a husband, father, son, employee, friend? How should one cope with the successes and disappointments of life and deal with laziness, anxiety, and ambition? The answer to the first question is that one ought to be a good husband, good father, good son, good employee, good friend. The answer to the second question is that one ought to be wise and moderate and courageous and industrious and considerate and patient, etc. In short, one should be a wise and good person.

So we have ascertained that what would make a person mentally healthy is being wise and good. But what is a wise and good person? Curiously, this is the key question in the branch of philosophy called ethics. The aim of ethics is to explain what it is about certain people that justifies their being called good people or bad people—not good mechanics or teachers, but good people. What we have discovered, then, is a surprisingly close link between mental health and ethics.

It matters not at all that some Mafia boss may strike us as "psychologically" well adjusted, although his life is full of evil deeds. The superficial and misleading impression of mental health might arise from the air of calmness with which he can enter upon a large drug deal or order the elimination of a rival. It is part of mental health to suffer the pangs of remorse for evil done. The Mafia boss's very calmness and stolidity are themselves symptoms of maladjustment, of mental disorder. It is a serious error to confuse mental calm with mental health and mental pain with mental illness.

Since personality disorders may well lessen ability to control behavior, it is important to add that what is at stake here is not the moral responsibility or guilt of mentally disturbed persons. I am certainly not saying that all neurotic behavior is morally evil. What I am saying is that neurotic and psychotic attitudes and behavior cannot in themselves be described as either mentally healthy or as morally good. Certainly it is not enough to say that they cannot be described as morally evil. But neither can they be described as mentally healthy, for the simple reason that mental health is what moralists are driving at under the rubric of moral goodness. Ethics, we should be clear, aims to describe good attitudes and good behavior; it is another matter altogether whether or not it is within the power of certain classes of persons to adopt those attitudes and behave in that manner. In other words, the issue of guilt is another matter altogether. To say that certain attitudes and behavior are morally evil is of a piece with saying that they are the opposite of mental health, indeed, that they are injurious to mental health.

When I have discussed this with various people, some have objected that in questions of actions the issue of guilt always arises. Their claim is that it is not possible to consider the notion of moral goodness without at the same time considering guilt. This observation may perhaps be justified in relation to the concrete actions of real people. It seems irrelevant to the matter of *conceptualizing* the nature of moral goodness. Galileo distinguished in the motion of a cannonball a vertical component from a horizontal component, although there cannot be a vertical motion in a gravitational field without a vertical component. I merely beg a similar liberty in the conceptualization of moral goodness and of mental health.

Grasp the relation indicated above between ethics and mental health, and you can begin to understand why Freud, consciously or unconsciously, shied away from questions of mental health, and why he excommunicated Adler for becoming occupied with the normal. That he really did shy away is amply documented. He explicitly ruled that ethics and psychoanalysis are distinct. Psychoanalysis, he claimed, is a "new and deeper science of the mind" (Freud, 1946, 86). On the other hand, in *Psychoanalysis and Faith* he says that it is "unreasonable to expect science to produce a system of ethics" (1963). Psychoanalysis is science, the claim is; ethics is not. It follows, in this frame of mind, that ethical considerations are debarred from psychoanalysis, and with them the whole consideration of mental health.

Other explicit statements of Freud lead to the same conclusion. Moralists assess the goodness or badness of actions in the first instance by appealing to intuition, albeit an intuition informed by experience and reflection. Some actions, when we have discovered their true nature, strike us immediately as morally admirable or as morally repulsive. The film maker expects audiences to recoil in moral horror from the portrayal of certain actions, and members of the audience are aware that they have so recoiled. Such awareness is an example of moral intuition. Freud will have nothing to do with intuition. In his *New Introductory Lectures on Psychoanalysis* he says, "Intuition and divination . . . may safely be reckoned as illusions" (1933, 159). Intuition, mark you, he places on the same footing as the reading of tea leaves. In rejecting intuition, he was depriving moralists of a voice. In place of intuition he set psychoanalytic science, which he saw as being of a piece with biology, biochemistry, and the other natural sciences. In adopting for psychoanalysis the language and stance of the natural sciences, he was distancing himself from philosophy and protecting psychoanalysis. In his *Autobiographical Study* he says that even when, with age and infirmity, "I have moved away from observation, I have carefully avoided contact with philosophy proper" (1946, 109). Moreover, in the same book he insists that psychology is a natural science on a par with other natural sciences (1946, 106). No place for a privileged intuition.

Ethics has no place in the theory of a science like biology (as opposed to the actions of biologists or the uses to which biological findings are put). It makes no sense to be morally indignant at the squirrel who eats your tulip bulbs or at the gene that made you bald. It follows that questions of normality in biology prescind from ethics. Adopt a biological stance in psychology (as do physiological psychologists in their study of the brain) and in that perspective ethical questions have no place in the formulation of theory. Freud's adopting the language and stance of the natural sciences secured him from philosophy and ethics, but at a price. The move also prevented him from developing a deeper understanding of mental health and ultimately from achieving his goal, which was to understand and cure neurosis. This is all rather tragic, for it is a major muddle.

What is most strange is that Freud could not leave ethics alone. Unlike the true natural scientist, for whom ethical issues do not arise in the formulation of theory, Freud saw himself as developing a new ethics, a new morality. Paul Roazen, who has made a lifelong study of Freud and his circle, quite rightly says that Freud "helped to change modern ethics" (1993, 205). Roazen quotes a letter of Freud's: "I stand for an infinitely freer sexual life" (1993, 111). That was certainly the impact of Freud's work. What is odd about the whole thing is the tension between Freud's seeking to influence ethical thinking and his scientific stance. Freud was simply trying to have it both ways.

The deeper reason Freud could not leave ethics alone is that the subject is essentially related to questions of mental health. He claimed that his exclusive study of neurosis revealed aspects of mental health. If he was right in this, it follows that he was discovering aspects of what it is to be a good person. From this it follows that he was discovering answers to ethical questions but, strangely, without engaging in ethics. He thus claimed to be able to run around the astonished community of moralists. To complete the trick, he deprived them of the right to comment, because they were mere philosophers trapped in the illusions of their ethical intuitions. Many seem to have been too bamboozled to notice that in assuming the mantle (if not the reality) of the natural sciences, Freud had surrendered the right to derive any ethical conclusion whatever from his psychological observations. Freud, on the face of it, seems to have pulled off one of the hoaxes of the century.

Has psychoanalysis produced experts on the human soul, people who can tell us how we ought to live? I see no evidence that it has. It's not that psychoanalysis has not had enough time; if the line taken here is right, it is that it was radically ill conceived. To adapt a phrase of Kant's, from timber so crooked as that of psychoanalytic theory, nothing straight can be fashioned. I fear that this will be the view of anyone who adverts to the relation between ethics and mental health.

And yet people have been helped by psychoanalysis. True, but people seem to have been helped to an equal degree by any form of psychotherapy, many of which owe nothing to Freud. The truth of the matter is that the intelligent sympathy of any fellow human being helps. This often seems to be what is at work in successful mental therapy. There is no substitute for humility, compassion, respect, love, and intelligence. The great thing about these qualities is that they enhance courage, independence, and a sense of worth in persons to whom they are directed. They guard against the danger that the therapist can all too easily deprive patients of dignity and self-reliance. I sometimes wonder whether any professional training lays enough stress on those qualities. They sound so old-fashioned, so unscientific—and so right.

The world is full of the most appalling mental suffering, and it is rapidly filling up, at least in the parts I know, with professionals to deal with it. I do not want anything that I say to discourage people from trying to help the mentally ill, and I certainly believe in the therapeutic efficacy of intelligent sympathy. Moreover, there seem to be some who are more intelligent, compassionate, and insightful than others, and for all I know, these qualities can be developed under the guidance of experienced masters. I also believe that the judicious use of certain drugs can sometimes relieve mental distress to a significant degree. But then the use of drugs places one in a rather different context from that in which Freud was working. He concentrated on hysterias and on what some call problems in living, these being the type of problems that arise from such factors as tensions in the family or the work place. In the treatment of people suffering from such problems, drugs seem to be less effective. I do not envy present-day therapists having to treat the type of problems that Freud addressed with the therapeutic means in which they have been schooled. I also believe that therapists are unlikely to improve those means significantly if they continue to ignore the very nature of mental health. I am not sure that if they do take due account of mental health, they will then develop a science of the soul on a par with any of the natural sciences, but perhaps they will be more successful in their main purpose.

Bibliographical Note

The works of Freud referred to include the following:

Freud, S. (1923/1927). *The Ego and the Id*. Translated by J. Riviere. London: Hogarth Press.

Freud, S. (1933). *New Introductory Lectures on Psychoanalysis*. Edited by E. Jones and translated by W. J. H. Sprott. London: Hogarth Press.

Freud, S. (1946). *Autobiographical Study*. Translated by J. Strachey. London: Hogarth Press.

Freud, S. (1948). *The Psychopathology of Everyday Life*. Translated by A. A. Brill. London: Ernest Benn.

Freud, S. (1963). *Psychoanalysis and Faith: Dialogues with the Reverend Oskar Pfister*. Translated by E. Mosbacher. New York: Basic Books.

Other books referred to include these:

Grünbaum, A. (1993). *Validation in the Clinical Theory of Psychoanalysis*. Madison, Conn.: International Universities Press.

Popper, K. R. (1983). *Realism and the Aim of Science*. Totowa N.J.: Rowmann and Littlefield.

Roazen, P. (1993). *Meeting Freud's Family*. Amherst: University of Massachusetts Press.

25

John B. Watson and the Behaviorists

Biographical Note

John Broadus Watson (1878–1958), a Californian, studied at Furman University and later at Chicago University. There he was attracted by the psychologist J. R. Angell and the biologist Jacques Loeb, one of the leading reductionists in the biology of the day. His doctoral thesis for Chicago was "Animal Education: The Psychical Development of the White Rat." In 1908 he joined the faculty of Johns Hopkins University. He wrote the seminal paper for behaviorism in 1913. In 1915, as president of the American Psychological Association, he introduced to psychology the physiological work of Ivan Pavlov on conditioned reflexes. After a period working for the U.S. Army on tests for the selection of pilots, he returned to Johns Hopkins. He had an affair with a graduate student of his, whom he later married. The affair, however, led to divorce proceedings and, in the climate of the time, he was obliged to resign his university post. For the rest of his life he worked in advertising, where he was successful and became rich.

In an America disillusioned with the introspectionist methods of E. B. Titchener and others and intent on putting psychology to practical use, especially in the domain of education, John B. Watson (1913) offered an alternative approach that proved immensely attractive. (For the background of behaviorism in America, see O'Donnell, 1985.) Here was a bold and entirely new approach to psychology. Not only was introspection banned, but with it intuition. A biologist cannot hope to get at the intuitions of a fruit fly (if it has any), much less those of a gene. Later in his career Watson made his preference for the biologists' approach fully explicit: "With animals I was at home. I felt that in studying them, I was *keeping close to biology* with my feet on the ground" (Watson, 1936,

276; emphasis added). This is another example, in the long line stemming from Hobbes, of attempts to do psychology on the model of some discipline that is not psychology.

The opening words for his 1913 paper are these:

Psychology as the behaviorist views it is a purely objective experimental branch of natural science. Its theoretical goal is the prediction and control of behavior. Introspection forms no part of its methods, nor is the scientific value of its data dependent upon the readiness with which they lend themselves to interpretation in terms of consciousness. The behaviorist, in his efforts to get a unitary scheme of animal response, recognizes no dividing line between man and brute. (Watson, 1913.) [See the definition of *behavior* in the Glossary.]

The article goes on to say that introspection had not produced solid results—a comment that was justified.

The introspectionists were not the only psychologists who were repudiated. Look at the words Watson used: "a purely objective experimental branch of natural science." This brushes aside both Wundt and Brentano, who claimed that at least an important part of psychology is not among the natural sciences, is not purely experimental, and is not purely objective, at least if this term was meant to exclude intuition. Later in the article Watson also says that when one tried to determine the elements of consciousness (both Wundt and Brentano recommended that we should), one found little agreement among researchers and little indication about how to resolve the disagreement. This too he said with a good deal of justice!

In this context what is behavior, as opposed to consciousness? This is not an easy question. The main idea was to fasten onto what was publicly observable in the activity of an animal and somehow demarcate a portion that was relevant for psychology. Donald Hebb later defined behavior as "the publicly observable activity of muscles or glands of external secretion as manifested in movements of parts of the body or in the appearance of tears, sweat, saliva and so forth" (1958, 2). I believe that Watson would have accepted this, particularly for its emphasis on public observability rather than private intuition. I do not believe that he would have been perturbed by the extension of the publicly observable with the arrival of ultrasound, PET scans, and other imaging devices. The main thing is that in using these devices, one need make no appeal to one's own intuition or to that of the person being observed.

Watson seems to have worried about such core aspects of psychology as knowledge, belief, thought, and reasoning. He hit upon an idea that he believed was promising from a behaviorist point of view, but he set it out, tentatively, in a footnote:

The hypothesis that all the so-called "higher thought" processes go on in terms of faint reinstatements of the original muscular act (including speech here) and that these are integrated into systems which respond in serial order (associative mechanisms) is, I believe, a tenable one. (1913, 174)

I think it is fair to say that this suggestion was a blind alley and that behaviorism never succeeded in giving an interesting, even if implausible, account of these cognitive functions. One result was that for a period the higher processes of mind were neglected in psychology or, to say the least, lost their central role. It is not so much that they were thought to be unimportant as that the field was preoccupied with external stimuli and publicly observable responses.

In time things began to right themselves. Inside the behaviorist framework there was talk of mental set. In due course some behaviorists, in an effort to take some of the higher processes more seriously, posited the existence of intervening variables or "associative mechanisms" between an observable stimulus and an observable response. These intervening variables were thought of as mental echoes of observable stimuli and responses. The move created some tension, because the original inspiration for behaviorism was to stick to the publicly observable, and intervening variables were not publicly observable. Of course, psychologists who posited them could reasonably appeal to practice elsewhere in science, where invisible particles, for example, are posited to explain visible effects. In the long run this idea of associative mechanisms proved inadequate, but we are getting ahead of ourselves.

One learning theorist who rejected all talk of intervening (invisible) variables was B. F. Skinner (1904–1990). He studied the effect of rewards on spontaneously occurring behavior, thus developing what came to be known as operant conditioning. Conditioning of this type has had an important impact on clinical psychology, where it goes under the name of "behavior modification" or "behavior therapy." This is one of the lasting benefits of the behaviorist movement. Interestingly, J. Konorski, in Poland, seems to have foreshadowed some of Skinner's most important ideas.

The theory that results from the movement as a whole is called "learning theory." While learning theorists, acknowledging that the term is vague, were cautious about giving a general definition of learning, it seems that we can take the following as a rough guide to what they had in mind: any change in behavior that is due to antecedent behavior or to environmental factors, especially if those factors included punishment or reward. Everything I say here has been the subject of controversy. With that in mind, this description will serve as a useful characterization of the main tendencies in the movement. A central idea was that punished or unrewarded behavior tended to disappear, whereas rewarded behavior tended to be repeated and to build up habit strength.

This offers a solution, even if not a convincing one, to Plato's problem of inquiry or learning. Learning theorists could claim to have solved the problem by saying that learning simply follows the pattern of rewards and punishments. Undoubtedly, this contains an important kernel of truth relating to the building up of habits, although the rewards and punishments for humans, being long-term, may often be present only through imagination. At the same time, rewards and punishment seem to relate but remotely to the learning of the slave boy in Plato's *Meno*. Recall that the task Socrates set the slave boy was to find a line whose square was eight square units of a given unit of length. Socrates seemed successful in leading the boy to reach insights showing a certain conclusion to be necessarily correct. There was no talk at all of reward and punishment in the process.

Learning theory, as an enterprise aimed at explaining learning in general, no longer occupies the central position in psychology that it did 40 years ago. Serious problems in many areas were discovered by learning theorists themselves, and the movement was subjected to a philippic by Noam Chomsky (1959) in a lengthy review of B. F. Skinner's *Verbal Behavior* (1957). I will not rehearse the lines of Chomsky's criticism. In the intervening years many psychologists have become convinced that the behaviorists seriously underrated the special preparedness of human infants for dealing with the phonology, lexicon, morphology, syntax, and semantics of a natural language. This preparedness is the core element in the psycholinguist response to Plato's problem of learning, but I will not here pursue the matter. Many psycholinguists also became convinced that chains of associations were too unwieldy to handle everyday creativity with language, as well as the ability of people to follow and understand sentences that they had never heard before.

To concentrate on these inadequacies, however, is to miss the real contributions of learning theory. Among the contributions I will mention just two. In the area of clinical psychology and health psychology, whenever there is need to break a habit or remove an unfortunate association, behavioristic methods can be applied, often with success. For example, many people who have had to undergo chemotherapy for cancer develop an uncontrollable negative reaction to the thought of having to return to hospital, even for a checkup. They may, for instance, develop upset stomachs and vomit on the morning of a hospital visit. This condition can be alleviated by desensitization, which derives from the study of how learned associations can be extinguished.

To my mind, the most valuable benefit that the learning theorists bequeathed to psychology is a technique for posing questions to creatures who cannot understand questions posed in a natural language or respond in one. Learning techniques are standard in physiological psychology, where one trains an animal to discriminate one pattern of events (or objects) from another and subsequently modifies the animal's brain in the hope of discovering what areas or what neural transmitters are involved in the original discrimination. This has led to work of considerable refinement and fruitfulness.

Learning methods have also proved effective with human infants. A typical paradigm is to present some stimuli repeatedly to infants, who are allowed to control the presentation by sucking on a nonnutritive nipple. When the infants start losing interest, as indicated by a fall off in sucking, stimuli of a new sort are shown to some infants (experimental), whereas other infants (control) continue to see examples of the old stimuli. If sucking revives in the experimental group as compared with the control group, there is an indication that infants are sensitive to the differences between the two classes of stimuli.

Over a period of some 40 years learning theorists explored in depth the most effective means of carrying out such investigations and the snags that can all too easily lead the unwary to draw unwarranted conclusions. The result is a finely tuned technique to be applied in psychological research.

In the 1940s and 1950s associations and habits seemed to be central in psychological theorizing. Then in the 1960s and 1970s they seemed to disappear, at least in experimental psychology. They have, however, made a reappearance under the rubric of connectionism or parallel distributed processing (PDP). The idea is to take a computer net with connections among the nodes representing associations and to program it to adjust the weights on various connections in accordance with the outcome of certain decisions, which are seen as modeling experience. The whole is seen as modeling the build-up of habit strengths with experience without appeal either to rule following or to logical insight. While advocates of PDP claim to be able to model a surprisingly large range of mental phenomena, other psychologists dispute their claims, especially in the areas of rule following and problem solving. The issues are highly technical and as yet unresolved. To my mind this much is clear: there are large areas of psychology where rules of various sorts are important, and there are large areas where habits play some part. For example, when one learns a language like French after early childhood, one is usually given many rules to follow. So there are the rules. But one needs practice at applying them. Even when one makes no mistakes, one's early attempts are halting. With practice one's performance in all its aspects becomes smoother. What is needed, then, is a theory that handles both rule-governed performance and the building up of habit strength in the application of rules. It seems to me that there is room for both sets of considerations, and that it should not be a question for either side of "conquering" territory.

I want to conclude by making an observation that many psychologists may regard as heretical. Psychology across the ages did not aim to *explain behavior*. It aimed to understand the nature and source of human knowledge and knowledge-informed desires, and other aspects of human experience only insofar as they relate to these. We here have paid most attention in these reflections to perception and cognition. Externally observable muscle activity and glandular secretions are related to the central concerns of psychology only insofar as they can be taken as indicative of perceptual and cognitive functioning, that is, only insofar as they can be construed as actions. To take behavior as the focus of attention for psychology is as big an error as to take tracks in cloud chambers as the main object of study in particle physics. Such tracks are interesting only as clues to the existence of certain particles and to their properties.

There is in this connection a confusion of terminology. "Behavior" can be taken in the sense the behaviorists intended, a technical sense. It can also be taken as roughly synonymous with "action," where actions are understood as being individuated by the beliefs and desires that motivate the agents. Behavior so understood falls within the purview of traditional perception and cognition psychology, although even in this sense I do not believe it was the main object of attention. To repeat what was said before, traditional psychology concentrated on the apparatus of the human mind rather than on the uses to which it was put. It did not attempt to explain behavior, no matter how the term is interpreted.

Physiological psychologists, who work with animals other than humans, naturally take "behavior" in the technical sense defined by Hebb. Their concern is to explain animal behavior by means of the neurological structures and activities that underlie it. On the other hand, clinical psychologists may also claim that they are seeking to explain behavior. When their explanations appeal to the motives of their patients, the agreement in aim with physiological psychologists is nominal only. Though both may use the same words, they mean different things by them. It is, then, tendentious to say that the aim of psychology is to explain behavior. It depends on what one means by "behavior" and on the type of psychology.

Although we paid most attention to the origins of behaviorism, this chapter brings us well along toward the present day. We saw that Watson advocated behaviorism as an escape from introspection, intuition, and consciousness. He was attracted to the behaviorist approach because he thought it brought psychology into line with biology. One problem was that behaviorism had serious difficulties in dealing with "higher mental functions." One enduring contribution of behaviorism, we saw, was a technique for addressing questions to creatures that cannot understand or respond in the sentences of a natural language. I mentioned two types of such creatures: brains and infants. Another enduring contribution is behavior therapy. I ended by noting that the word "behavior" is ambiguous, having a technical sense (observable activity of muscles and glands of external secretion) and an everyday one (roughly equivalent to action). It follows that psychologists who seem to agree that they are studying behavior may mean different things. We also saw that, physiological psychology apart, psychology does not now, nor did it in the past, take behavior as its main object of study, as what psychology undertakes to explain. It follows that only in a quite limited sense can psychology be described as a "behavioristic" or "behavioral science."

Key terms of this reflection were the following:

Behavior   Behavior is "the publicly observable activity of muscles or glands of external secretion as manifested in movements of parts of the body or in the appearance of tears, sweat, saliva and so forth" (Hebb, 1958, 2).

Action   An action is an event that has a true explanation in the agent's beliefs and desires. Actions are individuated by the beliefs and desires that inspire them.

Learning   Learning, as most behaviorists saw it, is any change in behavior that is due to antecedent behavior or to environmental factors, especially if those factors include reward or punishment.

Bibliographical Note

Watson, J. B. (1913). Psychology as the behaviorist views it. *Psychological Review* 20: 158–177.

Chomsky, N. (1959). Review of *Verbal Behavior* by B. F. Skinner. *Language* 35: 26–58. Reprinted in J. A. Fodor and J. J. Katz (eds.), *The Structure of Language: Readings in the Philosophy of Language,* pp. 547–578. Englewood Cliffs, N.J.: Prentice-Hall, 1964.

Hebb, D. O. (1958). *A Textbook of Psychology: A Neuropsychological Theory.* New York: John Wiley.

O'Donnell, J. M. (1985). *The Origins of Behaviorism: American Psychology, 1870–1920.* New York: New York University Press.

Skinner, B. F. (1957). *Verbal Behavior.* New York: Appleton-Century-Crofts.

26

Some Notes on the Gestalt Movement

Biographical Notes

Christian von Ehrenfels (1859–1932), an Austrian, was a student of Brentano's at the University of Vienna and took his doctorate in Graz under Alexius Meinong, another student of Brentano's. He was *Privatdozent* at Vienna (1886–1896) when he wrote his seminal paper on gestalt psychology. Later he went to the Charles University, Prague, as professor, where he spent the rest of his academic career. He was a gifted musician and composer.

Max Wertheimer (1880–1943) was born in Prague, where he studied under Ehrenfels and was greatly influenced by him. He later worked for two years in Berlin under Carl Stumpf, another student of Brentano's, although he took his doctorate at the University of Würzburg under Oswald Kulpe in 1904. For the next six years he wandered from one laboratory to another, supported financially by his father. In 1910 he began to work at Frankfurt, where in due course he met Köhler and Koffka. After Hitler came to power, he moved to the New School for Social Research in New York, where he ended his career.

Kurt Koffka (1886–1941) was born in Berlin and obtained his doctorate under Carl Stumpf in 1908. He then moved to the University of Würzburg and, a year later, to the Academy at Frankfurt am Main. In due course he came to Smith College.

Wolfgang Köhler (1887–1967) was born in Estonia but grew up in Saxony. He took his doctorate under Carl Stumpf at the University of Berlin, 1909. He then moved to Frankfurt and in 1913 accepted a government post in Tenerife (Canary Islands), returning to Berlin only after the end of the First World War in 1920, where he succeeded Stumpf as professor of psychology. He resigned in protest against Nazi treatment of a Jewish member of his staff and took a post at Swarthmore College, in 1934, where he remained for the rest of his career.

These biographical notes suggest that the Gestalt movement—for these are the principal figures—owes something special to Franz Brentano. In particular, Christian von Ehrenfels, who wrote the first paper on gestalt qualities in 1890, had been a student of Brentano's and of Meinong's (another of the Brentano circle, although personally estranged from Brentano) and was back at the University of Vienna when he wrote the seminal paper. Ehrenfels does acknowledge a debt to Brentano. Brentano, strangely, does not refer to Ehrenfels in his own book on perception (1907), although most of it was written in the decade following Ehrenfels's paper. Matters are not clarified by Brentano's faithful editor, Oskar Kraus, who wrote a monograph on Brentano in 1919. Kraus, who to my mind did not understand the originality of Ehrenfels's work, was dismissive of the Gestalt movement. It is important to try to set the record straight, not merely for reasons of historical truth but also for the light thus cast on important psychologists. It may be an exaggeration that would leave the psychophysicists restless, but it is not a caricature, to claim that from the last quarter of the nineteenth century the only substantive contribution to the theory of experimental (as opposed to physiological) psychology that is incorporated in today's psychology is gestalt psychology. By "substantive" here I mean to rule out such (important) adjuncts to psychology as mental tests, statistical procedures, and experimental research methods (e.g., reaction times). Gestalt psychology has simply been absorbed into the theory of perception. I begin by looking at Ehrenfels's concept of a gestalt, seeking, as we go along, to determine what is original in it and what is derived from Brentano. To end, I have a quick look at what happens to the idea in the hands of Wertheimer, Koffka, and Köhler.

For Ehrenfels, a gestalt quality is a perceptual property attaching to a number of distinguishable perceptual elements. The perception of the elements grounds the gestalt quality, which is distinct from the elements. The gestalt quality is not a summation of the elements or of the percepts to which they give rise; it is something over and above the elements and their related percepts. His definition is this:

By a gestalt quality we understand those positive perceptual contents that are linked in awareness with the presence of perceptual complexes consisting of separable elements (that is, each element can be perceived in the absence of the others).

We call the perceptual complex, which is essential to the existence of a gestalt quality, the *foundation* of the quality. (1890/1988, 262–263)

So we have the gestalt as a perceptual individual comprising several subaspects (e.g., color, texture, perhaps musical notes) as its foundation. But the gestalt is not identical with the foundation. Indeed, the main test for gestalt status is that the foundation can be changed, leaving the gestalt unaltered, or nearly so. The lead example is a melody, which can be played on different instruments in different keys, so that from one presentation to the next there is not a single physical element in common, and yet the melody is recognizably the same melody. It is important to note that from one presentation to the next it not merely *is* the same melody but also is so presented perceptually.

The possibility of varying the foundation while holding the perceptual individual constant is a sure sign that the individual is a gestalt. Ehrenfels allows, however, that the test may not always work, as for example when one has to do with a smell. It may happen that one is not always aware what foundational elements are contributing to a gestalt. Ehrenfels mentions musical chords and the timbre of certain sounds as examples of gestalts whose foundation may not be distinctly perceived. It is often difficult to distinguish the component notes contributing to a chord and impossible, without the aid of scientific instruments, to discern the elements that contribute to a particular timbre. In such cases the elements can be discerned only through a process of abstraction. It seems that what he has in mind is an experimental process of some sort. On hearing a chord on the piano, we may attempt to reproduce it, adding and subtracting notes until it sounds just right. Here the choice of elements is guided by the gestalt quality, but at the same time the particular set of elements, or better still, a set with the appropriate mutual relations, determines the gestalt quality. Moreover, a single note on its own sounds different from the same note played in a chord. In this connection Ehrenfels would only have to have remembered Brentano's extensive discussions of color mixing. For example, Brentano's *Untersuchungen zur Sinnespsychologie* deals with the color purple as appearing to have blue and red components. Yet there can be no question that the red component of purple looks different in a purple patch than it would if seen on its own.

The picture that emerges is of gestalt qualities distinct from their foundations with constraints running in both directions: top down, from gestalt to elements of the foundation, and bottom up, from the elements to the gestalt. It is only fair to say, however, that Ehrenfels concentrated more on the bottom-up constraints.

One may wonder about the ontological status of gestalt properties: whether they exist in the environment independent of the mind or whether their existence is wholly due to the operations of the mind. This is not a question, so far as I know, that Ehrenfels asked, although it certainly perplexed others. The reason may well have been that he accepted Brentano's teaching about external perception. In his *Psychology* Brentano makes it clear that he regards the perceptual properties of external objects as secondary qualities: "Knowledge, joy and desire really exist. Color, sound and warmth have only a phenomenal and intentional existence" (1874/1973, 92). In a later chapter we read, "But that which these mental activities refer to as their content and which really does appear to be external is, in actuality, no more outside of us than in us. It is mere appearance" (1874/1973, 175–176). There is, then, a strong element of idealism in Brentano's thought, and this may explain why Ehrenfels did not feel obliged to discuss the ontological status of gestalt properties. They have, he could have argued, whatever ontological status their foundation has. This was unlikely to satisfy a great many psychologists, who implicitly rejected idealism and tended towards realism. I may be permitted to remark en passant that if we lay aside illusory gestalt properties, as in the illusion of seeing a moving object (e.g., in a film), Ehrenfels would be justified in equating the ontological status of gestalt properties and their foundations. In my opinion, such gestalt properties are just as real as are the more elemental colors, textures, brightnesses, etc. None of the gestalt properties that Ehrenfels studied was illusory.

The main job of psychology proper for Brentano, recall, was to discern the elements of consciousness and their interconnections and combinations. This can also be taken as Ehrenfels's understanding of his task in connection with gestalt qualities. He saw himself as presenting a new element of consciousness, a gestalt, and as specifying its connections with other elements of consciousness, the elements of its foundation. Let us try to be clearer about this gestalt and its possible origins in Brentano's teaching.

I do not believe Ehrenfels's idea of gestalt is to be found in Brentano, but there is, prominently, the related Aristotelian concept of substance at the conceptual level. Substance in the Aristotelian tradition is opposed to accidents, as dog (substance) is opposed to sick or moving (accidents). Substance individuates accidents. What distinguishes Freddie's running from that of Spot is that it is the running of a dog that is different from Spot. The main test for substance status was that while we can predicate attributes of a substance, we cannot predicate the substance of anything. We say of Freddie, the dog, that he is sick. But of no other substance, Spot say, do we predicate the substance that is Freddie.

With this in mind, turn to Ehrenfels's favorite example, the gestalt of a melody. A particular presentation of a melody may strike us as gay or pensive. In other words, a gay or pensive quality may attach to the gestalt of the melody, and at the conceptual level this quality will justify the observation that the melody sounded gay, or sad. But the melody gestalt is not part of the foundation of any other gestalt. This is part of what Ehrenfels meant by the term "a perceptual individual." Do not become confused here. A gestalt quality, like any quality, can be predicated of a substance. What is special about a gestalt quality is that while other qualities may be predicated of it, it may not be predicated of any other perceptual object or quality. This is precisely what Ehrenfels meant to convey by speaking about gestalt qualities ("quality" because perceptual); he intended to draw attention to a perceptual phenomenon carved out from the rest of perception (hence "*Gestalt*," which is the German word for figure, as opposed to ground).

This is truly an original notion of great importance. It is a transposition to the perceptual level of the Aristotelian notion of substance. A gestalt has variable subaspects, its foundation, just as a substance has variable accidents. Moreover, a gestalt individuates its subaspects, its foundation. Yet there can be no gestalt without some foundation. The melody cannot be perceived at all unless it is played on some particular instrument(s) in some particular key. Gestalt and foundation somehow form one perceptual object, just as a substance and its accidents form one conceptual object. I am convinced that the importance of this notion for the theory of perception and how perception relates to cognition has hardly begun to be explored, but this is not the place to develop the subject. Suffice it to indicate that gestalts at the perceptual level prefigure the work of providing for individuation and identity that at the conceptual level is performed by kinds for the substances that are its members.

In Ehrenfels's work there are constraints working in both directions: a melody gestalt constrains the perception of a physical note, whether for example it is the basic tone of the key or a fifth above, but then the tones in a certain order with certain temporal relations also constrain the perception of that melody. This is parallel to the mutual constraints, at the syntactic and semantic levels, between sentences and their constituents. The word "hand" can be either a noun or a verb. Which it is on any occasion is determined by the sentence it is in: "Hand your cup" versus "Cup your hand." But then the sentence itself is determined by those words in those structural arrangements. This sort of dialectical relation is ubiquitous, and our minds are designed to handle it at both the conceptual and perceptual levels.

Ehrenfels saw this, and so did the (mainly) Austrian psychologists who followed up his ideas, e.g., Meinong and Benussi. The Berlin school of gestalt psychology—actually founded in Frankfurt—did not see this. They took the gestalt to be basic and dominant and the foundation to be quite secondary. We should try to understand why the difference came about and whether it is serious.

It seems to me that the difference came about in the following manner. The first work of the Berlin group was that of Wertheimer (1912). He presented subjects a line followed after a brief interval by another line in, say, a slightly different orientation. If the time interval was brief, but not too brief, subjects thought they were looking at a single object in motion. The best results were when the interval was about 1/15 of a second. Now Ehrenfels would be inclined to say that the two distinct lines appearing in rapid succession were the foundation and the movement a gestalt quality founded on the two lines. Wertheimer does not appear to have been happy with that, because subjects thought they saw only a single object. In what sense, then, were the two lines parts or aspects of the perceptual experience when they were not noticed at all, or at least not as distinct stationary lines? Impressed by Wertheimer's observation and many other related ones, the Berlin School diminished the importance of the foundation, claiming that one saw the foundation only to the extent

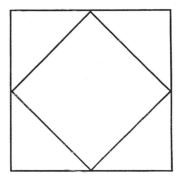

Figure 26.1
Köhler's diamond-in-a-square gestalt

that it was permitted, or mediated, by the gestalt. In other words, the Berlin School recognized constraints in only one direction: from gestalt to parts or aspects; not the other way about. This is quite explicit in the following remark by Wertheimer:

Is it really true that when I hear a melody, I have a *sum* of individual tones (pieces), which constitute the primary foundation of my experience? Is not perhaps the reverse of this true? What I really have, what I hear of each individual note, what I experience at each place in the melody, is a *part*, which is itself determined by the character of the whole. What is given to me by the melody does not arise . . . as a *secondary* process from the sum of the pieces as such. Instead, what takes place in each single part already depends on what the whole is. (1925, 5)

Here is another example, taken from Köhler (1947, 195) and slightly simplified. Consider figure 26.1. It strikes us as a diamond (or square) inscribed in a symmetrical manner in a larger square. This gestalt permits us to see the lines that form the sides of the two squares. It does not, however, permit us to see the letter "K," which is present four times over in different orientations. Once again, the gestalt dominates and, the Berlin School would say, mediates the perception of certain subobjects, but not of others. Evidence of constraints working in one direction and not another!

This difference in theory does not seem to have pronouncedly influenced the sort of experiment done by the two schools. For example, Koffka is able to accept all the experimental data collected by Benussi of the Austrian School. Koffka just interprets them differently. This agreement in practice, if not in theory, seems to me important, because it emphasizes the continuity across the schools and the contrast with the behaviorist school, founded almost simultaneously by J. B. Watson. Both gestalt schools are true to Brentano's descriptive psychology, being guided by intuition about the perceptual properties of objects.

Wertheimer's experimental methods were to vary the visual stimuli, vary the spatial and temporal intervals between them, and study the effect on perception. Ehrenfels would have been justified in saying that, like Wertheimer, he was varying the foundation and studying what happened to the gestalt. Ehrenfels had pointed out that sometimes the gestalt quality so dominated that special analytic methods were necessary to discover the foundation. It seems to me that the Berlin School should have allowed that there were bottom-up constraints at work too, because what else did it mean to say that certain changes in the stimulus conditions were associated with certain changes in the gestalt quality? The constraints run both ways. True, subjects are not always aware of the precise form of the foundation. But no foundation, no gestalt!

Both gestalt schools were opposed to British associationism, of the type advocated by John Stuart Mill and of the type that assumed such importance for behaviorists. Ehrenfels insisted that a gestalt was not the summation of its constituents or a tissue of associations among the members of its foundation; Wertheimer says repeatedly that a gestalt is not the product of "and-associations" (*und-Verbindungen*). Both are opposed to Ernst Mach's idea that a gestalt could be reduced to the elements of its foundation.

The indebtedness of both gestalt schools to Brentano becomes most apparent when we compare them with the behaviorists. Behaviorists, modeling themselves consciously on biological methods, as they understood them, rejected intuition. Brentano insisted that intuition is the main guide to psychology proper. Now it is by intuition that one is aware that there are gestalt properties over and above the physical elements of the foundation, although once they have been discovered, it is possible to show that nonhuman animals are also sensitive to them. It seems to me that it is this attentiveness to intuition that is gestalt psychology's main debt to Brentano. I believe that this is the reason for the enduring value of gestalt theory and experiment. How enduring can be seen in the recent work of Albert Bregman (1990), who transposes to audition all the major effects that the gestalt psychologists discovered in vision. Bregman's work, following closely in the footprints of the gestalt psychologists, lays solid new foundations for the theory of audition.

In one respect the Berlin School went against the spirit, if not the letter, of Brentano's work. They sought to explain and justify the gestalt perceptual effects by an appeal to what they called "dynamic fields" in the brain, conceived on the model of electromagnetic fields. It seems that this was an entirely fanciful approach to the neuropsychology of vision, and it has been dropped.

In this chapter we studied an application to perception of Brentano's descriptive psychology, which is guided mainly by intuition. We saw something of how solid and enduring the results were. In particular, we saw that Ehrenfels probably struck upon the idea of a gestalt by transposing Aristotle's notion of a substance from the conceptual level to the perceptual level. Aristotle's notion of substance was prominent in Brentano's theory of whole and part, into which we did not go. We saw how the later Berlin School followed the experimental practices of the Austrian School, while claiming to depart from the Austrian School in theory. The Austrian School claimed there were bottom-up constraints of foundation on gestalt as well as top-down constraints of gestalt on foundation; the Berlin School allowed only the top-down constraints. The claimed difference in theory, at least that part of it relating to constraints, appears to be a muddle, but not an important one. One moral to be drawn from the enduring success of the gestalt movement is the importance of intuition for psychology. Intuition is what sets experimental (as opposed to physiological) psychology apart from other scientific disciplines.

There were two important key terms that we encountered in this reflection:

Gestalt [The Berlin school of gestalt psychology, which included Wertheimer, Köhler, and others, did not use von Ehrenfels's expression "gestalt quality" (see below). They did not think of a gestalt as merely a separate quality of the stimulus but used the word to describe the "wholeness" of the stimulus pattern. While the whole was made out of parts, it was more than a structure built out of those parts. In addition to having properties that the parts taken individually did not have, it also gave roles and meanings to the individual parts. For example, when a series of wiggles drawn on paper are seen as a cartoon of a face, the curvature of a line is seen not as a mere curvature but as a smile. So this part is given properties that it would have had if it weren't part of a face.]

Gestalt quality   [According to Christian von Ehrenfels, a gestalt quality is the "property of the whole" that is perceived when a set of elements forms a pattern. The gestalt quality is an extra perceptual element in addition to the elements that are the parts of the pattern. A prime example is a melody. The quality of the melody itself is grounded on the individual parts (notes) that form it, but it is distinct from the parts. This distinctness is shown by the fact that the melody can be transposed to a different key, so that different notes are now creating the same melody.]

Bibliographical Note

I list works here in chronological order.

Brentano, F. (1874/1973). *Psychology from an Empirical Standpoint.* Translated by A. C. Rancurello, D. B. Terrell, and L. L. McAlister. London: Routledge and Kegan Paul.

Ehrenfels, C. von (1890). Über "Gestaltqualitäten." *Vierteljahrschrift für wissenschaftliche Philosophie* 14: 249–292.

Ehrenfels, C. von (1890/1988). On "gestalt qualities." In B. Smith (ed. and trans.), *Foundations of Gestalt Theory,* pp. 82–117. Wien: Philosophia Verlag.

Brentano, F. (1907/1979). *Untersuchungen zur Sinnespsychologie.* Hamburg: Felix Meiner.

Wertheimer, M. (1912). Experimentelle Studien über das Sehen von Bewegung. *Zeitschrift für Psychologie und Physiologie der Sinnesorgane* 61: 161–265.

Wertheimer, M. (1925). *Über Gestalttheorie: Vortrag gehalten in der Kant-Gesellschaft, Berlin, am 17. Dezember 1924.* Erlangen: Philosophischen Akademie.

Köhler, W. (1947). *Gestalt Psychology: An Introduction to New Concepts in Modern Psychology.* New York: Liveright.

Bregman, A. S. (1990). *Auditory Scene Analysis: The Perceptual Organization of Sound.* Cambridge: MIT Press.

Macnamara, J., and Boudewijnse, G.-J. A. (1995). Brentano's influence on Ehrenfels's theory of perceptual gestalts. *Journal for the Theory of Social Behavior* 25, no. 4: 401–418.

27

Extroduction

The earlier chapters offered a variety of perspectives on certain psychological themes: the relation between perception and cognition, Plato's problems of learning and truth, and Augustine's problem of access to ideals. I was not, however, content to outline how an author dealt with one or more of these issues; I attempted to evaluate the success of each particular treatment. My evaluations were guided by my own views. In this concluding chapter I would like to offer a systematic sketch of the position from which I was working and to bring together certain ideas that are scattered through the different chapters. One reason for doing so is to demonstrate, by personal example as it were, the lasting relevance for contemporary psychology of the authors we have reviewed. Gonzalo E. Reyes and I worked together to develop the theory I sketch, his being the lion's share of the work. Later we were joined in close collaboration by Marie La Palme Reyes and Houman Zolfaghari. We had the constant help and encouragement of Michael Makkai, and Bill Lawvere was always a source of inspiration and a beacon of light when the confusion seemed impenetrable.

Perhaps the most fundamental stance psychologists take is on the relations between perception and cognition. Aristotle thought that the theories of the two should be kept distinct, whereas the British empiricists, following Hobbes, ran them together with one another and with the theory of the physiological basis of perception. I believe that Aristotle was right to distinguish perception and cognition, the most obvious reason being this. We can vary the concept we correctly apply in connection with a given percept; we can vary the percept in connection with which a given concept is correctly applied. For example, given the percept of a particular dog, it may be appropriate to apply any of the concepts *poodle, dog, quadruped, mammal, animal, domestic animal, pal, pest,* etc. The single concept *animal* is correctly applied in connection with the perceptual presentation of a dog, a worm, a bird, a fish, a fly, a jellyfish, a lobster, a caterpillar, etc. It follows that perception does not determine cognition, nor cognition perception. This is not to deny, however, that there are important constraints, in both directions, between the two. [An example of such a constraint was given by the gestalt psychologists. The percept 13 does not determine a unique kind to which it belongs; it may be either a number (13) or a capital letter (B). If we find the percept in the array [A 13 C], we are inclined to say that it belongs to the kind LETTER. On the other hand, if we find the percept in the array [11 13 15], we are inclined to say that it belongs to the kind NUMBER.]

It is possible to make the same point more vividly. We cannot help perceiving the shadow cast by a physical object as a perceptual individual, even though we *know* that a shadow is not an object on the same footing as the physical object that casts it. In other words, perception and cognition draw apart, and their distinctness is thus revealed. The same applies to rainbows. These are cases where there is the perceptual impression of an object despite the knowledge that there is no object. There are also perceptual impressions of two objects when we know there is only one, as for example when we cross the two middle fingers of one hand and run a pencil in the cleft between them. Even though we know, and see, that there is only one pencil, we have the tactile impression that there are two. This, as well as the whole array of perceptual illusions, indicates a decoupling of perception and cognition. A more "modern" way to put the same point is to say that perceptual systems are modular. This is not, however, a satisfactory way of describing things, since it suggests that perception and cognition are independent of each other.

Perception and cognition do not determine one another, nor does one reduce to the other. That is, the primitive expressions in the theory of one cannot be defined in terms of the primitives of the other. To grasp this, notice that what gives rise to a visual percept of a dog, say, is part of the surface of its body; what one *knows* on the basis of this perception is the presence of a dog. But a dog is not a dog's surface. Most of a dog consists of invisible interior parts. This much we know, even if we have never seen the interior parts of any dog or even if we have little idea as to what they might be. Similar remarks may be made in connection with the other sensory modalities: dog sounds, dog smells, the feel of a dog, and so forth. A dog is not an assembly of dog percepts, nor is the concept of a dog constructed just from dog percepts. A device giving rise to the normal range of dog percepts but run by an electronic computer would not be a dog.

The import of recognizing that the theories of perception and cognition are distinct is that we are thereby invited to develop the theories of perception and cognition separately, and also to consider the mutual constraints that they exercise on one another. We have found that the mathematical theory of categories is an indispensable tool for working on these two theories, though I should say at once that we have worked more on the cognition end of things and that in keeping with the main interests of this book, I will concentrate here mainly on cognition.

An appeal to mathematics will surprise no one who knows anything of the writings of Plato, Aristotle, Descartes or Leibniz. Aristotle, for instance, created (discovered) logic for the purpose of handling fundamental problems in cognition and metaphysics. A suitable mathematical system is required, not only for making the theory precise but also to unify the different segments of the theory—the perception and cognition segments, for instance. To attempt to handle all this without adequate mathematical tools is like trying to dig a hole with one's bare hands.

A word about category theory in particular. Almost all work on cognition up to the present—in cognitive psychology, cognitive science, philosophy of mind, philosophy of language, the semantics of natural languages—appeals exclusively to set theory for models if it appeals to mathematics at all. There is a growing awareness that this has not paid off. The root problem is that from the point of view of a set, each member is a structureless atom. Now the mind is everywhere occupied with structure. At the perceptual level (for vision alone) there are perceptual figures standing out from a background, each figure with a complex structure of color, luminance, texture, edges, etc. In cognition there are dogs, bicycles, houses, families, schools, etc., again each with a complex internal structure as well as structural relations among them: dogs, bicycles, and houses belong to families, which send their children to schools.

Category theory, which treats Sets (the capital indicates that the category is intended) as just one category, in fact the most impoverished one, makes provision for building as much structure as is required into the mathematical model of psychological objects and operations. This line of thought and work leads me to propose the following relation: calculus is to physics as category theory is to psychology. Calculus is the language of preference to express the theory of physics, and it is the main conceptual tool for exploring the properties of physical objects and systems of such objects. I claim that category theory plays a similar role in psychology (for further detail, see Macnamara, 1994). It is interesting to note that this general standpoint was shared by Jean Piaget, who constantly appealed to mathematics, especially mathematical logic, to express and develop his theories, although the theories he developed and his use of mathematics differ substantially from what I propose. Curiously, towards the end of his life he began to apply category theory in his work, though once again there is a considerable difference between his use of it and mine.

Another reason for relegating Sets to a secondary role is that the logic of Sets is inescapably simplistic, precisely because a set sees its members as atoms. In Set theory every statement is either simply true or false. Human thought, however, is not usually so simple. If asked whether a movie was good, one may want to say "Yes and no," meaning perhaps good in acting and photography but weak in plot. In keeping with this, the negations of natural language—there are two, by the way (*not happy* versus *unhappy*)—are neither of them in general the single negation that is possible in Set theory. Category theory provides means for handling in a precise and satisfactory manner the interpretation of the two distinct natural-language negations (see La Palme Reyes, Macnamara, Reyes and Zolfaghari, 1994). This helps to clarify some basic operations of the human mind, operations, by the way, that were first distinguished and drawn to attention by Aristotle. (Nonmathematical readers interested in an introduction to category theory will find one in Magnan and Reyes, 1994.)

With all this in mind, let us return to a recurrent theme in our reflections: causal interactions are not given directly in experience. This surfaced first in our study of Aristotle, where we saw that to provide for learning about the structure of causally interacting components, he posited an active intellect that can reach beneath perceptual properties. This general position was roundly rejected by the British empiricists. Now, the layman (in biology) has the belief that a dog, say, is an intricate arrangement of causally interacting components. Biologists attempt to understand and spell out what the lay person can only gesture toward. To exclude or make inadequate provision for causality in psychology is to miss the core of the human mind, for the human mind is almost always concerned with the causal structure beneath appearances. This applies as much to the parent who tries to understand the reactions and behaviour of children as to the biological scientist. The main trouble with the Hobbesian and Lockean line in psychology is that it failed to make anything like adequate provision for knowledge of structure—a fact that became abundantly clear in our study of Berkeley and Hume. The root of the trouble was failure to distinguish in the appropriate way between perception and cognition, which in turn entailed failure to give any account of cognition as distinct from perception.

Brentano, following a line first noted by Aristotle, brought out what is distinctive about cognition, namely reference. Reference, however, is so common, so ubiquitous, an event in our mental lives that we cannot but wonder what might make it so special. The first thing to note is that reference occurs only in the context of a sentence, and sentences express truth conditions (or more generally, satisfaction conditions), where the truth conditions for a sentence are, as Ockham put it, what is needed and at the same time suffices for the sentence to be true. I wish not to spend time on truth conditions but to move on to the problem of accounting for the individuation and identity of the thing referred to. To gain the appropriate sense of wonder here, imagine that you are looking at a friend. The perceptual experience could evoke the concept of a friend, a woman, a wife, a mother, a teacher, or what not. [Each of these nouns refers to a kind.] Note that these kinds all handle identity differently. The woman was a woman before she was a wife, a mother, a teacher, or (perhaps) a friend of yours. If in her lifetime she ceases to be a wife or friend or teacher or mother, she will not cease to be a woman. And similarly for each of the kinds mentioned. Yet each kind individuates and traces identity in its own way. For example, it makes sense to ask whether the teacher of little Jane is *the same teacher* as the teacher Tim had last year. If you refer to the person in question as Leslie, something must individuate and handle the identity of what bears the name "Leslie." None of the categories mentioned will do, because Leslie was Leslie before she was a woman, a wife, a mother, a teacher, or a friend. What does the job for the bearer of the name is the kind PERSON.

The moral to draw is that the work of individuation and identity tracing for all the cases we have considered is done by kinds. This suggests the following Fundamental Postulate:

Fundamental Postulate   No reference without a kind to provide for individuation and identity of what is referred to. This means that to have an individual as the object of thought or desire, one must appeal, at least implicitly, to a suitable kind to individuate the object and handle its identity. Now kinds are abstract objects, in the sense that they do not enter the story of causal interactions taking place in space and time. What makes reference so special is the fact that it presupposes appeal to such abstract objects. Abstract objects cannot be perceived, for they give rise to no sights or sounds or any other perceptual signals, but they can be talked about. The ubiquitous appeal to abstract objects is what is special about reference, and hence cognition. [It is interesting to note that the entry in *Webster's Dictionary* for "individuate," namely "to distinguish from others of the same species," agrees with the fundamental postulate, "species" in the dictionary entry corresponding with "kinds" in the fundamental postulate. (See the postscript to this chapter. For an explanation, see the preface.)]

The Fundamental Postulate intimates an answer to the puzzle of universals and individuals that became particularly acute in the chapter on Duns Scotus and Ockham. The postulate says that what handles the problem of individuation is a kind. But then what individuates the kinds, distinguishing one from another, are their members. Kinds and their members mutually determine each other, just as sentences determine the grammatical category and interpretation of their constituent words, while sentences themselves are determined by their constituent words in particular syntactic categories with particular senses.

Following this line of thought, we discover that the question Duns Scotus asked, which he inherited from antiquity, was ill posed. Duns Scotus asked how, starting from a universal, one can have an individual that falls under the universal. This is to take universals (best conceptualized as descriptions of essential structure) as basic, and individuals as derivative. It is a mistake to take universals as primitive in this sense for a reason that can be presented by means of a familiar example. To express the universal for dogs, one would have to appeal to another kind: dogs are *animals* of a particular sort, that is, animals that satisfy certain conditions. This in turn leads to the notion that animals are *living creatures* of a certain sort, that is, that satisfy certain conditions. And so on up the scale until one runs out of kinds altogether and individuation and identity are not provided for or, what is virtually the same, one appeals to a universal kind, say THING. Now we have no grasp of the supposed kind THING. If asked to count the things in a room, should I count as one thing a book, or each word in the book on the grounds that a word is a thing, or the letters, or the corners of the pages, etc.? Since there is no answer, it follows that the word "thing" in the supposed sense fails to individuate. The upshot is that one has run out of manageable kinds, and this at the highest and most comprehensive level. It follows from the Fundamental Postulate that universals cannot be constitutive of kinds in the way in which Duns Scotus thought. Instead, they are logically secondary to kinds: they are descriptions of the individuals in a kind, descriptions that presuppose the individuals they purport to describe.

But what is the relation between all the kinds that may be associated with a particular person: GIRL, WOMAN, WIFE, MOTHER, TEACHER, FRIEND, and so on? If there are guests coming to supper, there may be among them members of all these kinds. The number of places to be laid at table, however, corresponds to the number of persons: one place for one person. This means that for certain purposes we identify a particular wife, woman, mother, teacher, and friend with a particular person. For other purposes we may need to distinguish [them in different ways]. For example, only teachers may be allowed to teach and use the teachers' room; it is not enough to be a person. These operations of identifying and distinguishing are basic operations of the human mind.

The psychological literature almost universally treats the relevant relations among kinds as set-theoretic inclusions. It says, for example, that GIRL and WOMAN are both included in PERSON. This has to be wrong.

Take g in GIRL, and let w in WOMAN be the woman she grows up to be. If the relations in question really were inclusions, g would have to be equal to a certain p in PERSON, and w would have to be equal to the same p. That is, $g = p$ and $w = p$, which inescapably yields that $g = w$. But this cannot be, since a girl is not a woman, nor a woman a girl. The problem disappears if we replace inclusions with maps: u: GIRL $\rightarrow$ PERSON and u': WOMAN $\rightarrow$ PERSON. These maps associate a person with each girl and a person with each woman. Naturally, we require that any situation of which g is a constituent should also have $u(g)$ as a constituent. In other words, the domain of existence of the underlying person should be at least as extensive as that of the associated girl. There is no problem in having $u(g) = u(w)$, because it does not imply that $g = w$.

The same move enables us to handle the somewhat different relation between kinds like PASSENGER and PERSON. If a person travels three times with Air Canada, for purposes of the annual report the company will count three passengers in association with the one person. Each of these passengers is a person, but while there are three passengers, there is only one person. The relation between the two kinds is therefore not an inclusion. With maps in place of inclusions, there is no problem, because several passengers can be mapped onto a single person. We can make a related point dramatically by calling the person Leslie. Each passenger is Leslie [i.e., each passenger has the property of being Leslie], yet while there are three passengers, there is only one Leslie. It follows that we need to distinguish in cognition between "Leslie" in subject position in a sentence and "to be Leslie" in predicate position. The transformations of subjects into predicates and predicates into subjects are fundamental operations of the human mind that Aristotle was fully aware of. They become apparent when, in the manner of Aristotle, one is attentive to intuitions about the rules for interpreting terms in varying grammatical positions. (Those interested in reading more about these ideas will find a nontechnical account in La Palme Reyes, Macnamara, and Reyes, 1994.)

There are other transformations that are equally fundamental. Take the kind CHICKEN. A chicken is an atomic object in the sense that cutting it in two does not yield two chickens, whereas dividing a quantity of water yields two quantities of water. One transformation of CHICKEN yields the plural CHICKENS, where the objects, being groups of chickens, are no longer atoms. A group of chickens can usually be divided into two groups of chickens. This transformation is performed by an operator similar to the power-set operator of Sets, with the difference that it must make provision for domains of existence. Another transformation yields the portion of meat associated with a chicken; yet another yields the portion of food, which may be larger than the portion of meat, since besides the meat there is the chicken content in the soup that can be obtained; and yet another transformation yields the portion of biological matter, which is larger than the food, since it includes the beak and feathers. This time the transformation has the added complication that the size of the portions of meat, food, and matter depend on when the chicken is killed. Chickens usually put on weight as they grow older. These facts must be handled appropriately in the theory, but I will not go into detail beyond saying that it seems unlikely that they can be handled without recourse to category theory.

Everywhere we find an interdependence of the physical objects of cognition on the abstract, and that gives us a clue as to how to handle one of our problems, Plato's problem of truth. Plato wondered how perceptual contact with a fleeting and changeable world should give rise to permanent and unchanging truths. The main part of the answer seems to be that when perceptions are interpreted, the immutable abstract objects enter to freeze things.

We were less interested in the metaphysical question of what makes truth permanent than in the psychological one of how we come to appreciate the permanence of truths that we grasp in connection with impermanent presentations. It seems that all our thinking presupposes that time does not change facts. We are as alive to the unchanging as to the changing. This, in turn, indicates that we somehow appreciate that we interpret the changing against an unchanging background. The unchanging background is supplied by the abstract objects.

The problem of truth is intimately connected with that of learning. Children who are learning the name "Freddie" for a particular dog must specify a kind, the kind DOG, to individuate the bearer of the name "Freddie" and handle his identity. When they learn the word "dog," they must specify the same kind DOG, but now as the reference of "dog." In addition, children must also specify the kind WORD to individuate the words "Freddie" and "dog" as linguistic entities and handle their identity, noting that the one is a proper name, the other a count noun. Otherwise, they would be unable to use them with appropriate syntax. This is not to say that they must know the relevant English words ("word," "proper name," "count noun"), but they should have available to them some symbols that can perform the same functions. Bringing together language and cognition in this way draws attention to the relation between the two. Words are combined into structures that we call sentences, and sentences describe structured relations among structured objects. The mutually inverse operations of interpreting sentences and encoding information about the world must respect the structure of the objects on which they operate. An operator that can do this is precisely what in category theory is known as a functor. Once again, we see the need for category theory if our understanding of cognition is to advance.

Since abstract objects play a crucial role in learning and since they are not perceptible, we see once again that learners must go beyond the purely perceptual. This in turn indicates that learning is not controlled by the environment in anything like the manner supposed either by the British empiricists or by the behaviorists.

What is the explanation of this reaching beyond perception and of the logical resources that are involved in doing so? The reader who has followed attentively this far will have concluded that the explanation has to include unlearned logical resources. The argument for them is perfectly straightforward. Allow with Brentano that all cognitive states and events involve reference, and allow that reference can occur only in an appropriate context. A proper name, for example, refers only in collaboration with a count noun to specify the kind to which the bearer belongs, and proper name and collaborating count noun must be in subject position in a sentence [e.g., "The dog Freddie died in 1991"]. Do not be misled here: a word that features many times as a proper name (e.g., "Nixon" in "Nixon was President of the United States") may also feature as a common noun (e.g., "Don't try to do a Nixon on me") or as an adjective (e.g., "That's a Nixon idea if I ever heard one"). What determines things is the sentence in which the word occurs. Now consider the first word a child learns, and consider the sentence that constitutes its context. The other constituents in the sentence cannot have been learned, since by hypothesis this is the first word learned. It follows that the remaining constituents cannot have been learned and therefore that there are unlearned logical resources.

The argument is readily extended to other representational systems. If in the system there are learned logical resources, consider the first one to have been learned. From here the argument we have just seen can be repeated mutatis mutandis.

The problem of learning, to which Plato points, can only be handled by compensating for the logical indeterminacy of learned responses with psychological preparedness. That is, learners must come to their task well prepared for an appropriate response. Such preparedness may well be guided in part by prior experience and training, but ultimately one must depend on unlearned operations, hypotheses, constraints, especially at the initial stages of learning.

A good theory of learning specifies the unlearned resources that are necessary for a particular domain. We have seen that there have to be some. When one has specified all that is necessary for learning a particular item, one can choose the unlearned elements by means of two criteria. (a) The item to be learned is not associated with a distinctive perceptual characteristic. For example, there is something perceptually distinctive about dogs—difficult though it may be to specify what that is—so that one can learn that there is the kind DOG. There being nothing perceptually distinctive about proper names, one cannot learn the existence of the kind PROPER NAME on the basis of perceptually distinctive features. (b) The item to be learned is primitive in our conceptual lives, or one has reason to believe that it is. This means that the item cannot be defined, and so the second avenue to learning is closed. The two criteria, jointly applied, indicate those elements that are unlearned. For example, if you agree that morally good actions are not perceptually distinct from actions that are not morally good and that moral goodness cannot be defined, you will probably agree that there is important unlearned content in the concept of moral goodness. This is not to deny, of course, that there are also environmentally inspired elements in this concept (see Macnamara, 1991).

What about access to ideals, which I specified as Augustine's problem? Since an ideal is a limit that some series tends to but never in our experience reaches, it follows that a grasp of ideals cannot be attributed to experience. This means that the ability to posit ideals must be a capacity that the human mind brings to experience rather than one that it derives from experience. The ideals in question include ideals of measurement, of the straightness of lines and the smoothness of surfaces, of personal charm and personal beauty, of justice, of knowledge, of goodness of action, and so forth. Augustine himself attributed ability to grasp such ideals to divine illumination operating within the mind. Aquinas took it to be part of natural endowment, and of course he must be right, but it is not easy to situate the ability in a general theory of cognition.

We saw that Kant attempted to make a radical division of labor, assigning ideals to some discipline other than psychology and assigning to psychology the "facts" about the operation of the human mind. For example, he assigned to logicians/philosophers the ideals of errorless interpretation and reasoning; to psychologists he assigned the "facts" of how people interpret and reason. We saw, however, that the distinction is unsustainable. Either it is a fact that we have access to logical ideals or it is not. If it is a fact, the ideals are also the concern of psychologists; if it is not a fact, we should forget all about them, for they are an illusion. On the assumption that we do have access to ideals, it follows that psychologists should be on the track of a single theory to handle both logical ideals and sometimes logically erroneous performance.

The division is responsible for much mischief in psychology. Its detrimental effects are to be seen not only in the psychology of reasoning but also in the psychology of decision theory and the psychology of mental health, which, as we noted in the chapter on Freud, usually ignores ethical ideals.

It seems to me that it was Hobbes's decision to do psychology in the model of something that is not psychology, namely kinematics, that started the trend of neglecting the mind's access to ideals. Hobbes was followed in this by those who modeled psychology on mechanics, chemistry, thermodynamics, telephone exchanges, biology, and computers. The result is the discounting of an essential property or set of properties of the human mind, with a consequent distortion of psychological theory. An influential voice raised against this whole way of doing things is that of Noam Chomsky, who in the area of linguistics insists that linguists and psychologists alike should combine in the effort to account for linguistic competence, that is, errorless ideal knowledge of grammar. In this work I follow his lead. Indeed, he advocated that his basic ideas should be applied in areas other than psycholinguistics. Evidence of an attempt to deal with the relevant ideals is a test of the seriousness of any psychological theory proposed for our consideration.

Colin McLarty's definitions of category and functor will be helpful (McLarty, 1992):

Category [A category has *objects A, B, C, . . .* and *arrows f, g, h, ...* Each arrow goes from an object to an object. To say that g goes from A to B, we write *g: A → B,* or say that A is the *domain* of g, and B the *codomain.* We may write $\text{Dom}(g) = A$ and $\text{Cod}(g) = B$. Two arrows f and g with $\text{Dom}(f) = \text{Cod}(g)$ are called *composable.* If f and g are composable, then they must have a *composite,* an arrow called *f ∘ g.* Every object A has an *identity arrow,* 1_A. The axions read as follows. For every composable pair f and g, the composite *f ∘ g* goes from the domain of g to the codomain of f. For each object A, the identify arrow 1_A goes from A to A. Composing any arrow with an identity arrow (if the two are composable) gives the original arrow. And composition is associative.]

Functor [A *functor* F from a category **A** to a category **B**, written **F: A → B**, assigns to each object A of **A** an object **F** A of **B**, and to each arrow f of **A** an arrow F*f* of **B**, meeting the following conditions. (1) It preserves domains and codomains: given $f: A → B$ of **A**, we have F*f*: FA → FB. (2) It preserves identities: for any A of **A**, $\text{F}(1_A) = 1_{FA}$. (3) It preserves composition: if f and g are composable in **A**, then $\text{F}(g \circ f) = \text{F}g \circ \text{F}f$, where the second composite is formed in **B**.]

Postscript

Is there, then, no reference in perception? In this connection, recall Berkeley's idea that visual perception should be conceptualized as a language. If we go along with this, as I am tempted to, the question of reference becomes pressing. But why go along with it? While this is not the place for a full treatment of the idea, I will indicate one line of motivation, connected with intentionality. We saw that perceptual experiences can be as intentional as cognitive ones. We have as little chance of discerning the forms of perceptual representations by introspection as of discerning those of cognitive representations. The reason is that in perception what are presented are perceptual objects and their perceptual properties; just as in cognition what are presented are objects and their properties. Brentano explains the intentionality of cognitive states and events by appealing to reference, reference being the property that establishes the "aboutness" of such states and events. Since this is the only explanation of intentionality that seems remotely plausible, it is tempting to employ it also in the explanation of perceptual intentionality. This is to conceptualize visual representations as sentences in a language of vision, but now as interpreted sentences, sentences whose terms are interpreted into perceptual objects and their perceptual properties and relations. For the record, this seems to have been Brentano's own move, for he came to treat both perception and cognition as mental, as involving reference to something as an object. This does not mean, however, running the two together in the manner of the radical empiricists, because, as we have seen, perceptual objects and their perceptual properties are not the objects and properties of cognition. Yet it does mean that the Fundamental Postulate applies also in the domain of perception, and that abstract objects (different ones) play a role in perception similar to the role they play in cognition. That will have to suffice for the purposes of this chapter.

Bibliographical Note

La Palme Reyes, M., Macnamara, J., and Reyes, G. E. (1994). Grammatical role and functoriality in syllogisms. *Notre Dame Journal of Formal Logic* 35: 41–66.

La Palme Reyes, M., Macnamara, J., Reyes, G. E., and Zolfaghari, H. (1994). The non-Boolean logic of natural-language negations. *Philosophia Mathematica* 3: 45–68.

Macnamara, J. (1991). The development of moral reasoning and the foundations of geometry. *Journal for the Theory of Social Behavior* 21: 125–150.

Macnamara, J. (1994). Logic and cognition. In J. Macnamara, and G. E. Reyes (eds.), *The Logical Foundations of Cognition*, pp. 11–34. Oxford: Oxford University Press.

Magnan, F., and Reyes, G. E. (1994). Category theory as a conceptual tool in the study of cognition. In J. Macnamara and G. E. Reyes (eds.), *The Logical Foundations of Cognition*, pp. 57–90. Oxford: Oxford University Press.

Notes

Chapter 3

1. ["Contradiction" is here used in the Hegelian sense, not in the logical sense, of the word. To understand the difference, consider arithmetic. When we say that there is no contradiction in arithmetic, we mean that it cannot be that both a sentence and its contradiction are theorems. This is the logical sense. On the other hand, according to Lawvere, the main contradiction of arithmetic is the law of distributivity, $a(b + c) = ab + ac$, which transforms a product into a sum and is the motor of further and deeper developments, for instance the introduction and development of categories of spaces. This is the Hegelian sense.]

Chapter 6

1. [Chapters 6 and 7 are not exegesis in the strict sense. The Bible has been read in the Christian tradition, and this is what Macnamara does. He is studying Genesis and John's Gospel in the light of the whole tradition. Technically, this is what scholars call *Wirkungsgeschichte*. The ideas about the image of God in Genesis have had a long history. Augustine developed them. For him, the principal image of the Trinity was the human mind: memory, intellect, and will. He also developed, however, a social analogy: lover, beloved, and love (book VIII of *De Trinitate* in Augustine, 1872). The social image was especially important for Richard of St. Victor in his *De Trinitate*, book III (1979). One can read about this in William Hill, *The Three-Personed God* (1982). I wrote an article entitled "The Trinity as divine community" in 1988.

The part about naming the animals, below, is stretching it a bit. The main point exegetically seems to be that God gives Adam stewardship over the creation. Still, the type of reflection found in the present book has some basis if one takes Genesis in the light of the whole tradition. It does seem that the Bible's belief in the creator grounds faith in the orderedness of the world.

One of the critical remarks in reviews of the manuscript was that Macnamara was trying to harmonize his faith in the Bible with his beliefs about human nature.

This seems to me a valid point. It is also quite classical: faith seeking understanding. So in summary, chapters 6 and 7 present for the most part a valid point of view, but they are reading the Bible spiritually, *lectio divina,* in the light of the whole tradition, not just as a scientific exegetical study.—John M. O'Donnell, S.J.]

Chapter 10

1. [We think that what Macnamara wanted to say was that a theory can describe (i.e., define) its own syntax if it contains arithmetic (technically, primitive recursive arithmetic suffices). Of course, the syntax is defined in the language of the theory, whence his rather clumsy statement. Furthermore, the author somewhat obscures the issue by bringing in semantics and talking of "a system that the language describes," when Gödel's theorem is purely "syntactical." Another factual error of the author is to confound, in one statement, two theorems. The negative statement about the nondefinability of semantical notions (in particular, "truth") is a famous theorem of Alfred Tarski and should be credited to him. In the light of this clarification, the second statement of Macnamara's could be formulated as follows: "The semantics of the theory of the brain cannot be defined in the language of that theory." This formulation requires that the theory of the brain, whatever that is, should be axiomatizable.]

Glossary

Abstract object An abstract object is an immutable object, an object that is neither causally active nor affected by the causal activity of other things. Examples are numbers, computational rules, proofs, plans, and so forth.

Accident Accidents are (mostly) variable attributes of substances. For example, a dog may be sitting at one time and not at another. So, to be sitting is an accident. Accidents do not exist on their own; they are individualized by the substances to which they belong. An accident is typically described by a predicable (a verb or adjective).

Action An action is an event that has a true explanation in the agent's beliefs and desires. Actions are individuated by the beliefs and desires that inspire them.

Active intellect Although this term does not occur in Aristotle, it is traditionally used in expositions of Aristotle's psychology. The active intellect is the intellect in its function of accepting perceptual information (describing accidents) as input and discovering substantial form beneath the accidents. The output of the active intellect is a mental representation of the substantial form, without the matter. Since this representation is true of all the members of the relevant species, it is a *universal.*

A posteriori A concept or a belief is said to be known a posteriori if it is derived from experience, rather than brought to experience. "A posteriori" and "a priori" are contrasting and complementary notions.

A priori A concept or a belief is said to be known a priori if it is brought to experience by the mind, rather than derived from experience.

Aristotle's problem [How can we gain knowledge of a substantial form when all we have direct access to is accidental, perceptual properties?]

Association The associations that particularly interest psychologists are mental associations. These are thought of as relations among mental objects where the evocation of one tends to evoke the other with which it is associated. For example, the occurrence of a mental representation of the word *boy* may evoke a mental representation of the word *girl,* or the mental representation of a person's name may lead one to imagine the person. It is important to appreciate that only mental objects are related by mental associations. There cannot be a mental association between a person and the person's name, for instance, neither being a mental object.

Augustine's problem   Since ideals are not fully realized in the objects or actions that one experiences, how can we explain the mind's access to them?

Behavior   Behavior is "the publicly observable activity of muscles or glands of external secretion as manifested in movement of parts of the body or in the appearance of tears, sweat, saliva and so forth" (Hebb, 1958, 2).

Category   [A category has *objects A, B, C, . . .* and *arrows f, g, h, ...* Each arrow goes from an object to an object. To say that g goes from A to B, we write $g: A \rightarrow B$, or say that A is the *domain* of g, and B the *codomain*. We may write $\text{Dom}(g) = A$ and $\text{Cod}(g) = B$. Two arrows f and g with $\text{Dom}(f) = \text{Cod}(g)$ are called *composable*. If f and g are composable, then they must have a *composite*, an arrow called $f \circ g$. Every object A has an *identity arrow*, 1_A. The axioms read as follows. For every composable pair f and g, the composite $f \circ g$ goes from the domain of g to the codomain of f. For each object A, the identity arrow 1_A goes from A to A. Composing any arrow with an identity arrow (if the two are composable) gives the original arrow. And composition is associative.]

Concept   A concept is a mental representation of structural relations in isolation from any perceptual properties that may be associated with them. When the structure to be represented is a substantial form, the related concept is an *intelligible outline*, which we construed as a blueprint.

Essence   The most basic meaning of "essence" is substance, which is, according to Aristotle, substantial form individuated by matter. But "essence" denotes substance in opposition to existence, whereas "substance" denotes the same thing in opposition to accidents. Essence limits existence and makes it one sort rather than another. Because "essence" denotes substance, it developed a secondary meaning: what is indispensable or, as we say, essential.

Functor   [A *functor* F from a category **A** to a category **B**, written $F: \mathbf{A} \rightarrow \mathbf{B}$, assigns to each object A of **A** an object FA of **B**, and to each arrow f of **A** an arrow Ff of **B**, meeting the following conditions. (1) It preserves domains and codomains: given $f: A \rightarrow B$ of **A**, we have $Ff: FA \rightarrow FB$. (2) It preserves identities: for any A of **A**, $F(1_A) = 1_{FA}$. (3) It preserves composition: if f and g are composable in **A**, then $F(g \circ f) = Fg \circ Ff$, where the second composite is formed in **B**.]

Fundamental Postulate   No reference without a kind to provide for individuation and identity of what is referred to. This means that to have an individual as the object of thought or desire, one must appeal, at least implicitly, to a suitable kind to individuate the object and handle its identity. Now kinds are abstract objects, in the sense that they do not enter the story of causal interactions taking place in space and time. What makes reference so special is the fact that it presupposes appeal to such abstract objects. Abstract objects cannot be perceived, for they give rise to no sights or sounds or any other perceptual signals, but they can be talked about. The ubiquitous appeal to abstract objects is what is special about reference, and hence cognition.

Gestalt   [The Berlin school of gestalt psychology, which included Wertheimer, Köhler, and others, did not use von Ehrenfels's expression "gestalt quality" (see below). They did not think of a gestalt as merely a separate quality of the stimulus but used the word to describe the "wholeness" of the stimulus pattern. While the whole was made out of parts, it was more than a structure built out of those parts. In addition to having properties that the parts taken individually did not have, it also gave roles and meanings to the individual parts. For example, when a series of wiggles drawn on paper are seen as a cartoon of a face, the curvature of a line is seen not as a mere curvature but as a smile. So this part is given properties that it would not have had if it weren't part of a face.]

Gestalt quality   [According to Christian von Ehrenfels, a gestalt quality is the "property of the whole" that is perceived when a set of elements forms a pattern. The gestalt quality is an extra perceptual element in addition to the elements that are the parts of the pattern. A prime example is a melody. The quality of the melody itself is grounded on the individual parts (notes) that form it, but it is distinct from the parts. This distinctness is shown by the fact that the melody can be transposed to a different key, so that different notes are now creating the same melody.]

Idea   In the period from the Renaissance to the present time, "idea" is generally taken as denoting mental representation. Many of the writers we study, including Descartes, take an idea to be the immediate object of awareness. Our awareness of other things is mediated by ideas. This is what I call "getting the intentionality wrong."

Ideas of reflection   Ideas of reflection are representations of the internal operations of the mind, such as thinking, desiring, wondering, and the like. Ideas of reflection are contrasted with *ideas of sensation,* that is, mental representations of external objects.

Intentionality   Etymologically, the word "intentionality" means to strain toward. It was frequently employed in the Middle Ages to register the fact that in perception and cognition we are not aware of internal representations of the objects perceived or thought about; we are aware of those objects themselves. The metaphor is meant to suggest that the mind ignores mental representations of objects and "strains toward" the objects themselves.

Introspection   Introspection is the supposed activity of attending to one's own mental states and operations with a view to learning (1) the form of a representation or the internal structure of an operation, (2) the causal origins in the mind of a mental state or operation, or (3) the content of a mental state or the object of a mental operation.

Kind   [A kind is a way of referring to, or grouping, individuals that allows one to individuate the members of the kind (distinguish them as individuals), to trace their identity over changes, and in principle to count them. Prototypical examples are the so-called *natural* kinds, such as DOG, ANIMAL, and in general the things referred to by count nouns. Kinds allow us to interpret expressions such as "two . . . ," "some, but not every . . . ," "this is the same . . . as that," etc. What I call the Fundamental Postulate says that there is no reference without the support of a kind. To understand this, assume that I point to a mannequin in a shop window and say, "I like that." What do I mean? Without further clues you cannot know whether I am referring to the mannequin itself, its clothes, the way that it has been placed in the window, etc. However, if I say I like that MANNEQUIN, or I like those CLOTHES, then I am able to convey my meaning by first getting the reference right (these two words refer to kinds).]

Learning   Learning, as most behaviorists saw it, is any change in behavior that is due to antecedent behavior or to environmental factors, especially if those factors include reward or punishment.

Matter   Matter in the Aristotelean view is itself a structureless constituent of a physical substance but is capable of being structured by a substantial form. Being formless, matter in itself is unintelligible. Matter is the principle of individuation. Matter accounts for the possibility of there being many individuals in a single species. Substantial form is a principle of sameness across the members of a species; matter is a principle of difference, of individuation.

Nature   "Nature" means the same as "substance," but nature is viewed as the source of activity. To keep things straight, I should note the following: "Nature" means substance as the source of activity. "Essence" refers to substance as opposed to existence. "Substance" itself is used in opposition to accidents.

Nominal essence   Nominal essence for Locke is an abstract idea of a kind. It is abstracted from perceptual experiences and represents just those properties of the experiences that were distinctive of members of the kind. Nominal essences are opposed to *real essences,* which, for Locke, are unknown.

Passive intellect   The passive intellect is the intellect in its function of grasping and understanding mental representations of substantial forms. It is a mistake to think of the active and passive intellects as two distinct intellects; rather, they are distinct functions of a single intellect.

Platonic ideas   Plato proposed that some abstract objects serve as the perfect prototypes of the objects we experience in perception. Knowledge, as opposed to mere opinion, is of these ideas, and they account for the immutability of truth. All abstract objects can be taken as corresponding to Platonic ideas. Platonic ideas must be distinguished from the ideas we have in our minds.

Plato's problem of learning   [A man cannot try to discover either what he knows or what he does not know. He would not seek what he knows, for since he knows it, there is no need of the inquiry, nor what he does not know, for in that case he does not even know what he is looking for.]

Plato's problem of truth   [How from changeable objects can one grasp unchanging truths about their nature?]

Primary and secondary qualities   "Qualities" in this context means perceptual properties. Qualities are said to be primary if they resemble the ideas to which they give rise; otherwise they are said to be secondary.

Radical empiricist A radical empiricist is a person who runs together perception and cognition, and claims that concepts consist of distinctive features abstracted from the perceptual array.

Rationalist A rationalist is a person who, making a principled distinction between perception and cognition, claims that concepts represent structure that is not given immediately in the perceptual array. Rationalists also believe in unlearned concepts and unlearned operating principles as a basis for all human thought.

Sense that is common In the Aristotelean view, sense that is common is an inner perceptual system. It deals not with information coming directly from the environment but with the outputs of the external perceptual systems. It has two special functions: (a) to coordinate the information coming from different external perceptual systems, (b) to register which external system is the source of some item of information.

Substance A substance is an individual, such as a dog, a person, or a rock. *Substance* emphasizes what remains constant throughout the existence of the individual. The most immediate answer to the question about "what is an individual?" is the substantive (or common noun) that has a special relation to the individual's substance.

Substantial form A substantial form is the basic structure or organization in a substance. It determines the substance to be of some particular type: a dog, a person, or a stone. It is the basic source of intelligibility in a substance. Accidents are secondary determinations of a substance.

Universal A universal is a representation that is true of many individuals. For Thomas Aquinas, universals are always mental representations.

References

Aquinas, T. (ca. 1252/1949). *On Being and Essence.* Translated by Armand Maurer. Toronto: Pontifical Institute of Mediaeval Studies. A translation of *De ente et essentia.*

Aquinas, T. (1265–73/1964–). *Summa Theologiae: Latin Text and English Translation.* New York: McGraw-Hill.

Aquinas, T. (1269/1984). *Questions on the Soul.* Translated by James H. Robb. Milwaukee, Wis.: Marquette University Press. A translation of *Quaestiones disputatae de anima.*

Aquinas, T. (1951). *The Soul: A Translation of St. Thomas Aquinas' De Anima.* St. Louis: B. Herder Book Co.

Aristotle (1941). *Basic Works of Aristotle.* Edited by R. McKeon. New York: Random House.

Augustine (ca. 397/1961). *Confessions.* Translated by R. S. Pine-Coffin. London: Cox and Wyman.

Augustine (1872). *The Works of Aurelius Augustine, Bishop of Hippo: A New Translation.* Edinburgh: T. and T. Clark.

Berkeley, G. (1709–13/1965). *Berkeley's Philosophical Writings.* Edited by D. M. Armstrong. New York: Collier-Macmillan.

Berkeley, G. (1734/1901). *The Analyst, or A Discourse Addressed to an Infidel Mathematician.* In *The Works of George Berkeley,* vol. 3, *Philosophical Works, 1734–52,* edited by Alexander Campbell Fraser. Oxford: Clarendon Press.

Boring, E. G. (1929). *A History of Experimental Psychology.* New York: Appleton-Century-Crofts.

Bregman, A. S. (1990). *Auditory Scene Analysis: The Perceptual Organization of Sound.* Cambridge: MIT Press.

Brenon, A. (1991). *Le vrai visage du Catharisme.* Editions Loubatières.

Brentano, F. (1874/1973). *Psychology from an Empirical Standpoint.* Translated by A. C. Rancurello, D. B. Terrell, and L. L. McAlister. London: Routledge and Kegan Paul.

Brentano, F. (1907/1979). *Untersuchungen zur Sinnespsychologie.* Hamburg: Felix Meiner.

Brentano, F. (1977). *Die Abkehr vom Nichtrealen.* Edited by F. Mayer-Hillebrand. Hamburg: Felix Meiner.

Brentano, F. (1982). *Deskriptive Psychologie* (Descriptive Psychology). Edited by R. M. Chisholm and W. Baumgartner. Hamburg: Felix Meiner.

Chomsky, N. (1957). *Syntactic Structures.* The Hague: Mouton.

Chomsky, N. (1959). Review of *Verbal Behavior* by B. F. Skinner. *Language* 35: 26–58. Reprinted in J. A. Fodor and J. J. Katz (eds.), *The Structure of Language: Readings in the Philosophy of Language,* pp. 547–578. Englewood Cliffs, N.J.: Prentice-Hall, 1964.

Chomsky, N. (1966). *Cartesian Linguistics: A Chapter in the History of Rationalist Thought.* New York: Harper and Row.

Darwin, C. (1859/1993). *The Origin of Species by Means of Natural Selection, or The Preservation of Favoured Races in the Struggle for Life.* New York: Random House.

Darwin, C. (1871/1989). *The Descent of Man and Selection in Relation to Sex.* New York: New York University Press.

Descartes, R. (1968). *The Philosophical Works of Descartes.* Vols. 1 and 2. Translated by E. S. Haldane and G. R. T. Ross. Cambridge: Cambridge University Press.

Duns Scotus, John (1964). *Philosophical Writings.* Translated by Allan Wolter. Indianapolis: Bobbs-Merrill.

Ehrenfels, C. von (1890). Über "Gestaltqualitäten." *Vierteljahrschrift für wissenschaftliche Philosophie* 14: 249–292.

Ehrenfels, C. von (1890/1988). On "gestalt qualities." In B. Smith (ed. and trans.), *Foundations of Gestalt Theory,* pp. 82–117. Wien: Philosophia Verlag.

Einstein, Albert (1956). *Lettres à Maurice Solovine.* Paris: Gauthier-Villars.

Fodor, J. A. (1975). *The Language of Thought.* New York: Thomas Y. Crowell.

Frege, G. (1884/1950). *Foundations of Arithmetic: A Logico-mathematical Enquiry into the Concept of Number.* Translated by J. L. Austin. Oxford: Basil Blackwell.

Freud, S. (1923/1927). *The Ego and the Id.* Translated by J. Riviere. London: Hogarth Press.

Freud, S. (1933). *New Introductory Lectures on Psychoanalysis.* Edited by E. Jones and translated by W. J. H. Sprott. London: Hogarth Press.

Freud, S. (1946). *Autobiographical Study.* Translated by J. Strachey. London: Hogarth Press.

Freud, S. (1948). *The Psychopathology of Everyday Life.* Translated by A. A. Brill. London: Ernest Benn.

Freud, S. (1963). *Psychoanalysis and Faith: Dialogues with the Reverend Oskar Pfister*. Translated by E. Mosbacher. New York: Basic Books.

Goodman, N., and Quine, W. V. (1947). Steps toward a constructive nominalism. *Journal of Symbolic Logic* 12: 105–122. Reprinted in N. Goodman (1972), *Problems and Projects*, pp. 173–198.

Grünbaum, A. (1993). *Validation in the Clinical Theory of Psychoanalysis*. Madison, Conn.: International Universities Press.

Hebb, D. O. (1949). *The Organization of Behavior: A Neuropsychological Theory*. New York: John Wiley.

Hebb, D. O. (1958). *A Textbook of Psychology: A Neuropsychological Theory*. New York: John Wiley.

Hill, William J. (1982). *The Three-Personed God: The Trinity as a Mystery of Salvation*. Washington, D.C.: Catholic University of America Press.

Hobbes, T. (1651/1962). *Leviathan, or The Matter, Forme, and Power of a Commonwealth Ecclesiasticall and Civil*. Edited by M. Oakeshott. New York: Collier.

Hume, David (1738–40/1967). *A Treatise of Human Nature*. Edited by L. A. Selby-Bigge. Oxford: Clarendon Press.

Hume, David (1748/1962). *Enquiries concerning Human Understanding and concerning the Principles of Morals*. Edited by L. A. Selby-Bigge. Oxford: Clarendon Press.

Husserl, E. (1900). *Logical Investigations*. Vols. 1 and 2. Translated by J. N. Findlay. London: Routledge and Kegan Paul.

Jackendoff, R. S. (1992). *Languages of the Mind: Essays on Mental Representation*. Cambridge: MIT Press.

Jahoda, G. (1993). *Crossroads between Culture and Mind: Continuities and Change in Theories of Human Nature*. Cambridge: Harvard University Press.

Jefferson, T. (1943). *The Complete Jefferson, Containing His Major Writings, Published and Unpublished, except His Letters*. New York: distributed by Duell, Sloan, and Pearce.

Kant, Immanuel (1781/1929). *Critique of Pure Reason*. Translated by N. Kemp Smith. London: Macmillan.

Kant, Immanuel (1800/1974). *Logic*. Edited by G. B. Jäsche and translated by R. Hartman and W. Schwarz. New York: Bobbs-Merrill.

Köhler, W. (1947). *Gestalt Psychology: An Introduction to New Concepts in Modern Psychology*. New York: Liveright.

La Palme Reyes, M., Macnamara, J., and Reyes, G. E. (1994). Grammatical role and functoriality in syllogisms. *Notre Dame Journal of Formal Logic* 35: 41–66.

La Palme Reyes, M., Macnamara, J., Reyes, G. E., and Zolfaghari, H. (1994). The non-Boolean logic of natural-language negations. *Philosophia Mathematica* 3: 45–68.

Leibniz, G. W. (1765/1981). *New Essays on Human Understanding.* Translated and edited by P. Remnant and J. Bennett. Cambridge: Cambridge University Press.

Locke, J. (1690/1894). *An Essay concerning Human Understanding.* Edited by A. C. Fraser. New York: Dover.

Lyons, W. (1986). *The Disappearance of Introspection.* Cambridge: MIT Press.

Macnamara, J. (1991). The development of moral reasoning and the foundations of geometry. *Journal for the Theory of Social Behavior* 21: 125–150.

Macnamara, J. (1994). Logic and cognition. In J. Macnamara, and G. E. Reyes (eds.), *The Logical Foundations of Cognition,* pp. 11–34. Oxford: Oxford University Press.

Macnamara, J., and Boudewijnse, G.-J. A. (1995). Brentano's influence on Ehrenfels's theory of perceptual gestalts. *Journal for the Theory of Social Behavior* 25, no. 4: 401–418.

Magnan, F., and Reyes, G. E. (1994). Category theory as a conceptual tool in the study of cognition. In J. Macnamara and G. E. Reyes (eds.), *The Logical Foundations of Cognition,* pp. 57–90. Oxford: Oxford University Press.

Maier, A. (1982). *On the Threshold of Exact Science: Selected Writings of Anneliese Maier on Late Medieval Natural Philosophy.* Philadelphia: University of Pennsylvania Press.

Mates, B. (1986). *The Philosophy of Leibniz: Metaphysics and Language.* Oxford: Oxford University Press.

McLarty, C. (1992). *Elementary Categories, Elementary Toposes.* Oxford: Clarendon Press.

Mendelson, M. J., and Marshall, M. (1976). The relation between nonnutritive sucking and visual information processing in the human newborn. *Child Development* 46: 1025–1029.

Michotte, A. (1946/1963). *The Perception of Causality.* Translated by T. R. Miles. New York: Basic Books.

Mill, J. S. (1843). *System of Logic.* London: Longman's.

Mill, J. S. (1865). *An Examination of Sir William Hamilton's Philosophy and of the Principal Philosophical Questions Discussed in His Writings.* Boston: W. V. Spencer.

Mill, J. S. (1924/1944). *Autobiography of John Stuart Mill.* New York: Columbia University Press.

Morgan, M. J. (1977). *Molyneux's Question.* Cambridge: Cambridge University Press.

Murray, D. J. (1988). *A History of Western Psychology.* Englewood Cliffs, N.J.: Prentice-Hall.

O'Daly, G. (1987). *Augustine's Philosophy of Mind.* Berkeley: University of California Press.

O'Donnell, J. (1988). The Trinity as divine community. *Gregorianum* 69, no. 1: 5–34.

O'Donnell, J. M. (1985). *The Origins of Behaviorism: American Psychology, 1870–1920.* New York: New York University Press.

Ockham, W. of (ca. 1349/1974–80). *Summa logicae.* Part 1, translated by M. J. Loux. Part 2, translated by A. J. Freddoso and H. Schuurman. Notre Dame: University of Notre Dame Press.

Ockham, W. of (1957). *Philosophical Writings.* Edited and translated by P. Boehner. London: Nelson.

Plato (1961). *The Collected Dialogues of Plato.* Edited by E. Hamilton and H. Cairns. Princeton: Princeton University Press.

Popper, K. R. (1968). *The Logic of Scientific Discovery.* 2nd ed. New York: Basic Books.

Popper, K. R. (1983). *Realism and the Aim of Science.* Totowa N.J.: Rowmann and Littlefield.

Quine, W. V. (1960). *Word and Object.* Cambridge: Technology Press of the Massachusetts Institute of Technology.

Reid, Thomas (1764/1817). *An Inquiry into the Human Mind on the Principles of Common Sense.* Glasgow: W. Folcener.

Richard of St. Victor (1979). *The Twelve Patriarchs; The Mystical Ark; Book Three of The Trinity.* New York: Paulist Press.

Roazen, P. (1993). *Meeting Freud's Family.* Amherst: University of Massachusetts Press.

Sarna, N. M. (1970). *Understanding Genesis: The Heritage of Biblical Israel.* New York: Schocken.

Shipley, T. (1961). *Classics in Psychology.* New York: Philosophical Library. Contains a translation of the Introduction to Wundt (1862).

Skinner, B. F. (1957). *Verbal Behavior.* New York: Appleton-Century-Crofts.

Sober, E. (1984). *The Nature of Selection: Evolutionary Theory in Philosophical Focus.* Cambridge: MIT Press.

Titchener, E. B. (1898). The postulates of a structural psychology. *Psychological Review* 8: 449–465.

Watson, J. B. (1913). Psychology as the behaviorist views it. *Psychological Review* 20: 158–177.

Watson, J. D. (1968). *The Double Helix: A Personal Account of the Discovery of the Structure of DNA.* New York: Atheneum.

Weimer, W. B. (1973). Psycholinguistics and Plato's paradoxes of the *Meno*. *American Psychologist* 28: 15–33.

Wertheimer, M. (1912). Experimentelle Studien über das Sehen von Bewegung. *Zeitschrift für Psychologie und Physiologie der Sinnesorgane* 61: 161–265.

Wertheimer, M. (1925). *Über Gestalttheorie: Vortrag gehalten in der Kant-Gesellschaft, Berlin, am 17. Dezember 1924.* Erlangen: Philosophischen Akademie.

Wills, Gary (1978). *Inventing America.* New York: Doubleday.

Wittgenstein, L. (1963). *Philosophical Investigations.* Oxford: Basil Blackwell.

Wundt, W. (1862). *Beiträge zu Theorie des Sinneswahrnehmung.* Leipzig: Winter.

Wundt, W. (1888). Selbstbeobachtung und innere Wahrnehmung (Introspection and inner perception). *Philosophische Studien* 4: 292–309.

Wundt, W. (1889). Über die Einteilung der Wissenschaften (On the division of the sciences). *Philosophische Studien* 5: 1–55.

Wundt, W. (1893–1895). *Logik: eine Untersuchung der Principien der Erkenntniss und der Methoden wissenshaftlicher Forchung.* Stuttgart: F. Enke.

Wundt, W. (1904–1923). *Völkerpsychologie: eine Untersuchung der Entwicklungsgesetze von Sprache, Mythus und Sitte.* 10 vols. Leipzig: W. Engelmann.

Wundt, W. (1907). Über Ausfrageexperimente und über die Methoden zur Psychologie des Denkens (On interrogations in experiments and on methods for [studying] the psychology of thought). *Psychologische Studien* 3: 301–360.

Wundt, W. (1913/1916). *Elements of a Psychological History of the Development of Mankind.* Translated by Edward Leroy Schaub. New York: Macmillan Co.

Wundt, W. (1921). *Probleme der Völkerpsychologie.* Stuttgart: Alfred Körner.

Index

Abstraction, critique of Mill's account of, 186
Abstract objects
defined, 23, 94 (*see also the Glossary*)
Hobbes dispensed with, 112
kinds as, 258
role of, in learning, 262
Accident, 31, 36
defined, 33 (*see also the Glossary*)
Action
vs. behavior, 241
defined, 242
Active intellect, 31–32
absence of, in Hobbes's theory of mind, 106
Aristotle on, 68
defined, 34 (*see also the Glossary*)
not needed by Berkeley, 149
Albigensianism, 46
Altruism, 173
American Sign Language, 40
A posteriori, defined, 165. *See also the Glossary*
A priori, defined, 165. *See also the Glossary*
Aquinas, Thomas, 6
and Aristotle, 74, 82
on being and essence, 80
biographical note on, 73
on concepts, 147
on divine illumination, 78
on existence as energy, 81
on intelligible outlines, 147
on intentionality, 79
on passive intellect, 88–89
rejected substance dualism, 85
relation of, to Aristotle, 82
on role of perception, 82
on the soul, 86–87
on *species intelligibilis*, 80, 147
Aristotle
on active intellect, 68
and Aquinas, 74, 82
biographical note on, 25
on central problem of cognition, 30
on common perceptual system, 38, 40, 43
on criterion of cognition, 27
on kinds, 197
Physics of, 1–3
psychology of, 1–3
on sense that is common, 38, 40, 43 (*see also the Glossary*)
on substantial forms, 30, 31
Aristotle's problem, 68
Association, defined, 201. *See also the Glossary*
Association of ideas vs. reasoning, 196
Augustine
biographical note on, 63
compared with Descartes, 70–71

Augustine (cont.)
  on divine illumination as source of
    immutable truths, 68, 69
  on dualism, 69–70
  on innate knowledge of contradic-
    tion, 67
  on knowledge vs. wisdom, 66
  on mind as noncorporeal, 69
  on perception, 65
Augustine's problem, 66, 68, 138
  and access to ideals, 263–264
  Kant's approach to, 181
Axioms, 138

Behavior
  vs. action, 241
  defined, 236, 242 (*see also the Glos-
    sary*)
  as erroneous focus for psychology,
    241
Behaviorism, 235–237
  contributions of, 239
  intervening variables in, 237
Behavior therapy, 237
Benevolence, 173
Benussi, Vittorio, 249
Berkeley, George
  on abstract ideas, 146
  active intellect not needed by,
    149
  biographical note on, 145
  blind man with sight restored as a
    test of theory of, 152
  on causality, 148
  on concepts, 147
  on God as agent for perceptual expe-
    riences, 150
  got intentionality wrong, 153
  Hume accepted arguments of, 162
  idealism of, 154
  on ideas, 147
  Principles of Human Knowledge of,
    146
  rejected the distinction of primary
    vs. secondary qualities, 149

  rejected the notion that perception is
    the coordination of information
    from different senses, 150
  rejected substances, 148
  on visual perception, 145
Blind man with sight restored as a
    test of Berkeley's theory, 152
Blueprint metaphor for Aquinas's in-
    telligible outlines, 147–148
Boring, E. G., 204
Brain and mind, 91
Bregman, Albert, and the Gestalt tra-
    dition, 251
Brentano, Franz Clemens, 266
  biographical note on, 213
  on descriptive psychology as re-
    stricted to humans, 219
  Deskriptive Psychologie of, 214
  on dualism, 220
  idealism in, 246
  influence of, on the Gestalt move-
    ment, 244, 250
  on inner perception as "intuition,"
    216
  introspection distinct from inner per-
    ception of, 207
  on mental as distinct from physical,
    219
  on mental as not reducible to physi-
    cal, 220
  on mental states as referring to ob-
    jects, 220
  on reference, 257, 262
  on self-observation as inner percep-
    tion, 215
  as a teacher, 213
British associationism, Gestalt psy-
    chologists' opposition to, 250

Calvino, Italo, 93
Category, defined, 265. *See also the
    Glossary*
Category theory, 262
  and natural-language negation,
    256

as system for formalizing cognitive theory, 255, 256
Causality, 81
  Berkeley on, 148
  Hume on, 160
  Hume's annihilation of common concept of, 158
  Kant on, 180
  never revealed in perception (Hume), 158
Cause, Hume's definition of, 160
Chomsky, Noam, 13, 183, 208
  argues that language is specific to humans, 121
  review of Skinner's *Verbal Behavior*, 238
Christianity, 53
Christian love, 173
Christian Platonism, 98
Cognition
  Aristotle on central problem of, 30
  Aristotle's criterion of, 27
  computer models of, 29
  vs. perception, 26, 34, 113, 143, 253–255
  vs. perception, Kant on, 180
  vs. perception, Mill on, 188
Common perceptual system, Aristotle on, 38, 40, 43
Common sense (Aristotle). See Common perceptual system, Aristotle on
Community, wisdom of (Reid), 170
Complex ideas, Locke on, 128
Computer modeling, 22
Concept(s)
  absent in animals, 196
  as abstractions from sets of perceptual features, 113
  Berkeley vs. Aquinas on, 147
  Darwin on, 196
  defined, 83 (*see also the Glossary*)
  vs. divine ideas, 78
  errors in, 130
  formation of, 6

hierarchical relations among, as given by perceptual attributes, 74
  Ockham on, 99
  vs. perceptual objects, 79
  relation of, to kinds, 199
  taxonomies of, 77
  of thing, 188
  of thing, Mill's, 187
  unlearned, 136 (*see also* Principles, unlearned)
  unlearned, Leibniz on, 138
  unlearned, Locke on, 137
Connectionism, 240
Conscious states, awareness of, 131
Contingent laws vs. necessary laws, Kant on, 182
Contradiction
  innate knowledge of, Augustine on, 67
  and necessary truths, 141
  and perceptual experience, 141
Cultural communities, differences among (Wundt), 210

Darwin, Charles
  biographical note on, 193
  on concepts, 196
  influence of, on psychology, 200
  on kinds, 197
  materialism supported by theory of, 194
  on minds as comparable in animals and humans, 194
  natural selection in theory of, 194
  nominalism as consequence of theory of, 197
  on reasoning in animals, 195
Decision theory, 183
Declaration of Independence
  as a Christian document, 170
  Enlightenment background of, 168
Descartes, René, 108, 136
  biographical note on, 115
  compared with Augustine, 70–71
  on divine illumination, 117

Descartes, René (cont.)
  on dualism, 120–121
  exchanges between Hobbes and,
    109
  got intentionality wrong, 119
  influence of, on Locke, 128
  on machines vs. the human mind, 121
  skeptical crisis of, 117
  on substances vs. perceptible proper-
    ties, 116
Descriptive psychology restricted to
  humans (Brentano), 219
Divine ideas vs. concepts, 78
Divine illumination
  Aquinas on, 78
  Descartes on, 117
  doctrine of, 54
  as source of immutable truths (Au-
    gustine), 68, 69
Dualism
  Augustine on, 69–70
  Brentano on, 220
  Descartes on, 121
  Descartes's arguments for, 120
  of Plato and Socrates, 32
  psychological, 60
  substance, Aquinas's rejection of, 85
  Wundt on, 204
Duns Scotus, John
  biographical note on, 95
  on thisness (haecceitas), 96

Ego, Freud on, 226
Ehrenfels, Christian von
  biographical note on, 243
  on gestalt qualities, 244
  on gestalts as new elements of con-
    sciousness, 246
Elements of consciousness and their
  combination, Wundt on, 218
Empiricist, definition of, 136
Enlightenment, 167
Enthymeme, operation of, as analo-
  gous to that of reason (Leibniz),
  140

Epistemology, 4
Equality of mankind, Jefferson on,
  170
Equality of moral sensibilities, 170
Esperanto, 208
Essence, 78
  defined, 83, 103 (see also the Glos-
    sary)
  nominal vs. real, 129
Ethics
  algebra of (Hutchison), 169
  and mental health, 229
Evil vs. good, 58
Existence as energy, Aquinas on, 81
External reality, Hume's rejection of,
  162

Faith and science as compatible, 56
Fodor, Jerry A., 102
  as modern-day Platonist, 15
Folk psychology, 171
Folk tales as sources of knowledge
  about the human mind, 210
Free will, in Genesis, 50
Frege, Gottlob, 186
Freud, Sigmund, 209
  biographical note on, 225
  disavows ethical claims, 230
  disavows intuition, 231
  on the Ego, 226
  on God, 226
  on the Id, 225–226
  on the Oedipus complex, 226
  on psychology as a natural science,
    231
  on sexual freedom, 232
  on the Superego, 226
Functor, 262
  defined, 265 (see also the Glossary)
Fundamental Postulate, 258. See also
  the Glossary

Galileo Galilei, 107
Genesis
  free will in, 50

singleness of God in, 45
Geometry as nonperceptible, 67
Gestalt(s)
  and the concept of thing, 188
  constraints of, on their foundations
    and vice versa, 246
  defined, 251 (*see also the Glossary*)
  domination of whole over parts in,
    248–250
  independence of, from their founda-
    tions, 245
  musical chords as, 245
  as new elements of consciousness
    (Ehrenfels), 246
  primacy of, 248
Gestalt psychology
  Berlin school of, 248
  and dynamic field theory, 251
Gestalt qualities
  defined, 252 (*see also the Glossary*)
  and substances, 247
God
  as agent for perceptual experiences
    (Berkeley), 150
  Freud's view of, 226
  singleness of, in Genesis, 45
Gödel, Kurt, 90
Good and evil, 58
Goodman, N., 222

Habits and rules in mental life, 240
Haecceitas (Duns Scotus), 96
Happiness as measurable (Jefferson),
  169
Hebb, D. O., 236
Historical explanation, 199
Hobbes, Thomas
  active intellect absent in theory of
    mind of, 106
  biographical note on, 105
  dispensed with abstract objects,
    112
  exchanges between Descartes and,
    109
  ideals absent in psychology of, 108

  on mind as motion, 106
  on perception as the source of mind,
    106–107
  on psychology as part of kinematics,
    106
  on universals as names, 111
Hume, David, 5
  accepted Berkeley's arguments, 162
  annihilated common concept of cau-
    sality, 158
  biographical note on, 157
  on causality, 160
  on causality as never revealed in per-
    ception, 158
  consequences of ideas of, for sci-
    ence, 161
  definition of cause of, 160
  influence of, on Kant, 179
  rejected notion of external reality,
    162
  rejected notion of personal identity,
    162
Husserl, Edmund, 186
Huxley, T. H., 193

Id, Freud on, 225–226
Idealism of Berkeley, 154
Idealizations
  in everyday life, 110
  in science and mathematics, 21
Ideals
  absence of, in Hobbes, 108
  access to, 263–264
  Leibniz on, 138
  positing of, as basic ability of hu-
    man mind, 264
  studied by philosophy (Kant), 182
Ideas
  abstract, Berkeley on, 146
  Berkeley on, 147
  as content of the mind (Locke), 126
  defined, 122 (*see also the Glossary*)
  Locke on, 127
  as mental representations, 118
  as objects of thought, 127

Ideas (cont.)
  Platonic, 20, 23, 64
  of reflection, defined, 133 (*see also
    the Glossary*)
  simple vs. complex (Locke), 126–
    127
  unlearned, 136
Identity supplied by kinds, 48, 198
Individuation
  and identity, 187–188, 257
  handled by kinds, 198
  by matter, 36
  of words, 262
Inner perception, 222
  equated with Brentano's "intuition"
    and Locke's "reflection," 216
  objects of, 217
  Wundt on, 214–215
Inquiry, problem of, 15
Intelligibility of nature, 49
Intelligible outlines, Aquinas on, 80,
  147
Intentionality, 149, 215, 266
  Aquinas on, 79
  Berkeley got it wrong, 153
  defined, 43 (*see also the Glossary*)
  Descartes got it wrong, 119
  Kant got it wrong, 184
  Locke got it wrong, 127, 148
  Mill got it right, 189
  problem of, 42
Introspection, 131, 132
  conditions for validity of (Wundt),
    206
  defined, 133 (*see also the Glossary*)
  distinguished from Brentano's inner
    perception, 207
  Wundt on, 205–206
Intuition
  disavowed by Freud, 231
  important for cognitive psychology
    and logic, 218

Jackendoff, Ray, 55, 61
Jefferson, Thomas
  biographical note on, 167

  on equality of mankind, 170
  on happiness as measurable, 169
  on morality of blacks, 172
  on public service, 173
  Scottish Enlightenment reflected in,
    175
  on self-evident truths, 169
Judgment, 82
Jung, Carl, 209

Kant, Immanuel
  approach of, to Augustine's prob-
    lem, 181
  on a priori knowledge, 179
  biographical note on, 177
  on causality, 180
  on contingent laws vs. necessary
    laws, 182
  on division of labor between philoso-
    phy and psychology, 183
  got intentionality wrong, 184
  influence of Hume on, 179
  influence of Leibniz on, 178
  on learning, 181
  on logic, 181
  on perception vs. cognition, 180
  on philosophy as the study of ideals,
    182
  on relation of philosophy to psychol-
    ogy, 182
  on truth, 181
Kinds, 47–48, 257
  Darwin vs. Aristotle on, 197
  defined, 43 (*see also the Glossary*)
  vs. perceptual indices, 129–130
  purpose of (Mill), 189
  reference to, not reducible to physiol-
    ogy, 221
  relation of, to concepts, 199
Knowledge
  a priori, 159
  a priori, Kant on, 179
  Meno on, 10
  vs. perception, Plato on, 22
  Plato on, 17
  vs. wisdom, Augustine on, 66

Koffka, Kurt, biographical note on, 243
Köhler, Wolfgang, biographical note on, 243
Konorski, J., foreshadowed Skinner, 238

Language and truth, 18
Language of thought, 89
  Fodor on, 38–39, 102
  Ockham on, 101, 102
Learning. *See also* Unlearned basis of mathematics, language, and space
  defined, 242
  discovery of unlearned elements in, 263
  of first words, 262–263
  Kant's view of, 181
  need for unlearned resources in, 263
  Plato's problem of, 9–15, 68, 127, 238
  as recollection (Plato), 13
Learning that vs. learning how, 9
Learning theory, 238
  collapse of, 113
  rewards, punishments, and habits in, 238
Leibniz, Gottfried Wilhelm
  biographical note on, 135
  on ideals, 138
  influence of, on Kant, 178
  on natural logic, 139
  on operation of reason, 140
  on possible worlds, 141
  response of, to Locke's empiricism, 136
  on unlearned concepts, 138
Linguistic intuition, 217
  as empirical (Chomsky), 218
Locke, John
  biographical note on, 125
  Brentano equates inner perception with "reflection" in, 216
  on complex ideas, 128
  consequences of ideas of, for science, 161
  got intentionality wrong, 127, 148
  on ideas, 127
  on ideas as content of the mind, 126
  ideational theory of meaning of, 127
  influence of Descartes on, 128
  Leibniz on empiricism of, 136
  on powers of mind, 126
  on reflection, 126, 131
  on sensation, 126
  on simple vs. complex ideas, 126–127
  on simple ideas, 128
  on unlearned concepts, 137
Logic
  aim of, 182
  Kant's view of, 181
Logical necessity, 178
Logical positivism, 205

Machines vs. the human mind, Descartes on, 121
Maier, Annaliese, 100
Manichaeism, 46
Mankind in God's image, 46
Maps preferred to set inclusion for modeling relations among kinds, 260
Materialism supported by Darwin's theory, 194
Mathematics as key to universe, Galileo on, 107
Matter, defined, 33. *See also the Glossary*
Meaning(s)
  of adjectives, Mill on, 190
  ideational theory of (Locke), 127
  Mill ignores grammar in theory of, 191
  relation of, to concepts, 131
  of words, Mill on, 189
  of words are kinds, 190
Memory and recall, 14
Mental
  distinguished from physical (Brentano), 219

Mental (cont.)
  not reducible to physical (Brentano),
    220
Mental health, 183–184
  Christian view of, 57
  and doing good, 173
  and ethics, 229
  as foundation for understanding
    mental illness, 227–230
  is not calmness or lack of mental
    pain, 230
  neglect of, in psychoanalysis, 225
  and the wise and good person, 229
Mental illness
  and moral responsibility, 230
  and concept of mental health, 184
Mental representations as objects of
  awareness, 118. See also Representations
Mental sketches, abstract ideas as, 146
Mental states refer to objects (Brentano), 220
Mental therapy, 233
Metaphysics, 4
Michotte, Albert, 161
Mill, John Stuart
  on abstraction, 186
  biographical note on, 185
  on cognition vs. perception, 188
  on concept of thing, 187
  got intentionality right, 189
  ignores grammar in theory of mean-
    ing, 191
  on meanings of adjectives, 190
  on meanings of words, 189
  on Plato's problem of learning, 188
  on purpose of kinds, 189
Mind
  and brain, 91
  as motion, Hobbes on, 106
  as noncorporeal, Augustine on, 69
  identical with the brain? 89
  vs. machines, Descartes on, 121
  nonmateriality of, 90–91
  powers of, Locke on, 126

unlearned operating principles of,
  140
Minds comparable in animals and humans (Darwin), 194
Moral insight as genetically derived,
  50
Moral issues, expertise on, 170
Moral reasoning, children's development of, 171

Natural-deductive rules, 139
Natural-deductive systems, 138
Natural languages as part of Völker-
  psychologie, 207
Natural logic, Leibniz on, 139
Natural selection
  in Darwin's theory, 194
  relation of, to dualism, 194
Nature, defined, 103. See also the
  Glossary
Natures of things, 64
  immutable, 65
  individuated by matter, 90, 96
Necessary laws vs. contingent laws,
  Kant on, 182
Necessary truths, 136, 140, 178. See
  also Truth(s)
  and contradiction, 141
New Testament, 53
Nietzsche, Friedrich, 59
Nominal essence, 129
  defined, 133
Nominalism, 31, 98–99, 111, 131
  as consequence of Darwin's theory,
    197

Ockham, William of
  biographical note on, 95
  on concepts, 99
  influence of, on psychology, 100–
    101
  on language of thought, 101, 102
Oedipus complex, Freud on, 226
Operant conditioning, 237
Original sin, 58

Parallel distributed processing (PDP), 240
Particulars and universals, 96, 97
Passive intellect, 31
  Aquinas on, 88–89
  defined, 34 (*see also the Glossary*)
Perception
  of the act of perceiving, 42
  Augustine's theory of, 65
  as coordination of information from different senses, rejected by Berkeley, 150
  does not give essences, 78
  vs. knowing, Plato on, 22
  reference in, 265
  role of, Aquinas on, 82
  as the source of mind, Hobbes on, 106–107
  visual, Berkeley on, 145
Perception vs. cognition, 26, 34, 113, 143, 253–255
  approach of contemporary psychology on, 113
  Kant on, 180
  Mill on, 188
Perceptual figures and the concept of thing, 188
Perceptual indices vs. kinds, 129–130
Perceptual objects vs. concepts, 79
Perceptual properties vs. substances, Descartes on, 116
Perceptual systems, 35
  communication between, 38
Personal identity
  Hume's rejection of, 162
  not given in perception, 163–164
Philosophy
  relation of, to psychology, Kant on, 182
  as the study of ideals, Kant on, 182
PHYSICAL OBJECT (the kind), 188
Piaget, Jean, 256
Plato, 64
  dualism of, 32
  on ideas, 20, 23, 64

  on inability to define virtue, 13
  on knowledge, 17
  on learning as recollection, 13
  on perception vs. knowing, 22
  problem of learning of, 9–15, 68, 127, 238
  problem of truth of, 17, 78, 112, 261
Platonic ideas, 20, 64
  defined, 23
Platonism, Christian, 64
Plato's problem of learning, 9–15, 68, 127, 238
  in contemporary psychology, 113
  Mill on, 188
Plato's problem of truth, 17, 78, 112, 261
Popper, Karl, 11–12
Possible worlds, Leibniz on, 141
Principles, unlearned, 138. *See also* Concepts, unlearned
Problem of inquiry, 25
Problem of learnability in psycholinguistics, 113
Properties, primary and secondary, 116
Prototypes, 64
  Eleanor Rosch on, 98
Psychologist, defined, 3–4
Psychology
  concept of mental health neglected in clinical, 228
  Darwin's influence on, 200
  defined, 3–4
  descriptive vs. physiological, Wundt on, 214
  difficulty of, 2
  history of, reasons for studying, 5–7
  as a natural science, Freud on, 231
  as part of kinematics, Hobbes on, 106
  physiological, 199
  rejection of Kant's division of labor between philosophy and, 183
  as study of one's own mind, 70

Public service, Jefferson's conception of, 173

Qualities, primary, 37
Qualities, primary vs. secondary, 36
  Berkeley's rejection of distinction of, 149
  distinguished, 122 (*see also the Glossary*)
Quine, W. V., 222
  on learning of word meaning, 12
Quine's problem, 113

Radical empiricist, 76
  defined, 143 (*see also the Glossary*)
Rationalist, defined, 143. *See also the Glossary*
Reasoning
  in animals, Darwin on, 195
  vs. association of ideas, 196
  as operations on sentences, 195
Reference, 130
  as distinct from concepts, 131
  as distinctive aspect of cognition, 257
  in perception, 265
  as primitive in cognitive psychology, 221
Reflection, Locke on, 126, 131
Representations
  general, 147
  pictures as, 127
Reyes, Gonzalo E., 41, 253
Reyes, Marie La Palme, 41, 253
Rights
  basic, 174
  inalienable, 168, 174
Rosch, Eleanor, 98
Rules and habits in mental life, 240
Rules as operating principles of the mind, 139

Science
  consequences of Locke's ideas for, 161

and faith as compatible, 56
Sciences
  natural vs. mental, Wundt on, 205
  unification of, 204
Scottish Enlightenment reflected in Jefferson, 175
Self-evident truths, Jefferson on, 169
Self-observation as inner perception, Brentano on, 215
Sensation, Locke on, 126
Sense that is common (Aristotle), 38, 40
  defined, 43 (*see also the Glossary*)
Senses, coordination among, 41
Set theory rejected as model for logical relations among kinds, 259–260
Sexual freedom, Freud on, 232
Simple ideas, Locke on, 128
Skinner, B. F., 237
Social animals, humans as, 55
Social cognition, Jackendoff on faculty of, 55
Socrates
  dualism of, 32
  on virtue, 10–11
Soul
  Aquinas on, 86–87
  intellectual, infinite capacity of, 92
Species as abstract entities, 47
Species intelligibilis, Aquinas on, 80
Structure, knowledge of, and association, 257
Substance(s), 78, 129
  Berkeley's rejection of, 148
  defined, 33, 103 (*see also the Glossary*)
  and gestalt qualities, 247
  immutability of, in contrast to accidental properties, 66
  individuated by matter, 80
  vs. perceptible properties, Descartes on, 116
Substantial forms, 80, 88
  Aristotle on, 30, 31

defined, 33, 36 (*see also the Glossary*)
Superego, Freud on, 226
Syntax and the individuation of words, 262

Therapies, behavior-based, 239
Thisness (Duns Scotus), 96
Titchener, E. B., 204, 219
Tokens and types, 19
Trinity, God as, 54
Truth(s)
   and language, 18
   Kant on, 181
   necessary, 140
   Plato on, 17
   problem of, 17, 18, 78, 112, 261
   psychological version of problem of, 20
   unchanging character of, 18
Types and tokens, 19

Understanding, use of images for, 25–26
Universal Grammar (Chomsky), 39, 208
Universals, 90, 259
   defined, 94 (*see also the Glossary*)
   and the Fundamental Postulate, 258
   logically secondary to kinds, 259
   as names, Hobbes on, 111
   and particulars, 96, 97
Unlearned basis of mathematics, language, and space, 142
Utilitarianism, 185

Virtue
   definition of, 10
   inability to define, Plato on, 13
   learnability of, 10–11
   Socrates on, 10–11
Vision, language of, 152–154, 266
Völkerpsychologie of Wundt, 203, 207–211
   study of, via folk tales, 210

Watson, John B., 200
   biographical note on, 235
Wertheimer, Max, biographical note on, 243
Wilberforce, Samuel, 193
Wills, Gary, 168
Wisdom vs. knowledge, Augustine on, 66
Wittgenstein, Ludwig, 198
Word, the, as the personification of divine intelligence, 54
Words
   individuation of, 262
   learning meanings of, 12
Wundt, Wilhelm, 1
   biographical note on, 203
   on conditions for validity of introspection, 206
   on descriptive vs. physiological psychology, 214
   on differences among cultural communities, 210
   on dualism, 204
   on elements of consciousness and their combination, 218
   on inner perception, 214–215
   on introspection, 205–206
   on natural vs. mental sciences, 205
   Völkerpsychologie of, 203, 207–211

Zolfaghari, Houman, 253